LIBRARY OF NEW TESTAMENT STUDIES

643

Formerly the Journal for the Study of the New Testament Supplement series

Editor
Chris Keith

Editorial Board
Dale C. Allison, John M. G. Barclay, Lynn H. Cohick, R. Alan Culpepper, Craig A. Evans, Robert Fowler, Simon J. Gathercole, Juan Hernández Jr., John S. Kloppenborg, Michael Labahn, Matthew V. Novenson, Love L. Sechrest, Robert Wall, Catrin H. Williams, Brittany E. Wilson

Beyond Canon

Early Christianity and the Ethiopic Textual Tradition

Edited by

Meron T. Gebreananaye, Logan Williams
and Francis Watson

t&tclark

LONDON • NEW YORK • OXFORD • NEW DELHI • SYDNEY

T&T CLARK
Bloomsbury Publishing Plc
50 Bedford Square, London, WC1B 3DP, UK
1385 Broadway, New York, NY 10018, USA
29 Earlsfort Terrace, Dublin 2, Ireland

BLOOMSBURY, T&T CLARK and the T&T Clark logo are trademarks of Bloomsbury Publishing Plc

First published in Great Britain 2021
This paperback edition published in 2022

Copyright © Meron T. Gebreananaye, Logan Williams, Francis Watson and contributors, 2021

Meron T. Gebreananaye, Logan Williams and Francis Watson have asserted their right under the Copyright, Designs and Patents Act, 1988, to be identified as Editors of this work.

All rights reserved. No part of this publication may be reproduced or transmitted in any form or by any means, electronic or mechanical, including photocopying, recording, or any information storage or retrieval system, without prior permission in writing from the publishers.

Bloomsbury Publishing Plc does not have any control over, or responsibility for, any third-party websites referred to or in this book. All internet addresses given in this book were correct at the time of going to press. The author and publisher regret any inconvenience caused if addresses have changed or sites have ceased to exist, but can accept no responsibility for any such changes.

A catalogue record for this book is available from the British Library.

Library of Congress Cataloging-in-Publication Data

Names: Gebreananaye, Meron T., editor. | Watson, Francis, 1956– editor. | Williams, Logan, editor.
Title: Beyond canon : early Christianity and the Ethiopic textual tradition / edited by Meron T. Gebreananaye, Logan Williams, and Francis Watson.
Description: London ; New York : T&T Clark, 2020. | Series: The library of New Testament studies, 2513-8790 ; 643 | Includes bibliographical references and index. | Summary: "This book seeks to highlight the significance of a group of five texts excluded from the standard Christian Bible and preserved only in Ge'ez, the classical language of Ethiopia. These texts are crucial for modern scholars due to their significance for a wide range of early readers, as extant fragments of other early translations confirm in most cases; yet they are also noted for their eventual marginalization and abandonment as a more restrictive understanding of the biblical canon prevailed - everywhere except in Ethiopia, with its distinctive Christian tradition in which the concept of a "closed canon" is alien. In focusing upon 1 Enoch, Jubilees, the Ascension of Isaiah, the Epistula Apostolorum, and the Apocalypse of Peter, the contributors to this volume group them together as representatives of a time in early Christian history when sacred texts were not limited by a sharply defined canonical boundary. In doing so, this book also highlights the unique and under-appreciated contribution of Ethiopia to the study of early Christianity"– Provided by publisher.
Identifiers: LCCN 2020032584 (print) | LCCN 2020032585 (ebook) | ISBN 9780567695857 (hb) | ISBN 9780567697653 (paperback) | ISBN 9780567695864 (epdf) | ISBN 9780567695888 (epub)
Subjects: LCSH: Bible–Canonical criticism. | Bible–Canon. | Apocryphal books–Criticism, interpretation, etc. | Bible. Ethiopic–Versions.
Classification: LCC BS521.8 .B49 2020 (print) | LCC BS521.8 (ebook) | DDC 229/.9046—dc23
LC record available at https://lccn.loc.gov/2020032584
LC ebook record available at https://lccn.loc.gov/2020032585

ISBN:	HB:	978-0-5676-9585-7
	PB:	978-0-5676-9765-3
	ePDF:	978-0-5676-9586-4
	ePUB:	978-0-5676-9588-8

Series: Library of New Testament Studies, ISSN 2513-8790, volume 643

Typeset by RefineCatch Limited, Bungay, Suffolk

To find out more about our authors and books visit www.bloomsbury.com and sign up for our newsletters.

Contents

List of Contributors		vi
Introduction		1
1	The End-time in 1 Enoch, Paul and Matthew: Continuity and Discontinuity *Philip F. Esler*	9
2	Debating Daniel's Dream: The Synoptic Gospels and the Similitudes of Enoch on the Son of Man *Logan Williams*	23
3	Peter and the Patriarch: Eschatological Perspectives from 1 Peter and 1 Enoch *Sofanit T. Abebe*	39
4	Has Christian Tradition Influenced the Ge'ez and Greek Versions of 1 Enoch? *Loren T. Stuckenbruck*	55
5	Non-human Animals in the Primeval History of Jubilees *James R. Hamrick*	67
6	The Trial of Isaiah: On Alleged Jewish Backgrounds of the Ascension of Isaiah *Jan Dochhorn*	85
7	The *Vorlage* of the Ethiopic Version of the *Epistula Apostolorum*: Greek or Arabic? *Darrell Hannah*	97
8	The Apocalypse of Peter: The Relationship of the Versions *Eric J. Beck*	117
9	Gospel Writing in Transition: A Look at the Ethiopic *Ta-'ammərä 'Iyasus* *Meron T. Gebreananaye*	131
10	'The House of the Gospel': Text, Image and Sacred Space *Francis Watson*	145
Afterword *Michael A. Knibb*		163
Bibliography		167
Index of Authors		181

Contributors

Sofanit T. Abebe (University of Edinburgh)

Eric Beck (University of Edinburgh)

Jan Dochhorn (Durham University)

Philip Esler (University of Gloucestershire)

Darrell Hannah (All Saints' Church Ascot Heath)

James Hamrick (Ludwig-Maximilians-Universität München)

Michael A. Knibb (King's College London)

Loren T. Stuckenbruck (Ludwig-Maximilians-Universität München)

Meron T. Gebreananaye (Durham University)

Francis Watson (Durham University)

Logan Williams (Durham University)

Introduction

Within the modern collections of ancient texts labelled 'Old Testament Pseudepigrapha' or 'New Testament Apocrypha', there are at least five important texts preserved in full only in Ge'ez, the classical language of Ethiopia. These texts are important for modern scholars because of their significance for a wide range of early readers, as extant fragments of other early translations confirm in most cases. Those readers included pre-Christian Jewish communities, at Qumran and elsewhere, in the case of two of the five texts (1 Enoch and Jubilees); yet these works were also popular and valued among Christians. The other three (the Ascension of Isaiah, the *Epistula Apostolorum*, and the Apocalypse of Peter) are of Christian origin. For early Christian readers, the modern scholarly distinction between a Jewish and a Christian origin was unknown or irrelevant. For such readers, these texts were the work of the prophets and apostles of the Old and New Testaments respectively. The revelations contained in the post-resurrection dialogues recounted by the Twelve and Peter were already anticipated in the prophetic testimonies of Enoch (the inventor of the art of writing and so the author of the oldest of all written texts) and in Moses and Isaiah. By virtue of their prestigious authorship and the revelations they contain, all these texts lay claim to authoritative scriptural status. This claim would surely have carried greater weight with most of their early readers than rarefied elite discussions about the limits of the scriptural canon.

Nevertheless, advocates of a closed canon prevailed in the end, and an important function of the canonical lists they produced was to *suppress* texts now deemed to be non-canonical. Suppression need not involve deliberate physical destruction of manuscripts; all that is required is a climate of opinion that discourages the commissioning of new copies to replace worn-out older ones. Thus large numbers of once-popular texts were deemed 'apocryphal' and gradually faded from view. Not all of them, of course, and not everywhere all at once, yet evidence of increasing canon-consciousness is widespread, whether in the Latin west, the Greek east, or in Coptic Egypt. Ethiopia is the great exception. For reasons that are obscure but that may have to do with Ethiopia's relatively isolated position within the Christian world of late antiquity, the Ethiopic manuscript tradition persisted in copying ancient literature that had long been suppressed and forgotten elsewhere. In its Ethiopic form this literature is preserved in relatively recent manuscripts, typically dating from between the fifteenth and the twentieth centuries, testimony to a tradition that refused to let these texts die along with the lost older manuscripts that had been their bearers over a period of more than a millenium.

While there are significant intertextual links between 1 Enoch and Jubilees and between the *Epistula Apostolorum* and the Apocalypse of Peter, the five main texts covered in the present book form a coherent group only in the limited sense that they were all popular reading matter among early Christians but survive in full only in Geʿez. Yet there are advantages in taking them out of their modern categorizations within Old Testament pseudepigrapha and New Testament apocrypha. These categories are irrelevant to the Ethiopic reception of these works, where they are viewed as integral to a set of holy scriptures the extent of which remains undetermined. In their Ethiopic form these texts make it possible to reimagine a time in early Christian history when there were sacred texts – some in relatively stable and fixed collections – but no sharply defined sense of a canonical limit. These texts remind us that canons are contingent constructs specific to particular locations and contexts. That is, of course, to state the obvious. Yet it is easy even for otherwise responsible scholarship to assume that canonical status is integral to some texts while others are inherently apocryphal, and to establish one's interpretative priorities accordingly. The challenge posed by a more inclusive and open-ended conception of holy scripture may be salutary.

1 Enoch is a composite work comprising five major sections: the Book of Watchers (chapters 1–36), the Similitudes of Enoch (also known as the Book of Parables) (chapters 37–71), the Book of the Luminaries (chapters 72–82), the Dream Visions (chapters 83–90) and the Epistle of Enoch (chapters 91–105), with two additional concluding sections: the Birth of Noah (chapters 106–7) and the Eschatological Admonition (chapter 108). The Book of Watchers gives a detailed account of the fall of the Watchers, angelic beings who disobeyed God and came down to earth in order to mate with human women, and who thereafter taught humanity all kinds of forbidden secrets, such as metallurgy and divination. God responds to their disobedience by imprisoning the Watchers with a view to a still harsher punishment at the Last Judgement; Enoch's plea that they be given a chance of restoration is peremptorily rejected. Enoch is then taken on a tour of the cosmos in which he is shown the places of judgement, the mountain of God, Eden, and more.

Following on from this, the Similitudes describe a conflict between, on the one hand, Azazel and the 'kings' and the 'mighty', and, on the other hand, God's righteous people and a messianic figure who is identified (variously) as 'the Chosen One', 'the Righteous One' and 'the Son of Man'. Powerful kings have exploited and persecuted the righteous, and the Enochic author predicts that the Son of Man will remedy this situation by delivering retribution to those kings, casting away the demonic forces from their position of influence, vindicating the righteous, and bringing all to recognize the Son of Man.

The Book of the Luminaries presents Enoch as the recipient of revelation through the angel Uriel. In a vision Enoch learns about the various cosmological phenomena associated with the calendar. In the Dream Visions, Enoch recounts to his son Methuselah the two visions he had received in his youth, the first concerning the future flood, the much longer second pre-narrating the scriptural history and its goal with various animals representing its righteous or unrighteous human protagonists (thus it is often dubbed the 'Animal Apocalypse').

Lastly, the Epistle of Enoch is a final testament in which the prophet addresses his children and sets before them warnings and exhortations, outlining the negative fate of the unrighteous and the positive destiny of the righteous. Enoch emphatically predicts that God will necessarily repay all for what they have done, whether good or bad. We should note furthermore that within the Epistle is a discrete section called the 'Apocalypse of Weeks' (93.1–10; 91.11–17), which, like the Dream Visions, retells human history from creation to eschaton and the arrival of the 'new heaven'; all this is told within a temporal frame in which major sections of human history are referred to as 'weeks'.

The popularity of this Enochic literature at Qumran is attested by the survival of fragments of multiple copies (eleven in this case, written in Aramaic). The predominance of material from the Book of Watchers and the Animal Apocalypse may suggest that the book had not yet reached its now familiar 108-chapter form, and this is seemingly confirmed by the fluidity of the Qumran material related to the Book of Luminaries and by the presence of an Enochic 'Book of Giants' absent from the present form of the text. Like other Second Temple texts, 1 Enoch was readily adopted by Christian readers; indeed, it is quoted as authoritative scripture in the New Testament letter ascribed to Jude – although patristic authors are aware of some who have reservations about this work, or express reservations themselves. While the very fact that intellectual leaders felt the need to criticize this work demonstrates its popularity, it also heralds its eventual demise everywhere except Ethiopia. In the Ethiopic manuscript tradition 1 Enoch may be placed before the Octateuch on the assumption that it long predates the Mosaic texts, anticipating the end of salvation-history from the standpoint of the beginning. Christological readings of the second part of the book (the Similitudes of Enoch) both reflect and confirm its secure scriptural status within the Ethiopic Christian tradition.

Five of the chapters in this volume are concerned with this key apocalyptic text, with particular reference to its relationship to other early Christian literature. Philip Esler offers a comparative analysis of the depiction of the eschaton in 1 Enoch, Paul and Matthew, focusing especially on the theme of ethnic identities and their eschatological significance as depicted in 1 Enoch, Paul and Matthew. Logan Williams queries claims for direct dependence between early Christological concepts and 'Enochic Judaism', contrasting the reading of Daniel 7 discovered in the Synoptics and the image of the Son of Man in the Enochic Similitudes. Sofanit T. Abebe compares the eschatological expectations of 1 Enoch and 1 Peter and raises questions about the conventional assumption that 'realized eschatology' is a distinctively Christian phenomenon. Loren Stuckenbruck's text-critical analysis of selected passages investigates the possibility of Christian redactional influence – a further indication of the assimilation of this pre-Christian Jewish text to later Christian contexts. A similar point is made by quite different means in Francis Watson's interpretation of an Enochically inspired image in an ancient Ethiopic gospel book.

The book of Jubilees is a retelling of the scriptural narrative from creation through to the time of Moses, with a particular focus on the major figures of Adam, Noah, Abraham, Jacob and Moses. The text begins with Moses ascending Mount Sinai, where God commands the angel of the presence to write down the sacred history from the time of the 'first creation' onwards (Jub 1.27). Moses too is commanded to write (1.26), and here the reference may be to the Torah or Pentateuch itself – in which case the angelic writing of the book of Jubilees occurs in parallel to Moses' writing of the Torah. Although Jubilees was known to several patristic writers under the title 'The Little Genesis', it is much more than just a condensed version of its canonical counterpart. Jubilees goes well beyond Genesis: among many other supplementary elements, the narrative more explicitly incorporates the story of the Watchers and other angelic or demonic forces, it has a strong eschatological emphasis (even interpreting the flood as a form of eschatological victory which bestows a new 'nature' on humanity), and it ascribes special significance to the progression of time in history. Jubilees is deeply concerned with chronology in numerous regards, including the division of time, the qualitative evaluation of different days (i.e. some as sacred) and the length of time that has passed since creation. This meticulous focus on chronological matters is captured by its usual title, which derives from the opening lines of the work: 'This is the Account of the Division of Days of the Law and the Testimony for Annual Observance according to their Weeks (of years) and their Jubilees through all the Years of the World'. While Jubilees' retelling of history takes its structure and base content from Genesis and Exodus, it does so with a kind of interpretative engagement that in fact produces a truly new text. Jubilees is not just a parabiblical parasite of the Hebrew Bible but rather a text in its own right, a work which, through drawing upon and synthesizing numerous Jewish traditions and sources, constitutes itself as an impressive work of theological and literary imagination.

Longer or shorter passages from Jubilees are preserved in Hebrew, Syriac, Greek and Latin, attesting its popularity in both the Second Temple Jewish milieu – fragments of fourteen copies survive from Qumran – and later Christian contexts, where the emphasis on sabbath observance and other Jewish ritual practices seems not to have hindered its acceptance. Yet it is only in Ethiopia that complete texts are extant: the modern edition of James C. VanderKam lists twenty-seven of them, with dates ranging from the fourteenth to the twentieth century and thus representing a unique unbroken manuscript (and interpretative) tradition. In Ethiopic manuscripts, Jubilees sometimes occurs on its own or paired up with Enoch, but it is more usually to be found following the 'Octateuch', the eight texts from Genesis to Ruth that precede the four books of Kingdoms (= 1, 2 Sam; 1, 2 Kgs) in the conventional canonical sequence. This is, then, a 'scriptural' text no less than any other; the high claims it makes for its own authority are echoed and affirmed in its Ethiopic context. Thus the Ethiopian tradition preserves the early Jewish and Christian assumption that the number of sacred texts ascribed to prestigious figures of the (Jewish and/or Christian) past should not be prematurely limited.

In the present collection, James Hamrick focuses on the depiction of non-human animals in Jubilees, showing how this text can serve to inform historical, literary and ethical reflection on this topic. To this end, he particularly notes that the primeval history portrays animals as moral agents whose natures and behaviours are prone to change and development.

The Ascension of Isaiah is a Christian apocalypse which utilizes the prophet Isaiah as its central visionary figure. The first five chapters recount how, when Manasseh began to rule Israel, a false prophet named Belchira subjected Isaiah to false accusations that led to Isaiah being sawn in two with Manasseh's approval (this event is likely referred to in Hebrews 11.37). Chapters 6–11 describe Isaiah's journey up through the seven heavens. As he passes through the first six heavens he sees choirs of angels appearing in ever-increasing splendour, but when he arrives at the seventh heaven he sees 'all the righteous from the time of Adam' (9.7), then receives prophecies about Jesus Christ, and finally sees the Lord himself – an obvious echo of Isaiah 6, which has inspired this whole account. The Lord is later revealed to be Jesus, whom Isaiah sees descending through the various heavens in angelic form before causing himself to be born through the Virgin Mary. The narrative closes with Isaiah witnessing Jesus' re-ascent into heaven, and with his own return to earth. In the chronological scheme of this work, the Christological vision narrated in chapters 6–11 is the main reason for Isaiah's persecution and martyrdom as narrated in chapters 1–5.

The account of Isaiah's vision in the second part of the work survives in Latin and Slavonic translation, and Greek, Latin and Coptic fragments from different parts of the work confirm both its early popularity and the demise of the associated manuscript traditions. In Ethiopic manuscripts the Ascension of Isaiah is usually presented as a supplement to the prophetic book of Isaiah, analogous to the various short supplementary works that accompany the book of Jeremiah in manuscript traditions shaped by the Septuagint. In juxtaposing the two Isaianic texts, the Ethiopic manuscripts further enhance the role of Isaiah within Christian tradition as the most explicit of the prophetic voices that heralded the coming of Christ. This is in keeping with the Christian provenance of this text. As Jan Dochhorn shows in his contribution to this volume, the account of the martyrdom of Isaiah presented here lacks any credible Jewish background and is most likely of Christian origin.

Despite its (modern) title, the *Epistula Apostolorum* is not primarily an 'epistle' in the ordinary sense of the term. The work presents itself as an account of a revelation to the apostles from Jesus himself, in the form of a question-and-answer session on Easter Day that occupies the short interval between Jesus' resurrection and his ascension. The letter-opening is followed by a credal passage and a group of miracle stories in the style of a gospel, derived from earlier gospel traditions. These include the healing of the haemorrhaging woman, the wedding at Cana, and walking on water. After a brief reference to his death and burial, Jesus appears to three women when they visit his tomb (Sarah, Martha and Mary in the Ethiopic version), and the post-resurrection dialogue that ensues comprises the majority of the *Epistula*. A wide range of themes is at play here: the fleshly corporeality of Jesus is viewed as proof of the resurrection of both body and soul in the eschaton, and we also learn of the journey of Christ down through the lower heavens to become incarnate on earth, his further descent into Hades, and the future conversion of Saul or Paul, along with much else. The dating of the Parousia (after 150 years in the Ethiopic version, 120 in the Coptic) can plausibly be used to establish an approximate *terminus ad quem* for the composition of this work.

The pagination of the incomplete Coptic version of this text shows that it too once included passages now extant only in Ge'ez: these include the letter-opening, the credal passage, the collection of miracle stories, the prediction of Paul's conversion, and the ascension narrative with which the work concludes. The Ethiopic version has also acquired a long and clearly secondary opening section, set in Galilee, in which the risen Jesus informs his disciples about the events of the last days, culminating in the coming of the Antichrist and Jesus' own return in glory to save the elect and condemn the wicked. An analogous case of redactional expansion may be seen in the addition of 2 Esdras 1–2 (= 5 Ezra) to the apocalyptic text now known as 4 Ezra (= 2 Esdras 3–14). In the Ethiopic manuscript tradition the *Epistula* with its secondary Galilean prelude is usually placed after and assimilated to a still longer and later work that focuses on issues of church order, the Testament of our Lord and Saviour Jesus Christ, also extant in Syriac and Arabic translations from the original Greek.

Greek was also the original language of the *Epistula*, and Darrell Hannah argues that it was likely translated into the Ethiopic from Greek rather than from Arabic as has been commonly assumed. This suggests that the translation dates from around the middle of the first millenium rather than the first half of the second. The *Epistula* may conceivably have been available in Ge'ez for almost as long as the canonical gospels.

The Apocalypse of Peter is written from the standpoint of Peter, who reports Jesus' post-resurrection eschatological discourse on the Mount of Olives. As in the Synoptic parallels, Jesus describes and predicts imminent eschatological events, but this apocalypse includes numerous new dimensions, in particular an account in graphic detail of how the unrighteous will be punished in the eschaton. The unrighteous are to receive punishments corresponding to their particular sins: those who blaspheme will be hung up by their tongues, those who plait their hair as a means of seduction are hung by their neck and hair, men who have illicit sex with such women are hung by their thighs, murderers are cast into fire and endure waking torment forever, and those whose lies led to the deaths of the Christian martyrs have their lips cut away and are filled with fire. Evidently bodily resurrection is a prerequisite of eternal punishment as much as of eternal salvation. The angel Ezrael is identified as the 'angel of wrath' and plays a consistent role in preparing and enacting the different forms of punishment. After these detailed descriptions of various torments and their warrants, Peter and the other disciples accompany Jesus to a mountain, where Moses and Elijah appear – as in the Synoptic transfiguration story, which underlies this part of the text. Peter receives a vision of a garden, the dwelling-place of the patriarchs and the righteous. His proposal to construct three tabernacles is rejected, and Moses, Elijah and Jesus ascend to heaven in a cloud as a divine voice acclaims Jesus as the beloved Son.

The Apocalypse of Peter probably dates from the mid-second century and was known and cited by Clement of Alexandria and other church fathers. Although once widely regarded as a canonical text, it is now extant in full only in Ethiopic translation, incorporated into a larger work entitled 'The Second Coming of Christ and the Resurrection of the Dead'. In both of the two known manuscripts of this work – one in Paris, the other remaining in Ethiopia – it follows the Testament of our Lord Jesus Christ with the (extended) *Epistula Apostolorum* as its supplement (as mentioned above). Thus, both early Christian texts are assimilated to longer and later texts with which they share a post-resurrection narrative setting. Once again, it is the Ethiopic manuscript tradition alone that has preserved a work used and highly valued by many early Christian readers.

Part of the Apocalypse of Peter is also extant in a Greek version, discovered at Akhmim in Egypt. Eric Beck queries the contemporary scholarly consensus regarding the superiority of the Ethiopic text over the Akhmimic Apocalypse of Peter through a comparative analysis of the two recensions and their differing Christologies.

In addition to preserving the five early Jewish or Christian works featured in this volume, the Ethiopic tradition also produced a number of influential 'apocryphal' texts, that is, texts that presuppose and elaborate established scriptural texts such as the four canonical gospels. The *Ta-'ammərä 'Iyasus* (Miracles of Jesus) is a large-scale compendium of miracle stories attributed to John the evangelist, being one of the many books that he produced, so that this work is a gospel not only in form but also as regards its own self-identification. The text adds its own contributions to its sources, such as having Jesus identify the names of the various husbands of the Samaritan woman from John 4. In addition to the canonical gospels, sources include the Infancy Gospel of Thomas, the Protevangelium of James, and the Apocryphal Gospel of John. By grouping the miracles in discrete sections with introductions and benedictions, the *Ta-'ammərä 'Iyasus* reorganizes this diverse material into a coherent structured whole. In her chapter, Meron T. Gebreananaye examines the literary and hermeneutical processes by which gospel traditions are brought together and reworked to develop a new narrative. In view of the continuing popularity of this work, it is questionable how far the canonical/non-canonical dichotomy is necessary or appropriate in assessing its function and status.

In raising questions about conventional understandings of canon, the chapters in this volume also illustrate the importance of the Ge'ez language for the study of the literature valued by early Christian readers, whether this was created within or adopted into a Christian context. While much conventional New Testament scholarship can seemingly make do with a knowledge of Greek supplemented perhaps by Hebrew, a wider range of linguistic competences is required if the New Testament texts are to be properly understood as what they truly are: an anthology of early Christian literature selected out of a much wider body of texts over a period of several centuries. As a number of contributors to this volume demonstrate, our understanding of the New Testament texts is enhanced when they are put into dialogue with their closest literary neighbours, including a significant group of texts preserved only in Ge'ez.

1

The End-Time in 1 Enoch, Paul and Matthew: Continuity and Discontinuity

Philip F. Esler

The aim of this chapter is to compare and contrast the way in which the end is represented in a selection of texts from 1 Enoch, Paul and Matthew. All of these texts have in common a passionate concern with how God will bring to a successful conclusion his dealings with a humanity enmeshed in sin and create a new order in which the power of sin has been crushed forever. While Enochic influences upon Paul and Matthew will be set out, one basic point of distinction will prove to be the maintenance of ethnic identities, especially Israel's, as relevant to certain portrayals of end-time in 1 Enoch, contrasted with the relegation of ethnic identity by Paul and its elimination by Matthew at the end-time with respect to entry into the state of salvation. In what follows I will assume what I have repeatedly argued since the early 2000s, namely, that the *Ioudaioi* are best understood as members of an ethnic group (like the others of their world). In this context, ethnic identity (as originally presented by Fredrik Barth in 1969) is constructed, self-ascriptive, and flexible over time.[1] Nevertheless, it is also generally (and diagnostically) symbolized by a common proper name to identify the group; a myth of common ancestry; a shared history or shared memories of a common past; a common culture, embracing such things as customs, language and religious practices and beliefs; a link with a homeland (having a capital, a *mētropolis*, a mother-city), and a sense of communal solidarity.[2] In this framework, religious phenomena matter, but as one aspect of a larger sense of identity that is ethnic. It is anachronistic to speak of 'religion' in relation to this world,[3] and if 'Judaism' is understood as an instance of a religion in that context, it is a category error.

---

[1] Fredrik Barth, 'Introduction', in *Ethnic Groups and Boundaries: The Social Organization of Culture Difference*, ed. Fredrik Barth (London: George Allen and Unwin, 1969), 9–38.
[2] John Hutchinson and Anthony Smith, eds, *Ethnicity* (Oxford: Oxford University Press, 1996), 3–14, at 6–7.
[3] See Brent Nongbri, *Before Religion: A History of a Modern Concept* (New Haven and London: Yale University Press, 2015), and Carlin A. Barton and Daniel Boyarin, *Imagine No Religion: How Modern Abstractions Hide Ancient Realities* (New York: Fordham University Press, 2016).

Enochic understandings of the end-time

There are two main ways to differentiate end-time scenes in 1 Enoch. The first is based on who does the judging. In most parts of the text, including the Book of Parables (1 Enoch 37–71), there are scenes where God does the judging and there is no mention of some other figure with this responsibility, such as 'the Chosen One' or 'the Son of Man'. Other scenes found in the Book of Parables do contain such a figure. The second way to differentiate these scenes, which I will focus on here, is in relation to those scenes of judgement that are connected to ethnic Israel ('the first type') in contrast to those that are not ('the second type'). The connection to ethnic Israel is typically indicated by situating the judgement within the land of Israel and/or the temple (that is, in the ethnic homeland).[4] There are two passages of the first type, in 1 Enoch 26–27 and in 1 Enoch 90.20–38, but a considerably larger number of the second.

Two examples of the first type of end-time scene
The Book of Watchers (1 Enoch 1–36)

The first chapter of 1 Enoch offers (in vv. 4–9) the reader the reassurance that God will ultimately deal with evil in the world. The Great One will come forth from his dwelling and tread upon Mount Sinai with his army. Creation will be rent. He will make peace with the righteous and bless and protect them. Coming with his myriad of holy ones, he will execute judgement on all and destroy the wicked. This passage, however, only mentions the starting points for God's mission: first heaven and then Mount Sinai, but where next? At one point later in the text Enoch is brought to a place that is clearly the site for the future Jerusalem (1 Enoch 26–27). After the topography is described (chapter 26), Enoch asks about a valley that can only be Gehenna. It is a cursed place and will be the habitation for those cursed people who speak evil things against the Lord in the last times, 'in the days of righteous judgment in the presence of the righteous for all time' (27.2–3). Although the temple is not mentioned, the righteous are living in proximity to Gehenna, so they are in Jerusalem. The framework, therefore, is ethnic Israel, with the end-time situated on the site of what will be the capital city of the homeland.

The end-time in 1 Enoch 90.20–38 (the Animal Apocalypse)

Before considering the presentation of the end-time in 1 Enoch 90.20–38, which is towards the end of the Animal Apocalypse, it will help to set out some of the textual context. 1 Enoch 89.50 recounts the construction of 'a house that became large and broad' and 'a large and high tower that was built upon that house'. The house was low, but the tower was high. 'The Lord of the sheep stood on that tower, and they spread a

---

[4] For a detailed discussion of 1 Enoch 26–27 and Angus Pryor's 2m × 2m painting thereon (reproduced in colour), see Philip F. Esler and Angus Pryor, 'Painting 1 Enoch: Biblical Interpretation, Theology, and Artistic Practice', *BTB* 50/3 (2020): 136–153, at 143–145

table before him.' In context, the house is the Jerusalem of Solomon's time and the tower is the temple that he built. 1 Enoch 89.66 records the destruction of tower and the house; this is a reference to the destruction by the Babylonians in 587 BCE. 1 Enoch 89.72b–74a relates the return from exile and the rebuilding of the fallen parts of the house (no doubt referring at least to the walls of the city) and the tower (meaning the temple), with a table before it, together with the fact that the bread put on the table was polluted and impure and the eyes of the sheep and the shepherds were blind.

The very troubled period up to the end-time, which perhaps includes allusions to the actions of Judas Maccabaeus, ends with God taking up a staff to strike the earth so that all the beasts and birds attacking the sheep fall into the earth and it covers them (90.18). Then a large sword is given to the sheep, which go out against all the wild beasts to kill them, so that all the beasts and birds of heaven flee before them (90.19). Nickelsburg suggests that a sword being given to the sheep when the Lord has been active with this staff is not unsurprising, since we find the same pattern in the Apocalypse of Weeks (93.1–10; 91.11–17). In this latter text, after the judgement, a sword is given to the righteous to execute judgement on the wicked (91.11–12). The idea seems to be that the righteous participate in an action against a wider group of non-Judeans than those with whom they have been in immediate conflict.[5]

This material finds its climax in the details of two scenes of judgement and endtime renewal. In the first scene (90.20–27), a throne is constructed in the pleasant land and the Lord of the sheep sits upon it and opens the books. Judgement is executed upon the errant stars, the seventy leaders and the blinded sheep and they are thrown into the fiery abyss. The second scene (90.28–38) begins with the old house being dismantled. Its pillars, beams and ornaments are removed and put in a place in the south of the land (90.28). Although the tower is not mentioned, presumably since it was built 'on' the house (89.50), the removal of the house entails the removal of the tower. So, the built dimension of Jerusalem and the temple are dismantled and removed. Nickelsburg is probably correct in suggesting that the 'first city and temple were destroyed because of the sins committed there. The postexilic replacement of that temple was characterized by a polluted cult.'[6]

Then the Lord of the sheep brings a new house, larger and higher than the first (with all its pillars, beams and ornaments being new and larger than those in the old) and builds it on the site of the old one (90.29). All of it is new. No mention is made here of the tower and there is a lively scholarly discussion as to whether the new Jerusalem had a temple.[7] Since a temple was really, in effect, a portal to God in heaven,[8] and God will be present in the city (90.34), it is difficult to see why a temple would be needed and this probably explains its absence here. The statement 'All the sheep are within it' (90.29) must mean that all Israel will be present in the house/city. Other birds and

---

[5] George W. E. Nickelsburg, *1 Enoch 1: A Commentary on the Book of 1 Enoch, Chapters 1–36, 81–108* (Hermeneia; Minneapolis: Augsburg Fortress, 2001), 401.
[6] Nickelsburg, *1 Enoch*, 404.
[7] See Patrick A. Tiller, *A Commentary on the Animal Apocalypse of I Enoch* (EJL 4; Atlanta, GA: Scholars Press, 1993), 45–51 and 376.
[8] Philip F. Esler, *God's Court and Courtiers: Re-interpreting Heaven in 1 Enoch* (Eugene, OR: Cascade, 2017), 110–111.

animals worship the sheep (90.30). The narrator is set down among those sheep by three figures (sc. angels) clothed in white 'before the judgment took place' (90.31–32).

At this point there is a difficult passage, in which the text, after noting that the sheep were white with abundant, clean wool, states that all that had been destroyed and dispersed (the sheep presumably) *and all the wild beasts and all the birds of heaven* (wa-kʷəllu ʾarawit gadām wa-kʷəllu ʾaʿəwāf samāy) were gathered in that house, 'and the Lord of the sheep rejoiced with great joy because they were all good and had returned to that/his house (wa-gabəʾu labētu)' (90.33). This is very odd, because how could the wild beasts and birds (non-Judean ethnic groups) be described as good or as returning to the temple? Although the Ethiopian manuscripts unanimously read wa-kʷəllu ('and all'), at the start of this statement, Nickelsburg considers this to be a mistake for '*by* all the wild beasts and birds', thus referring to the agents of the destruction and dispersal of the sheep.[9] Further below I will discuss the situation, first on the assumption that the text is correct, and, secondly, on the assumption that it requires Nickelsburg's emendation.

The issue is an important one in view of what happens next. Finally, the three angels lay down the sword and seal the house and all the sheep are enclosed in the house, but it does not contain them. All their eyes are open. The house is large and full (90.34–36). Then there is a final, very enigmatic scene, with a white bull born and all the wild beasts and birds of heaven are afraid of it and they make petition and their species are changed and they all become white cattle. The first becomes a leader, being some type of animal lurking under the Ethiopic word *nagar*, with large black horns on its head.[10] The Lord of the sheep rejoices over it and over all the cattle (90.37–38).

According to Daniel Olson,

> Most scholars read this passage (sc. 90.37–38) as indicating a universal return of all humanity to a single, Adamic state; that is, a state of primordial integrity, a state of original goodness. The Jewish sheep and the Gentile wild animals become *white cattle*, the one species which represented all of humanity from Adam until the Flood (85.3–89.10), with the important difference that here at the end of all things, there are no more black cattle to commit crimes or red cattle to be victimized. Although the text is difficult, it would appear that the mysterious white bull who appears in verse 37 serves as some sort of catalyst or harbinger of the universal transformation.[11]

In his earlier commentary, Olson takes a very similar view: he emphasizes the universalism of the allegory, arguing that it ends with the abolition of the distinction between Jew and Gentile,[12] which is a surprising stance for an author writing in the beginning years of the Maccabean revolt and a supporter of Judas. Similarly, Patrick Tiller argues that the ending of the Animal Apocalypse is universal rather than

---

[9] So Nickelsburg, *1 Enoch*, 403.
[10] On the nature of the *nagar*, see Esler and Pryor, 'Painting 1 Enoch', 142–143.
[11] Daniel C. Olson, *A New Reading of the Animal Apocalypse of 1 Enoch: 'All Nations Shall be Blessed'*, (SVTP 24; Leiden: Brill, 2013), 19–20 (emphasis original).
[12] Daniel C. Olson, in consultation with Archbishop Melkesedek Workeneh, *Enoch: A New Translation* (North Richmond Hills, TX: Bibal Books, 2004), 16.

Judeocentric. All animals eventually become white cattle (90.37–38) and, as all of humanity is thus restored to a single Adamic species, the new age is one without nationalities and conflicts.[13] Nickelsburg is similar: he concludes, although without a detailed analysis of vv. 37–38, that 'all the species representing the diversity of nations and people return to the primordial unity from which they diverged ... all the species are transformed into white bulls.'[14] Let us now consider what the text says.

1 Enoch 90.37–38 on the assumption that wa-kʷəllu *is correct*. Here the universalist reading is aided by the fact that the wild beasts and birds are within Jerusalem; that is, they are at least in physical propinquity to the sheep. But the text still throws major, indeed insurmountable, difficulties in the way of this universalist interpretation. 1 Enoch 90.37 describes all the wild animals and all the birds of heaven reacting with fear to the birth of a white bull with large horns. That is, from a mixed group of animals in the city, only the wild animals and birds react to the birth of a white bull. The sheep do not react. The wild beasts and birds also 'continually' (that is, for a period of time) make petitions to the white bull. The sheep do not. Elsewhere in 1 Enoch people or entities (such as the earth) make petitions when they find themselves in a very difficult predicament and seek relief. Since the animals and birds fear this white bull, they presumably consider that it might attack them, and are beseeching it not to. Their fearful and agitated state is very different to the happy condition of the sheep in the house as previously described. This conclusion is not dependent on the identity of the person symbolled in the white bull, if indeed the author had a particular person in mind. The fear and petitioning of the wild animals and birds now find their answer: 'And I looked until all their species (kʷəllu 'azmādihomu) were changed, and they became white cattle' (90.38a). This transformation is tied to the particular situation in which the wild animals and the birds of heaven find themselves: the solution to the fear they feel for a white bull is to become white cattle themselves, whatever their species. This section of the text has nothing to do with the sheep in the large house. To try to force the sheep within the expression 'all their species' represents a manifestly untenable interpretation of the text. In short, in the expression 'all their species (kʷəllu 'azmādihomu)' the possessive adjective is necessarily limited to the wild animals and birds of heaven, since otherwise the author would have said 'all *the* species ('azmād)'. Supporting this interpretation is the final statement: 'the Lord of the sheep rejoiced over it (sc. the *nagar*) and over all the cattle', thus recognizing the existence of two groups of animals: sheep on the one hand and cattle led by the *nagar*. Olson says that no weight can be attached to describing God as 'Lord of the sheep' since this expression is used thirty times and 'it is doubtful that its continued use here can carry a great deal of special exegetical weight'.[15] This is a highly implausible objection: why would the author persist with a now redundant, indeed inaccurate description? On the contrary, this is a deliberate step by the author to keep in play both sheep and cattle. Thus, the end-time picture is of two types of human beings: sheep, standing for Israelites, and white cattle, standing for transformed non-Israelites. A broad ethnic division between

---

[13] Tiller, *Commentary*, 20.
[14] Nickelsburg, *1 Enoch*, 406.
[15] Olson, *A New Reading*, 2013.

Israel and not-Israel is thus maintained, although both are within the new Jerusalem. This result does not depend upon the character of the mysterious *nagar*.

Kathy Ehrensperger does not really reach a final view on whether the sheep are transformed into white cattle along with the wild animals and birds. On her view, even if that were the case, the point would not be the elimination of ethnic difference but rather the overcoming of violence and destruction. While hers is an argument sensitively attuned to the text, I cannot see how the elimination of ethnic difference can be avoided if all the wild animals were to become white cattle.[16]

1 Enoch 90.37–38 on the assumption that wa-k^{w}əllu *is incorrect*. On this assumption the same result flows, although with considerable extra force, since there is now not even physical propinquity between the sheep in Jerusalem and the wild beasts and the animals outside.

Examples of the second type of end-time scene

There are numerous examples of the second type of end-time scene in 1 Enoch, where there is no stated connection with ethnic Israel.

In 1 Enoch 38, a Righteous One appears in the presence of the righteous whose works depend on the Lord of Spirits. Here, then, we appear to have a figure additional to God. Then judgement will appear, but we are not told at whose instigation. Nor is any specific geographical location, including the ethnic homeland of the Israelites, mentioned. It appears to be a world-wide process where the righteous and chosen 'who dwell on the earth' (not just in Israel) are rewarded, while sinners (38.3), the mighty and the exalted (38.4), and the kings and the mighty will perish (38.5). The fact that 'kings' are mentioned solidifies the impression that a world-wide process is in view. The perspective here is rather similar to that which appears in Matthew 25.31–46 (see below). A short judgement scene that is similarly non-specific as to place is found in 1 Enoch 41.1–2.

Equally broad in scope is the judgement described in 1 Enoch 45.3–6. The passage begins with a statement very similar to Matthew 25.31:

> On that day, my Chosen One will sit on the throne of glory,
> And he will <test> their works,
> And their dwelling places will be innumerable.[17]

God will transform heaven and earth and make them a blessing, so the arena is the cosmos, not the Israelite homeland, and he will make his chosen ones dwell upon the earth.

In 1 Enoch 51.2–5 we learn that 'my Chosen One' will arise and choose the righteous and the holy from among them. He will sit upon his throne and wisdom will go forth from his mouth. Mountains and hills will rejoice, and the angels in heaven will be

---

[16] Kathy Ehrensperger, 'The Pauline Ἐκκλησίαι and Images of Community in Enoch Traditions', in *Paul the Jew: Rereading the Apostle as a Figure of Second Temple Judaism* (Minneapolis: Fortress Press, 2016), 183–216.
[17] Translation George W. E. Nickelsburg and James C. VanderKam, *1 Enoch: The Hermeneia Translation* (Minneapolis: Fortress Press, 2012), 59.

radiant with joy. The earth will rejoice, and the righteous will dwell on it and the chosen will walk on it.

A detailed example occurs in 1 Enoch 61–62. The Lord of Spirits sits the Chosen One on the throne of glory. There he will judge all the works of the holy ones in the heights of heaven (61.8–9). This is clearly not a judgement tied to the Judean ethnic homeland but is rather cosmic in nature. The holy ones will cry out in praise of God. Also, all the chosen will bless him (61.10–12). Then, once again, the Lord of Spirits is described as seating the Chosen One on the throne of his glory. He is given the spirit of righteousness to slay all the sinners by the word of his mouth (62.1–2). All the kings and great ones who possess the earth – not just whoever might be ruling Israel – will stand up there and recognize the Chosen One and righteousness will be judged in his presence. 'And one group of them will look at the other; and they will be terrified and will cast down their faces, and pain will seize them when they see the Son of Man sitting on his throne of glory' (62.5).[18] The Son of Man was hidden but he was revealed to the chosen (62.7). The kings and powerful ones will seek mercy, but to no avail. The Lord of Spirits himself will get rid of them and they will be shamed and delivered to the angels for punishment (62.9–12). But the righteous and chosen will be saved. They will eat with the Son of Man and they will have arisen from the earth and put on the garment of glory (62.13–16). There is a summary account of this scene in 69.26–29. The Son of Man is revealed, sits on his throne of glory and all judgement is given to him. He makes sinners vanish, and those who led the world astray are bound in chains and shut up. His word will go and prevail in the presence of the Lord of Spirits.

There are numerous other brief references to the final judgement in the Book of Parables or to events thereafter (including 1 Enoch 63), commonly with respect to the time when sinners (very often the wicked elites) will be punished and the righteous rewarded. This discussion thus illustrates the large amount of material of the second type of end-time scene in 1 Enoch.

Paul

Seeking to relate Paul to passages of the first and second types of end-time scene allows us to explore significant features of his thought.

Paul and the first type of end-time scene in 1 Enoch

A lively focus of discussion in the New Testament area at present concerning Paul's relationship with his own people is the 'Paul within Judaism' movement.[19] The central idea proposed, as ably articulated by Mark Nanos, is that 'the writing and community building of the apostle Paul took place *within* late Second Temple Judaism, *within* which he remained a representative after his change of conviction about Jesus being

---

[18] Translation Nickelsburg and VanderKam, *1 Enoch*, 80.
[19] See the essays in Mark D. Nanos and Magnus Zetterholm, eds, *Paul Within Judaism: Restoring the First-Century Context to the Apostle* (Minneapolis: Fortress Press, 2015).

the Messiah (Christ)'. This also means that the assemblies that he founded 'for non-Jews as well as for Jews' were '*within* Judaism'. In saying this, Nanos defines Judaism as 'the Jewish way(s) of life'.[20] This broad definition allows him, to an extent, to circumvent the current dissatisfaction with the more widespread view that 'Judaism' was a 'religion'. Such dissatisfaction is based on the increased acceptance that 'religion' is an anachronism for the first-century Mediterranean world – which makes 'Judaism' (meaning a religion) equally problematic – and that the ancient *Ioudaioi* of our sources were the representatives of an ethnic group, one of numerous such groups existing in that world. On this approach, someone who became a Judean did not undergo a 'conversion' but a process of ethnic transfer. In my view, while it is clear that Paul was steeped in Judean tradition and that he 'expounded his message by appealing to Jewish texts, practices and customs',[21] the 'Paul within Judaism' movement underestimates the extent to which Paul regarded himself as profoundly alienated from his Judean ethnic group. While this is not the place for a detailed discussion of this topic, Romans 9.1-15 and 2 Corinthians 3 seem to me to provide strong evidence for this alienation.

Leaving aside this general objection to the idea of Paul and the Christ-groups being 'within Judaism', one particular aspect of this approach is germane to the present discussion: the notion that Paul envisaged his Christ-followers as having an ultimate destiny that was firmly within the framework of 'Judaism', which I will modify to 'within the Judean ethnic group'. While this framework certainly seems to be in place in 1 Enoch 26-27 and 90.20-38, as we have seen above, is this true of Paul? The high point of this view is that Paul believed that at the end-time his non-Judean Christ-followers would experience a fate as set out in 'Jewish restoration theology', of which 1 Enoch 90.20-38 is certainly a representative. This theology feeds off the experience of exile; it looks to the reversal of the terrible sufferings of Israel and its restoration, with twelve tribes reinstated, the people brought back to the land, Jerusalem and the temple re-established and the Davidic monarchy restored. Of great interest is that non-Judean peoples figure in many of the biblical passages concerning these events, although in a variety of ways. Some of these passages predict a negative fate for the non-Judean nations. They will be defeated, destroyed and made subservient to Israel (Isa 45.14; 60.10, 12). Their cities will be devastated or repopulated by Israel (Isa 54.3; Zeph 2.2-3, 8-14). God will destroy them and their idols (Mic 5.9, 15). Foreign kings will lick the dust at Israel's feet (Isa 49.23). They will bring gifts and wealth to Jerusalem (Isa 18.7; 45.14; 60.5, 11). They will recognize the special status of Israel among the nations: 'Let us go with you, for we have heard that God is with you' (Zech 8.23). The non-Judeans will be ruled by a Davidic messiah (Isa 11.10).[22] Yet there are also passages portraying

---

[20] Mark D. Nanos, 'Introduction', in Nanos and Zetterholm, *Paul Within Judaism*, 1–29, at 9 (emphasis original).

[21] Paula Fredriksen, 'How Jewish is God? Divine Ethnicity in Paul's Theology', *JBL* 137 (2018): 193–212, at 212.

[22] For collections of these passages see Paula Fredriksen, 'Judaism, the Circumcision of Gentiles, and Apocalyptic Hope: Another Look at Galatians 1 and 2', *JTS* 42 (1991): 532–64, at 544–5, and Loren T. Stuckenbruck, 'The Eschatological Worship of God by the Nations: An Inquiry into the Early Enoch Tradition', in *With Wisdom as a Robe: Qumran and Other Jewish Studies in Honour of Ida Fröhlich*, ed. Károly Dániel Dobos and Miklós Kőszeghy (Sheffield: Sheffield Phoenix, 2009), 189–209, at 191–2.

a positive destiny for the non-Judean peoples. They will come to Jerusalem and worship God there (Isa 66.23; Zech 14.16–19; Ps 22.27; 86.9), at times with Israel (Isa 2.2–4; Mic 4.1–2). They will eat together the feast that God has prepared (Isa 25.6).

One aspect of these passages emphasized by Paula Fredriksen, and largely accepted by the 'Paul within Judaism' scholars, is that in the end-time these non-Judean nations would not be required to become Judeans – God would accept them as they were:

> When God establishes his Kingdom, then, these two groups will together constitute 'his people': Israel, redeemed from exile, and the Gentiles, redeemed from idolatry. Gentiles are saved as Gentiles: they do not, eschatologically, become Jews.[23]

In addition:

> Eschatological Gentiles, on the other hand, those who would gain admission to the Kingdom once it was established, would enter as Gentiles. They would worship and eat together with Israel, in Jerusalem, at the Temple.[24]

This seems a reasonable account of this biblical material, except to the extent that it is probably more accurate to speak of non-Judean nations, ἔθνη, rather than to refer to them simply as 'non-Judeans' ('Gentiles', in their usage), as if talking about loose collections of individuals. The position for which Fredriksen argues also coheres quite closely with the ultimate picture in 1 Enoch 90.20–38 as discussed above. Yet it is not at all clear that in all of these biblical passages the non-Judeans were dispensed from becoming Judeans. Nevertheless, the 'Paul within Judaism' scholars argue that Paul bought into this complex of thought to explain what would happen at the end. While I will argue below that Israelite restoration theology does not represent how Paul or Matthew understood the end-time, I will reiterate that these ideas do plainly seem to have been in the minds of the Enochic authors, at least as far as 1 Enoch 26–27 and 90.20–38 are concerned. Moreover, it is likely that Matthew and perhaps Paul were influenced by this tradition, but only in a manner that allowed them radically to differentiate their views from those of the Enochic scribes in relation to the first type of end-time scene.

To my mind, a fundamental problem with attempts by the 'Paul within Judaism' scholars to tie Pauline views of the end to Israelite restoration theology is that Paul very seldom quotes any of the Old Testament passages on that topic. Moreover, even on the infrequent occasions when Paul quotes these passages, he either makes significant changes or uses them in ways that do not necessarily have any connection with Judean restoration theology. While we really need detailed exegetical proof for Paul's alignment with Judean restoration, close exegesis pushes us in the opposite direction.

Here are a few examples, beginning with Romans 11.25–26:

> Lest you be wise in your own conceits, I want you to understand this mystery, brethren: a hardening has come upon part of Israel, until the full number of the

---

[23] Fredriksen, 'Judaism', 547.
[24] Fredriksen, 'Judaism', 548.

non-Judeans come in, and so all Israel will be saved; as it is written, 'The Deliverer will come from Zion, he will banish ungodliness from Jacob'.

RSV, modified

Paula Fredriksen suggests that the fullness of the non-Judeans means 'seventy' and refers to the seventy nations in Genesis 10. The non-Judeans will come in first and then all of Israel so that the aim of Jewish restoration theology will be fulfilled, so that 'Israel and the nations might worship together in Zion'.[25] In Romans 11.26 Paul cites Isaiah 59.20. The MT speaks of the redeemer coming 'to' Zion and to them that turn from transgression in Jacob. The LXX states that the redeemer will come on account of (ἕνεκεν) Zion and will turn transgressions from Jacob. Both versions have a strong ethnic dimension, with Mount Zion/Jerusalem and Jacob the loci and objects of the redeemer's actions. Indeed, Fredriksen specifically cites Romans 11.26 for the proposition that when the Judeans and non-Judeans gather, 'they gather not just anywhere, but in Jerusalem, at the temple'.[26] One problem with this creative view is that Paul makes a very significant alteration to the source: he has the deliverer coming out of Zion, not going to it or out of concern for it. In addition, Zion serves only to identify the redeemer's point of origin (it is similar to John's 'salvation is from the Judeans', 4.22); it has nothing to say concerning the location of the end-time events. Moreover, Fredriksen's argument cuts across the whole point of Romans 11.25–26, which is not to denote an eschatological shared worship but merely to insist that, in the end, Israel will get there too, but long after most of the non-Judean nations have entered. The focus is on entry, not on what happens thereafter. And the place of the redeemer's salvific work is no longer Jerusalem, so that a basic link to Judean ethnic identity is severed.

Although Romans 15.9–12 is also brought into the argument by Fredriksen,[27] the case is difficult to maintain, since this is not a passage about the end. Romans 15.10 cites Deuteronomy 32.43 (from the end of Moses' address which has nothing to do with the end-time): 'Rejoice, O you nations, with his people', but this is a way of speaking about the subject of good relations between Judean and Greek Christ-followers in Rome, not the end-time. Similarly, Isaiah 11.10, cited by Paul in Romans 15.12 and stating that there will be a root of Jesse in whom the non-Judeans will hope, does not align Paul with restoration theology. It is just a statement that the Messiah is a Judean and a descendant of David; it again says little more than John's 'Salvation is out of the Judeans'. (A trickier question is whether in Romans 10.13 we are to take in all of Joel 2.32, about deliverance for a remnant on Mount Zion and in Jerusalem; but even so, that does not include non-Judeans.) In short, it is hard to find evidence in the Pauline correspondence that lines up his thought with the position of non-Judeans portrayed in (some only of) the restoration of Israel passages.

From this discussion flows the result that Paul's relationship with the sort of Judean thought represented in 1 Enoch 26–27 and 90.20–38 is one of discontinuity, not

---

[25] Fredriksen, 'The Question of Worship: Gods, Pagans, and the Redemption of Israel', in Nanos and Zetterholm, *Paul*, 175–201, at 197 (see also 197n48).
[26] Fredriksen, 'The Question', 197–8.
[27] Fredriksen, 'The Question', 199.

continuity. But that is not the end of the story, for we still have the second type of Enochic end-time scene to consider.

Paul and the second type of end-time scene in 1 Enoch

Here we do seem to have a case of continuity. Paul's most extended account of the end-time is found in 1 Thessalonians 4.13–18, a letter that was written for a non-Judean audience (1.9: 'you turned to God from idols'). There is no mention in this passage of Jerusalem or Zion, or Israel or Israelites for that matter.[28] It describes the *parousia* of the Lord. It is quite an Enochic picture in many respects, but it lacks ethnic marking. The Lord will come down from heaven (not even from Zion or Sinai), with a command, at the voice of an archangel and the trumpet of the Lord. But he will not land anywhere on earth, not Jerusalem, not anywhere. For the dead will rise first, and then those who are alive at that time, who will be snatched up with them into the clouds to meet the Lord *in the air*! It is difficult to know what more Paul could do to signal the irrelevance of the ethnic homeland to the end than by having the Lord meet his people as they rise towards him in the air.

In this respect, however, the passage resonates with the second type of end-time scene in 1 Enoch, in particular with the notion of the Chosen One undertaking the final judgement in the 'heights of heaven' on this throne of glory (1 Enoch 61.8). This is not actually what we have in 1 Thessalonians 4.13–18, where there is no mention of a throne of glory (an idea absent from all of Paul's letters), but as the Lord has come down from heaven it is reasonable to assume that is where he will lead those who have risen to meet him in the air, where they 'will always be with the Lord' (1 Thess 4.17). A further point of connection is the statement in 1 Enoch 61.12 that 'all who sleep not in the heights of heaven will bless him'. But most significant is a description of the resurrection in 1 Enoch 62.14–15:[29]

> And the Lord of Spirits will abide over them,
> and with that Son of Man they will eat,
> and they will lie down and rise up forever and ever.
> And the righteous and chosen will have arisen from the earth,
> and have ceased to cast down their faces
> and have put on the garment of glory.

This looks very like the glorious fate that is implied for those who rise to meet the Lord in the air in 1 Thessalonians 4.13–18. In neither case is there any ethnic qualification specified for those to be saved.

---

[28] It is surprising that this passage is not cited by anyone in Nanos and Zetterholm, *Paul*, not even by Donaldson in his chapter in the volume providing a critique of the group.
[29] Translation from Nickelsburg and VanderKam, *1 Enoch*, 81.

Matthew

This brings us, finally, to Matthew, in particular to Matthew 25.31–46. As I have recently published a discussion of this text elsewhere,[30] I will merely summarize the contents of that discussion here. The opening verse of this passage evokes the following picture:

> When the Son of man comes in his glory, and all the angels with him, then he shall sit on his glorious throne.

In the passage that follows, the 'blessed' of his Father (v. 34), the righteous (v. 37), are separated from the 'cursed' (v. 41), with the former inheriting the kingdom and eternal life, and the latter being subjected to eternal punishment. This process is not called a judgement in the passage but that is what it must be – the 'day of judgment' mentioned earlier in the Gospel (Mt 10.15; 11.22, 24; 12.36) and also 'the judgment' (Mt 12.41, 42).

It is worth noting first how much Matthew 25.31 shares with 1 Enoch, which indicates use of that text or of other traditions very similar to it. As with 1 Enoch 1.4–9, we have a movement through space of a divine figure, accompanied by his angels, the implied arrival at a place and the process of differentiation into two groups, with eternal reward for the righteous and punishment for the unrighteous.

Although there is a (muted) ethnic dimension to 1 Enoch 1.4–9, in many other parts of the text there are end-time scenes where no such features are to be found and where, more like Matthew 25.31–46, an intermediate figure is engaged in the judgement. This is the case with 1 Enoch 38, 45.3–6, 51.2–5, 61–62 and 69.26–29. Moreover, in some of those texts (notably 1 Enoch 62.14, and 69.26–29) this intermediate figure is called the Son of Man and sits on a glorious throne. In all of these passages (unlike 1 Enoch 26–27 and 90.20–38) there is no ethnic marking in the form of a judgement that is localized in Israel, neither in Jerusalem nor anywhere else.

Thus the first general point to make about Matthew 25.31–46 is that, similar to this second type of end-time scene in 1 Enoch, there is no place specified in which the Son of Man will sit on his throne and for the other events described to occur. This is significant. Situating the events of the end-time in Jerusalem reflected the important role played by the homeland, and especially its capital city with the important temples, in the construction of ethnic identity. Matthew does not take this route.

Matthew 25.32 continues the passage by stating: 'And all the nations (ἔθνη, here meaning 'ethnic groups having their own polity') will be gathered before him.' In my view, the ἔθνη mentioned here include Israel. Some scholars have argued that Israel was not included among the ἔθνη mentioned as gathered in Matthew 25.32

---

[30] Philip F. Esler, 'Ethnic Identities in the Dead Sea Legal Papyri and Matthew: Reinterpreting Matthew 25:31–46', in Daniel Gurtner and Anders Runesson, eds, *Matthew Within Judaism: Israel and the Nations in the First Gospel*, Early Christian Literature (Atlanta, GA: SBL, 197–211, 2020).

since Israel was to be judged separately, by the Twelve.[31] This suggestion depends upon Matthew 19.28:

> Jesus said to them, 'Truly, I say to you, in the renewed creation (παλιγγενεσία), when the Son of Man shall sit on his glorious throne, you who have followed me will also sit on twelve thrones, judging (κρίνοντες) the twelve tribes of Israel.'

On this view, Israel was judged separately and therefore could not be in view in Matthew 25.32. This creative idea, however, encounters an insuperable obstacle in Matthew 19.28 itself, which provides a vignette not of a scene of judgement but of that blessed state of things, the παλιγγενεσία, the 'renewed creation', which will subsist *after* the righteous have been recognized and rewarded and the evil punished. 'Judging' rather has its sense of 'leading', as frequently in the Book of Judges. It is thus not possible to argue that Matthew envisaged a final judgement with different procedures for the Judean ethnic group as opposed to non-Judean ethnic groups, in which case the ethnic boundary between Israel and the other nations would remain in place.

Yet there is an even more notable sign that Matthew did not have a judgement based on ethnic identity in mind in this passage. Although Matthew 25.31–46 is often called the 'judgment of the nations', it is not 'nations' that are judged. Critical for understanding this passage are vv. 32–33:

> And all the nations (πάντα τὰ ἔθνη) will be gathered before him, and he will separate them (αὐτούς) from one another, just as a shepherd separates the sheep from the goats, and he will set the sheep on this right and the goats on his left.

The use of αὐτούς, masculine plural, in spite of the neuter plural antecedent, ἔθνη, is of the greatest import. The suggestion that the antecedent of αὐτούς is ἔθνη, in spite of the change of gender,[32] is irreconcilable with the way the narrative develops. For there is a sharp juxtaposition here: although the nations are gathered, it is human beings, not nations, who are separated into sheep and goats. This 'implies individual rather than national judgment'.[33] This view is developed by the sheep being described as 'the blessed (εὐλογημένοι) of my father' (v. 34) and the goats as 'cursed people (κατηραμένοι)' (v. 41), with the masculine plural used in each case. This view is confirmed later when we discover that the rationale for the differentiation has been how those in the respective groups responded to individuals needing help, with whom Jesus identifies himself. The Matthean Jesus identifies six needs that are mentioned

---

[31] See Daniel J. Harrington, S.J., *The Gospel of Matthew* (Sacra Pagina 2; Collegeville, MN: Liturgical Press, 1991), 358–9, and Anders Runesson, *Divine Wrath and Salvation in Matthew: The Narrative World of the First Gospel* (Minneapolis, MN: Fortress Press, 2016), 25–31.

[32] This is argued by S. W. Gray, *The Least of My Brothers: Matthew 25:31–46: A History of Interpretation*, (SBDLS 114; Atlanta, GA: Scholars Press, 1989), 353, and Donald A. Hagner, *Matthew 14–28*, WBC 33B (Dallas, TX: Word Books, 1995), 742.

[33] Robert H. Gundry, *Matthew: A Commentary on His Literary and Theological Art* (Grand Rapids, MI: William B. Eerdmans Publishing Company, 1982), 512; similarly John Nolland, *The Gospel of Matthew: A Commentary on the Greek Text* (Grand Rapids, MI: Eerdmans, 2005), 1025.

four times and in the same order: being hungry, thirsty, a stranger, naked, sick or in prison. The word ἑνί ('to one') in the expression 'to one of the least of my brothers' (v. 40) serves 'to bring into focus individual acts done in connection with individual needs'.[34]

The character of the particular assistance that particular individuals required excludes the idea that it is nations that are responsible either for offering that assistance or refusing it. No nation as such, not even Israel, finds itself on one side or another. It is only members of the nations who are differentiated into one or another group.

Thus, the factor responsible for people finding themselves in one group or the other – with the former, the righteous (δίκαιοι),[35] who are individuals not nations, destined for eternal life, and the latter for eternal punishment (v. 46) – is how they, as individuals, treated other individuals. Thus, salvation, even for Israelites, has nothing to do with one's ethnic identity. This means that the Matthean picture is aligned with the more general and cosmic descriptions of judgement evident in the abundant second type of such scenes in 1 Enoch. The Israelite author or authors responsible for these passages in 1 Enoch and Matthew have bequeathed to us representations of ultimate reward and punishment that do not depend upon one's ethnic identity.

---

[34] Nolland, *The Gospel of Matthew*, 1031.
[35] Righteousness is a favourite concept for Matthew (Hagner, *Matthew*, 744).

2

Debating Daniel's Dream: The Synoptic Gospels and the Similitudes of Enoch on the Son of Man

Logan Williams

The tantalizingly elusive section of Daniel that mentions 'one like a son of man' offers virtually no explanation of his background, history, or identity (Dan 7.13). This figure, however, possesses cosmic and eschatological significance: in the midst of pervasive chaos, the 'one like a son of man' receives glory, universal recognition, and a kingdom that stands impenetrable to the forces of destruction (Dan 7.14). The theological reception of this figure in Second Temple Judaism indicates that its ambiguity was enticing and inviting to the interpretative imagination. The Similitudes of Enoch (1 Enoch 37–71) and New Testament texts comprise a few of the texts that creatively develop the identity of Daniel's mysterious 'one like a son of man'. Numerous recent studies, accordingly, have sought to uncover the historical and theological relationship between the interpretation of this figure in the Similitudes and early Christianity. One growing thesis among these investigations claims that the theological community responsible for penning the Similitudes provides not just one but *the* decisive context of origin which explains the shape of early Christology. For example, Gabriele Boccaccini claims that the 'cohesion in the belief of Jesus as the "Son of Man", in an exalted heavenly Messiah, the forgiver on earth and the would-be eschatological Judge' indicates that 'Enochic Judaism' was 'the kind of Judaism to which the Jesus movement was born'.[1] After outlining some points of theological continuity between Paul and the Similitudes, James Waddell confidently asserts that '[n]ow we can say with a high degree of certainty from which stream of Jewish intellectual tradition Paul

---

[1] Gabriele Boccaccini, 'Jesus the Messiah: Man, Angel, or God? The Jewish Roots of Early Christology', *Annali di Scienze Religiose* 4 (2011): 193–220, at 213–14. Those who suggest that Jesus knew the traditions in the Similitudes include e.g. D. L. Bock, 'The Use of Daniel 7 in Jesus' Trial with Implications for his Self-Understanding', in *Who is this Son of Man? The Latest Scholarship on a Puzzling Expression of the Historical Jesus* (ed. Larry Hurtado and Paul Owen; London: T&T Clark, 2011), 78–100, at 90; James H. Charlesworth, 'The Date and Provenience of the Parables of Enoch', in *The Parables of Enoch: A Paradigm Shift* (Jewish and Christian Texts 11; ed. Bock and Charlesworth; London: T&T Clark, 2013), 37–57, at 53; idem, 'Did Jesus Know the Traditions in the *Parables of Enoch*? ΤΙΣ ΕΣΤΙΝ ΟΥΤΟΣ Ο ΥΙΟΣ ΤΟΥ ΑΝΘΡΩΠΟΥ; (Jn 12:34)', in *The Parables of Enoch*, 173–217.

developed his concept of the Messiah. It was Enoch.'² While Boccaccini and Waddell acknowledge some notable differences between the New Testament texts and the Similitudes, they both suggest that the strong similarities between them signal that early Christology directly derived from the Jewish group responsible for the Similitudes.³

But, as Samuel Sandmel memorably warned us, the movement from similarity to dependence is a dangerous and perilous step, and we need to remain deeply sceptical of a certain double mistake which consists in 'that extravagance among scholars which first overdoes the supposed similarity in passages and then proceeds to describe source and derivation as if implying literary connection flowing in an inevitable or predetermined direction'.⁴ Sandmel launches both a formal and material critique here: the formal problem consists in the presumptive jump from similarity to dependence; the material problem concerns overplaying similarities between texts to justify that jump. To apply the formal critique to the present topic, whereas assertions regarding 'similarity' between the Similitudes and the New Testament require minimal evidence (one must simply identify points of conceptual contact), claims about dependence have a much higher threshold. To conclude that New Testament Christology derived or evolved from the Similitudes, we would need to prove numerous claims: that this text is pre-Christian, that it was available to other theological communities, that the New Testament authors knew its traditions, and that they utilized them in their work. But we must acknowledge that, with the limited extant evidence, determining the provenance of the Similitudes will remain a notoriously thorny and necessarily speculative task.⁵ We can only ever say that it *might* be that the Similitudes preceded the New Testament texts, it *might* be that it was not a sectarian document, it *might* be that this text or its ideas were circulated widely, it *might* be that a New Testament author came into contact with these ideas, and it *might* be that New Testament

---

² James A. Waddell, *The Messiah: A Comparative Study of the Enochic Son of Man and the Pauline Kyrios* (Jewish and Christian Texts 10; London: T&T Clark, 2013), 209; similarly, Boccaccini claims that 'Paul never uses the term "Son of Man", yet his view of the Messiah Jesus as the *kyrios* so closely resembles the *concept* of the Messiah Son of Man of the Parables that one could look at the term *kyrios* as a convenient translation and development in Hellenistic terms of the Enochic concept' ('Finding a Place for the Parables of Enoch within Second Temple Jewish Literature', in *Enoch and the Messiah Son of Man: Revisiting the Book of Parables* (ed. G. Boccaccini; Grand Rapids: Eerdmans, 2007), 263–89, at 278). However, *pace* Boccaccini and Waddell, see Chris Tilling, *Paul's Divine Christology* (WUNT II/323; Tübingen, Mohr Siebeck, 2012), 206–30, esp. 227.

³ Differences are acknowledged in Boccaccini, 'Jesus the Messiah', 212–13; Waddell, *The Messiah*, 184–6.

⁴ Samuel Sandmel, 'Parallelomania', *JBL* 81 (1962): 1–13, at 1.

⁵ For those who support a Jewish provenance and first-century BCE to first-century CE date, see e.g. Boccaccini, 'The Enoch Seminar at Camaldoli: Re-entering the Parables of Enoch in the Study of Second Temple Judaism and Christian Origins', in *Enoch and the Messiah*, 3–16 and the chapters on dating in *Enoch and the Messiah*, 415–97. More support for this dating is found in Charlesworth, 'Date and Provenance' and George W. E. Nickelsburg and James C. VanderKam, *1 Enoch 2: A Commentary, Chapters 37–82* (Hermeneia; Minneapolis: Fortress, 2012), 58–62. However, Ted Erho has problematized the confidence of an early dating in various essays, namely 'Historical-Allusion Dating and the Similitudes of Enoch', *JBL* 130 (2011): 493–511; idem, 'Internal Dating Methodologies and the Problem posed by the Similitudes of Enoch', *JSP* 20 (2010): 83–103; idem, 'The Ahistorical Nature of 1 Enoch 56:5–8 and its Ramifications upon the Opinio Communis on the Dating of the Similitudes of Enoch', *JSJ* 40 (2009): 23–54.

authors appropriated these ideas into their work. Even if we considered all of these assertions to be *mostly* probable, the multiplication rule of probability means that when these numerous yet indeterminate possibilities are taken together, any confidence that the similarities between early Christological concepts and 'Enochic Judaism' indicate a relationship of direct dependence ends up standing on dangerously thin statistical ice.[6]

My intention here, however, is to concentrate Sandmel's material objection onto some of the recent comparisons between the Synoptic Gospels and the Similitudes. Sandmel's recognition of interpreters 'overdoing supposed similarity', I think, aptly captures some of the latest scholarship which attempts to connect the Similitudes to early Christology. While I would not deny the real similarity between these two texts (as noted, they comprise some of the texts which explicitly develop Daniel 7.13–14), I do want to problematize the extent of the stated similarity between them. The two edges of my thesis here are, first, that the interpretation of the 'Son of Man' figure in the Synoptics presents a reading of Daniel 7 which in some respects deeply contrasts with the image of the Son of Man in the Similitudes; but, second, these dissimilar elements have been downplayed because studies on the relationship between 1 Enoch and the canonical gospels regularly utilize a *religionsgeschichtlich* method which is unable to recognize such differences. Here I tackle these two claims in reverse order: I begin by reviewing the method of some select recent approaches and suggesting a new model which might deepen our understanding of the theological relationship between 1 Enoch and the Synoptics. I then illustrate instances in which the 'Son of Man' epithet in the canonical gospels directly conflicts with the theology proferred by the Similitudes.

A paradigm shift?

John M. G. Barclay suggests that New Testament scholarship has generally moved away from what he calls the 'genealogical' approach to the relationship between early Christianity and Judaism. In his own words,

> There was a time when Christian scholars saw the study of pre-Christian (including early Jewish) literature as the search for the roots of Christian language and ideas – a genealogical exercise concerned first and foremost with tradition-history, founded on the capacity to set texts in a clear chronological sequence ... The hermeneutical traffic in this exercise was always one-way: one travelled from earlier sources to illuminate later texts and traditions. There was always a temptation to *underplay* difference, in order to discover similarities and thus connection ...[7]

---

[6] Even if we attributed a generous 80 per cent probability for every item in this list, the resulting probability would be 32.768 per cent.
[7] John M. G. Barclay, 'Constructing a Dialogue: 4 Ezra and Paul on the Mercy of God', in *Anthropologie und Ethik im Frühjudentum und im Neuen Testament* (ed. M. Konradt and E. Schläpfer; WUNT 322; Tübingen: Mohr Siebeck, 2014), 3–22, at 4 (emphasis original).

Barclay recalls this approach as if it were from a bygone era of scholarship existing only in distant memory. While this might well be true for most subsectors of studies comparing Jewish and Christian texts, this genealogical method has been the default *modus operandi* deployed by many investigations into the relationship between the Similitudes and the gospels. For example, Leslie Walck's study comparing Matthew and the Similitudes sets out to 'to bring Literary, Redaction, Sociological and Narrative Criticism to bear on the question to elucidate the relationships', but the investigation into these relationships is explicitly limited to the 'positive relationship' between the two texts.[8] When Walck arrives at the Matthean material, he therefore deems any differences between the two texts hermeneutically irrelevant: 'The earthly sayings and the suffering sayings can be excluded a priori since the Enochic view of the Son of Man is of a future, non-suffering Figure.'[9] James D. G. Dunn introduces one essay by claiming that he is inquiring (only) into 'possible influence of the Son of Man imagery in the *Parables of Enoch* upon the Gospel of Mark'.[10] In the preface to *The Parables of Enoch: A Paradigm Shift*, James Charlesworth lays out a list of ten questions which the volume seeks to answer, but whereas two of them ask whether the Similitudes exerted any influence upon the historical Jesus, virtually *none* of their stated questions concern potential theological divergence between the texts.[11] Charlesworth takes this methodological approach because he 'consider[s] it paradigmatically important to discern "Who influenced whom?"'[12] These kinds of genetic, linear analyses which only look for positive similarities could be listed *ad nauseam*.[13]

The restricted scope of this genealogical method can produce two specific problems. First, the studies which concern themselves primarily or solely with drawing out the presence of 'similarities' or 'parallels' in order to discover 'influence' can end up eclipsing and avoiding most, if not all, other potentially fruitful lines of historical inquiry. If explaining the origin of a thing is never sufficient for understanding it (a contrary position would commit a historical version of the genetic fallacy), then the scope of these genetic investigations has problematically limited *a priori* the range of historical and theological questions and thereby also radically constricted the range of possible conclusions. Second, the narrow vision of this method can result in distorting the textual and theological relationship between the canonical gospels and the Similitudes. The confident assertion that early Christology derived from 'Enochic Judaism' can easily emerge from a self-confirming methodological feedback loop: investigations which only look for similarities or 'positive influence' are already on track to find no notable or significant differences. Screening out differences *a priori* from the scope of

---

[8] L. W. Walck, *The Son of Man in the Parables of Enoch and in Matthew* (Jewish and Christian Texts in Contexts and Related Studies 9; London: T&T Clark, 2011), ix, 2; cf. 252.
[9] Ibid, 165.
[10] J. D. G. Dunn, 'The Son of Man in Mark', in *The Parables of Enoch*, 18–34, at 18.
[11] Charlesworth, 'Foreword', in *The Parables of Enoch*, ix–xi, at x.
[12] Ibid, x; cf. his similar statement in 'Did Jesus Know', 173.
[13] For some more examples, see Walck, 'The Son of Man in the *Parables of Enoch* and the Gospels', in *Enoch and the Messiah*, 299–337; Charlesworth, 'Did Jesus Know'; G. Macaskill, 'Matthew and the *Parables of Enoch*', in *The Parables of Enoch*, 173–217; L. M. McDonald, 'The *Parables of Enoch* in Early Christianity', in *The Parables of Enoch*, 329–63.

an investigation, or considering divergence mostly irrelevant, can too quickly give way to announcing complete conceptual overlap between texts in places where there is, in fact, only superficial similarity or even none whatsoever.

The persistent genealogical approach exhibited by these studies thus calls into question the claim that the general acceptance of a Jewish provenance for the Similitudes at the 2005 Camaldoli Enoch Seminar inaugurated a 'paradigm shift'.[14] According to the seminal work by Thomas Kuhn, who coined this term, a paradigm shift signals that a change in *method* has occurred, not just a shift in *conclusion*.[15] Even if radically divergent from what preceded, the emergence of a 'new consensus' cannot automatically be equated with a new paradigm.[16] While the generally positive reception of the Jewish provenance of the Similitudes remains important for the study of Judaism and Christian origins, the fundamental methods utilized to evaluate the relationship between the Similitudes and early Christology have not changed: scholarship prior to this consensus also focused mostly on the question of influence.[17] Because most studies still utilize a *religionsgeschichtlich* approach which sets its eye only on similarity and downplays dissimilarity – put another way, because *there is no substantial methodological discontinuity between pre-2005 and post-2005 scholarship* – the 2005 Camaldoli Enoch Seminar did not trigger a paradigm shift, at least in the Kuhnian sense.

I am not suggesting that these kinds of genetic investigations are *ipso facto* inappropriate or unfruitful. But I am suggesting some of the scholarship on this issue has been unbalanced insofar as it has neither sufficiently considered the differences between the Similitudes and the gospels nor what possible conclusions these divergences might produce. To ask a new question with Charlesworth's words, might it not also be of 'paradigmatic importance' to press deeply into how the Similitudes and the gospels *differ*? And might these differences in fact help us understand each of these texts in more depth? To produce an affirmative answer to these questions requires an alternative method which can interpret and evaluate where the gospels theologically stand vis-à-vis the Similitudes. The model proposed below, I think, promises to yield some fresh interpretative results and might – to use Kuhn's words – push us towards a methodological 'crisis'.[18]

A dialogical model

The method of some of the studies on the Son of Man in the Similitudes and the gospels can be depicted as such:

---

[14] Charlesworth, 'Preface: The Books of Enoch: *Status Quaestionis*', in *The Parables of Enoch*, xiii–xvii, at xiii.
[15] T. S. Kuhn, *The Structure of Scientific Revolutions* (4th ed.; Chicago: University of Chicago Press, 2012), 43–53, 111–34.
[16] These are conflated in Charlesworth and Bock, 'Conclusion', in *The Parables of Enoch*, 364–72, at 364.
[17] See e.g. J. Theisohn, *Der auserwählte Richter: Untersuchungen zum traditionsgeschichtlichen Ort der Menschensohngestalt der Bilderreden des Äthiopischen Henoch* (Studien zur Umwelt des Neuen Testaments 12; Göttingen: Vandenhoeck & Ruprecht, 1975), 161–81.
[18] Kuhn, *Structure*, 52–76.

But investigating the holistic relationship between these two bodies of literature necessitates more than focusing solely on positive influence. We need, as Francis Watson suggests, to look beyond 'unilinear movement' by moving into the realm of 'interaction', into the world of *dialogue*.[19] Dialogue, of course, is only possible if two parties stand on some common ground, and in this case the shared space is the fact that the Similitudes and the gospels exist in a 'single intertextual field' as they receive, interpret and deploy the Son of Man figure from Daniel 7.[20] Placing them on this common hermeneutical territory thus positions them in enough proximity for us to construct a conversation between them regarding the meaning, significance and implications of Daniel's dream – to have them question, confirm, interrogate, and even object to one another. In this model, the gospels and the Similitudes have their own appropriation of the material from Daniel, which opens up the possibility to bring them to engage each other precisely *qua* interpreters of Daniel. A complex model that incorporates these aspects looks like this:

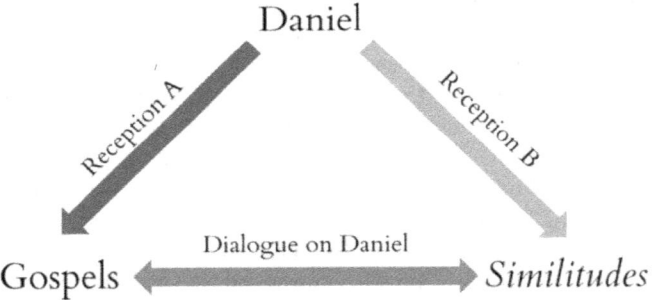

If Sandmel's objection regarding 'overdoing supposed similarity' applies to some of the scholarship on the Similitudes and the Synoptics, then this imbalance calls for a focus on the points of disagreement between them. To state the thesis of the rest of the chapter in Watson's language, the Similitudes and the gospels read the same text about the Son of Man in Daniel 7, but they read it differently, realizing the semantic potential of Daniel's dream in divergent directions and utilizing this figure for different purposes within their distinctive theological visions. To illustrate this, we can listen in on a hypothetical conversation between the Son of Man in the Similitudes and the gospels on three issues: 1) the function of the Son of Man's authority; 2) the nature of the Son of Man's representation of his people; and 3) the object of the Son of Man's salvific activity.

---

[19] F. Watson, *Paul and the Hermeneutics of Faith* (London: T&T Clark, 2004), 4; cf. the proposed dialogical method in Barclay, 'Constructing a Dialogue', and J. A. Linebaugh, 'Debating Diagonal Δικαιοσύνη: The Epistle of Enoch and Paul in Theological Conversation', *EC* 1 (2010): 107–28.

[20] Watson, *Paul*, 3.

The function of authority

As a textual reaction to horrific injustices, the Similitudes wrestles with the theological possibility of hope in the face of suffering. In this text, a group of elites identified variously as those who possess the land, the mighty (*ḥayyālān*), the kings (*nagaśt*), the strong (*ṣənu'ān*), the powerful (*'azizān*) and the exalted (*lə'ulān*) have committed acts of violence against the righteous and possess unjustly acquired land from which they exploit and persecute the author's community (1 Enoch 46.7; 47.4; 53.7; 55.4; 62.11; 63.10).[21] As Suter notes, the author speaks to a community that perceives a cosmic injustice in 'the world that does not seem to be structured according to the laws of their God' and that challenges 'their belief in a God who, as the divine lawgiver, rewards in concrete ways the community of his chosen ones when it is faithful to his law'.[22] Responding to the utter theological disorder presented in the prospering of the wicked over against the persecuted righteous, the Similitudes hopes, expects and predicts a soon-to-be massive political upheaval of cosmic proportions consisting in 'the overthrow or fall of the oppressive order and the establishment of a new society'.[23] In the midst of the theological tension between the disenfranchisement of the righteous and the success of those who exploit them, the promise of radical eschatological reversal provides hope for the righteous and a theological defence of divine justice: God will invert the fortunes of sinners by evicting the mighty from their place (38.2) and will thereby vindicate the righteous, enabling them to judge their oppressors and to dwell in their rightful land (38.4). In the end, God will neither abandon the righteous nor permit the victory of their oppressors.

The author of the Similitudes does not simply state that those who have committed such radical injustices and horrific acts of oppression will be judged; the author also explicates the means by which this judgement will come. Drawing from the deep well of the Jewish scriptural heritage, the text holds out the promise that the one to enact these eschatological upheavals will be the Danielic Son of Man (e.g. 46.4). One such section of the Similitudes that retrieves the vision from Daniel 7 is Enoch's vision in 52.1-9. The salvific figure here is called not 'the Son of Man' but 'the Chosen One' (*ḫəruy*), yet, since the author consistently weaves together scriptural lexemes and motifs to describe Daniel's Son of Man in various terms – such as 'his Anointed One' (*masiḫu*) or 'the Righteous One' (*ṣādəq*) – the lack of 'Son of Man' should not deter us from seeing Daniel's figure here.[24] One piece of evidence suggesting that this section

---

[21] For the various identifiers for these elites see 38.4-5; 48.8; 62.1, 3; 62.6, 9; 63.1, 12; 67.12. On this theme see Pierluigi Piovanelli, 'A Testimony of the Kings and the Mighty who Possess the Earth: The Thirst for Justice and Peace in the Parables of Enoch', in *Enoch and the Messiah*, 363-79, at 372-3.

[22] David W. Suter, *Tradition and Composition in the Parables of Enoch* (SBLDS 47; Missoula: Scholars Press, 1979), 164.

[23] Ibid, 164.

[24] On the identity between these figures, see VanderKam, 'Righteous One, Messiah, Chosen One, and Son of Man in 1 Enoch 37-71', in *The Messiah: Developments in Earliest Judaism and Christianity* (ed. Charlesworth; Minneapolis: Fortress, 1992), 169-201 (*pace* the questioning of Tilling, *Paul's Divine Christology*, 213-14). The use of the epithet 'The Son of the Offspring of the Mother of all Living' (62.7; 69.26, 27; 69.29; 71.17) is also equivalent to 'Son of Man'. On this see Jan Dochhorn, 'Die Menschen als 'Kinder der Mutter der Lebenden' – eine etymologische Parallele zu êm kol-chaj in Gen 3,20 aus dem Altäthiopischen', *Zeitschrift für Althebraistik* 12 (1999): 2-20.

pulls from Daniel 7 is that it imitates the language and structure of Daniel's judgement scene:

> And in those days, none will save himself either by gold or silver, and none will be able to flee. And there will not be iron for war, nor a garment for a breastplate; copper will be of no use, and tin will be reckoned as nothing, and lead will not be desired. All these will be rejected and be destroyed from the face of the earth, when the Chosen One appears before the Lord of Spirits (*soba yāstar'i ḫəruy ba-qədma gaṣṣu la-'əgzi' manāfəst*).
>
> 1 Enoch 52.7–9

The definitive moment when the Chosen One appears (*yāstar'i*) before the Lord of the Spirits draws from the scene in Daniel 7 in which the Son of Man 'comes' (מטה) to the Ancient of Days and 'they present' or 'offer' the Son of Man (הקרבוהי) before him (Dan 7.13; cf. 1 Enoch 49.2). To strengthen this connection, in both Daniel and 1 Enoch the presence of each figure before God is closely tied to divine judgement over the world and its injustice: in Daniel the offering of the Son of Man is preceded and followed by the judgement and dethroning of the beasts (7.11–12, 17–18) and thus parallels how in 1 Enoch the appearance of the Chosen One before the Lord of Spirits happens concomitantly with the Son of Man purging the cosmos (52.9).

The beginning of this scene in 1 Enoch 52 draws on a more specific element of Daniel 7 – the 'authority' of the Son of Man:

> And he said to me, 'These things which you have seen are for the authority of his Anointed One (*la-śəlṭāna masiḥu*), so that he will be powerful and mighty on the earth (*ya'azzəz wa-yəthāyyal diba mədr*).'
>
> 52.4

Although he is called 'his Anointed One' (*masiḥu*), the invocation of 'authority' (*śəlṭān*) in a scene which recounts the judgement of Daniel 7 hearkens back to the 'authority' (שלט [= same root]) given to the Son of Man in Daniel 7.14.[25] Two more points can be made about this. First, the 'authority' belonging to the Son of Man establishes his power and might *on earth* (*diba mədr*) (52.4); second, that this authority that makes him 'powerful and mighty (*ya'azzəz wa-yəthāyyal*)' strikes an intentional contrast to the unjust kings described as both 'powerful' (*'azzizān*) and 'mighty' (*ḫayyālān*). Applying these descriptors to the Son of Man signals that by receiving divine authority he will be 'powerful and mighty' so as to displace the sinful 'powerful and mighty' kings who have oppressed the righteous.[26] This becomes clearer in the repetition of this material in 1 Enoch 53, in which the author predicts that 'the kings of the mighty of the earth' will 'perish' (53.5) by the 'instruments of Satan' (53.3), which happens when 'the Chosen one will cause the house of this congregation to appear' (53.6), giving them 'rest from

---

[25] So also Nickelsburg and VanderKam, 1 Enoch 2, 189–90. However, the Ge'ez translations of Dan 7.14 use *makwannən* for שלט.

[26] Nickelsburg and VanderKam, 1 Enoch 2, 190.

the oppression of the sinners' (53.7). To reiterate, these elements from Daniel are retrieved to instil hope: the authority identified in Daniel 7.14 is not just an ambiguous, static authority; it is rather hermeneutically specified and applied to the author's present situation to promise that by this authority the Son of Man will vindicate the righteous from their present experience of oppression. The Similitudes here engages in a hermeneutic of theodicy by invoking Danielic authority to defend God's commitment to justice: the function of the eschatological authority of the Son of Man is to overturn sinful structures by destroying the unrighteous and reinstating the rightful prospering of the righteous. This brings us to Jesus' appeal to that very same authority in Mark.

In Mark 2 a paralytic man unable to access Jesus is let down from the roof just in front of him (Mk 2.4). Seeing this, Jesus declares that the paralytic's sins are forgiven (ἀφίενταί σου αἱ ἁμαρτίαι) (2.5), but the scribes and Pharisees accuse him of blaspheming. Jesus retorts to this challenge by exhorting his audience to 'know (εἰδῆτε) that the Son of Man has authority on earth to forgive sins (ἐξουσίαν ἔχει ὁ υἱὸς τοῦ ἀνθρώπου ἀφιέναι ἁμαρτίας ἐπὶ τῆς γῆς)' (2.10).[27] A few factors point to the conclusion that Jesus here appeals to Daniel 7.13-14. First, the phrase 'the Son of Man has authority', like 1 Enoch 52.4, strongly evokes the language of Daniel that the Son of Man 'was given authority'.[28] Second, the Similitudes claims that Daniel's Son of Man has authority *on earth (diba mədr)*; thus, there is another text that weaves together 'Son of Man', 'authority' and 'on earth', which points to Daniel 7. Third, an appeal to authoritative scripture fits the context of conflict here: given that Jesus elsewhere appeals to scripture when he is accused of wrongdoing (Mk 2.25-27), it would not be a stretch to suggest that he responds to the accusation of blasphemy by arguing that he can forgive sins because the Danielic Son of Man can forgive sins. Fourth, Jesus clearly appeals to Daniel 7.13 elsewhere (e.g. Mk 14.62), which strengthens the hypothesis that the language would also evoke Daniel 7 here.

Jesus asserts that his possession of this Danielic divine authority permits and enables him to forgive sins. It is possible, of course, to try to decipher how this interpretation of Daniel 7.14 in Mark 2.10 came about and what parallels or precedents there are for this reading.[29] But this way of interpreting the Son of Man is only one *possible* way of

---

[27] For a grammatical solution to the confusing ἵνα-clause here, see T. Daiber "Wisset!' Zu einem angeblichen Anakoluth in Mk 2,10 bzw. zum ὅτι recitativum', *ZNW* 104 (2013): 277-85, esp. 282, who suggests that ἵνα ... εἰδῆτε functions as an imperative; Daiber's analysis gives some grammatical foundations to the treatment in M. Wolter, "Ihr sollt aber wissen ...': Das Anakoluth nach ἵνα δὲ εἰδῆτε in Mk 2,10-11 parr', *ZNW* 95 (2004): 269-75.

[28] Some have doubted whether there is any appeal to Daniel here (e.g. Larry W. Hurtado, 'Summary and Concluding Observations', in *Who is This Son of Man?*, 159-77, esp. 166; R. Leicester, 'Exit the Apocalyptic Son of Man', *NTS* 18 (1971-72): 243-67; Geza Vermes, 'The Son of Man Debate Revisited: 1960-2012', *The Parables of Enoch*, 1-17. But see the critique in Crispin H. T. Fletcher-Louis, *Jesus Monotheism*, 120-3, 179-82). Those who do see an appeal to Daniel here include J. Marcus, 'Authority to Forgive Sins on Earth', *The Gospels and the Scriptures of Israel* (ed. C. A. Evans and W. R. Stegner; JSNTSup 104; Studies in Scripture in Early Judaism and Christianity 3; Sheffield: Sheffield Academic, 1994), 196-211; idem, *Mark 1-8: A New Translation with Introduction and Commentary* (AB 27; New Haven: Yale University Press, 2002), 208, 531; D. Boyarin, 'How Enoch can Teach us About Jesus', *EC* 2 (2011): 51-76, esp. 75-6; A. Y. Collins, *Mark: A Commentary* (Hermeneia; Minneapolis: Fortress, 2007), 187-9.

[29] So Marcus, 'Authority to Forgive Sins on Earth', 205-6.

theologically receiving and realizing the authority bestowed upon the Son of Man in Daniel 7.14, which is neither realized in the Similitudes nor demanded by Daniel in the first place. We cannot assert, as Walck does, that simply because 'authority' is mentioned in 1 Enoch, 'Authority to forgive must be assumed as part of the depiction [of the Son of Man] in the *Parables*'.[30] There is just no reason to state that any such appeal to 'authority' and judgement in the Similitudes automatically implies anything about the power to forgive, and we cannot assume that everyone would have found this interpretation of the 'authority' the Son of Man plausible and acceptable.

In fact, here the Similitudes and Mark radically diverge in their application of the authority from Daniel 7.14. The point of contention between the Similitudes and Mark's Jesus has less to do with the *location* of his authority – both texts say that the Son of Man has authority on earth – and more to do with the *shape* and *function* of that authority. In the Similitudes, the authority given to the Son of Man is the means by which he is empowered to vindicate the righteous and displace the kings and mighty on the earth by himself being powerful and mighty on the earth; in Mark, it is the basis for his ability to forgive such sinners.[31] My point here is not that the Similitudes has a theological stance against forgiveness (it does not) or that Mark's Jesus has nothing to do with judging sinners (he does). My point is that the use and explicated function of the Son of Man's 'authority' from Daniel 7.14 runs in a divergent direction in each text: whereas in the Similitudes this Danielic authority empowers the Son of Man to displace sinners, in Mark it permits him to forgive them. To the author of the Similitudes, the use of the Son of Man's 'authority' for the purpose of forgiveness would appear theologically superfluous. The Son of Man comes to solve the present empirical-theological mismatch of the suffering righteous and prospering oppressors. Jesus' invocation of Daniel 7 in Mark 2 stands within a theological contention agreeable to the Similitudes (namely, that God forgives), but the Enochic author might object to the use of Daniel 7 to argue for this point. Right doctrine, wrong text.

Representation or identification?

Daniel correlates the Son of Man with the 'holy ones of the most high' by claiming that the Son of Man and the people of God both receive the kingdom (7.14, 19).[32] This

---

[30] Walck, 'The Son of Man', in *Enoch and the Messiah*, 316. There is an offer for forgiveness in 1 Enoch 50.2, but the Son of Man does not participate in this scene. As for the kings and the mighty, their repentance and confession is met with rejection (63.1–12), and their faces are ashamed in the presence of the Son of Man (63.11). So Boccaccini recognizes that 'The Book of Parables does not attribute forgiveness to the Messiah, who remains the judge and destroyer of evil' ('Forgiveness of Sins: An Enochic Problem, a Synoptic Answer', in *Enoch and the Synoptic Gospels: Reminiscences, Allusion, Intertextuality* (EJL 44; ed. Loren T. Stuckenbruck and Boccaccini; Atlanta: SBL, 2016), 153–67, at 161).

[31] This contrasts with Savino Chialà's assertion that the point of contention in Mark 2 concerns the location of the Son of Man's authority ('The Son of Man: The Evolution of an Expression', in *Enoch and the Messiah*, 153–78, at 163–4).

[32] This should not, however, lead us to equate the 'Son of Man' with the people of God, especially since that reading of Daniel 7 is attested nowhere in early Jewish readings of Daniel, *pace* e.g. N. T. Wright, *The New Testament and the People of God* (Minneapolis, Fortress: 1992), 291–9.

correlation is taken up and expanded in the Similitudes as it consistently portrays the Son of Man as the 'heavenly representative' of the righteous: the Son of Man is called 'the Chosen One' (ḥəruy), and the community is called 'the chosen ones' (ḥəruyān) (39.6; 40.5; 45.3); when he appears before the Lord of Spirits, they appear as well (45.3; 52.9; 53.6); they will live together in the land (45.4-5) and the salvation of the righteous is contained within the eschatological victory enacted by the Son of Man (51.5; 61.4-5).[33]

Paul Owen suggests that the correlation between the righteous and the Son of Man implies that the Son of Man is also a 'suffering figure', especially given the association between the Son of Man and Wisdom (e.g. 46.3), the latter of which is sent into the world but finds no place in which to dwell (42.1-2).[34] But this stretches the text well beyond its breaking point, and the eagerness to suggest a suffering Son of Man in 1 Enoch likely exhibits a tendency to collapse this text into the theology of the gospels as opposed to respecting its own theological integrity. To reply to Owen, Wisdom responds to finding no place on earth by simply returning to heaven to dwell with angels, and this rejection does not hint toward any experience of suffering; on the contrary, those who reject the Lord of Spirits (38.1; 45.2; 67.8) and his messiah (48.1) bring God and his agent no grief. These sinners are simply obliterated by the Son of Man for rejecting him (52.9).[35]

In this connection, we should note how the Similitudes receives and interprets Isaiah's servant songs. Nickelsburg, VanderKam and Theisohn point out striking parallels between 1 Enoch and the Isaianic servant passages (specifically 1 Enoch 62-63 and Isa 52.13-53.12).[36] But, curiously, the Son of Man in 1 Enoch, albeit apparently identified with the Isaianic servant, shows no hint of suffering. Here we need to be cautious as to how we interpret one text's use of another. Utilizing the suggestion of Richard Hays - that if text A 'echoes' the language or themes of text B, it signals that text A is retrieving the broader context of text B - would in fact obscure the unique reception of Isaianic material in 1 Enoch.[37] It is always possible that the reception and use of one text in another will not be naturally intuitive. If we applied Hays' method here, should we not conclude that the multiple echoes of Isaiah 52-53 imply that the Son of Man is also the servant, who undeniably suffers in Isaiah 53? But what makes the interpretation of Isaiah in 1 Enoch so interesting is that the author identifies the Son of Man as Isaiah's servant *without* suggesting or even implying that he suffers. And we should not try to read this theme into the text where it is not.[38]

---

[33] This list and the phrase 'heavenly representative' are taken from H. S. Kvanvig, 'The Son of Man in the Parables of Enoch', in *Enoch and the Messiah*, 179-215, at 192.
[34] Owen, 'Aramaic and Greek Representations of the "Son of Man" and the Importance of the Parables of Enoch', in *The Parables of Enoch*, 114-23, at 123.
[35] So Nickelsburg rightly states that 'Wisdom not finding a home is not suffering' ('Did Jesus Know', 203).
[36] Nickelsburg and Vanderkam, 1 Enoch 2, 258; Theisohn, *Der auserwählte Richter*, 118-26.
[37] As suggested in R. B. Hays, *Echoes of Scripture in the Letters of Paul* (New Haven: Yale University Press, 1989).
[38] So rightly E. Sjöberg, *Der Menschensohn im äthiopischen Henochbuch* (Skrifter Utgivna av Kungliga Humanistika Vetenskapssamfundet i Lund 4; Lund: GWK Gleerup, 1946), 116-39, esp. 139; Nickelsburg and Vanderkam, 1 Enoch 2, 259; cf. Walck, 'The Son of Man in the Parables of Enoch and the Gospels', 319.

Thus, the Son of Man in the Similitudes, while he *represents* the righteous and acts on their behalf, does not *identify* with them by participating in the pain of their oppression (notwithstanding the numerous other correlations between the Son of Man and the righteous). In fact, it may be that the lack of a suffering Son of Man in the Similitudes fits perfectly within its theological logic: that the Son of Man will overcome but not experience their suffering gives readers hope that one day their oppression will be reversed when he victoriously triumphs in forcefully displacing the wicked rulers.

Luke, however, has a different vision. Although many have debated the presence of Isaiah 52–53 in Mark, that Luke interprets Jesus as the Isaianic servant is clear when he explicitly ties these Isaianic texts to Jesus' life (e.g. Lk 22.37; Acts 8.32–33).[39] What is peculiar, however, is that the theme of suffering, taken from the language and theology of Isaiah, is often connected with the epithet 'Son of Man' as opposed to 'servant' (9.22, 44; cf. 22.22). For example, Jesus claims that

> everything that is written about the Son of Man by the prophets will be accomplished. For he will be delivered over to the Gentiles and will be mocked and shamefully treated and spit upon. And after flogging him, they will kill him, and on the third day he will rise.
>
> 18.31–33

But where is it *written* that he will endure such suffering? Searching through the Hebrew Bible would produce no direct result; the Son of Man is never said to experience any adverse situation or hardship in Daniel 7. However, if Luke's Jesus has already identified the Son of Man from Daniel 7 with the suffering servant from Isaiah 53, then this claim makes sense: it is, in fact 'written' that the Son of Man will suffer (cf. Lk 24.25), because the figure from Isaiah 53 is also the Son of Man from Daniel 7.

In one section retrieving Isaianic material, Jesus claims that 'this scripture must be fulfilled in me, "And he was counted among the lawless"; and indeed, what is written about me is being fulfilled' (Lk 22.37). Because his suffering is portrayed as 'being counted with' sinners (Isa 53.12) – and this is precisely what happens when Jesus is crucified alongside two other criminals (Lk 23.32–33) – we can say that Luke's Jesus, as the figure from Isaiah 53 and the Son of Man, *identifies* with the lawless and thus shares with and participates in their experience of suffering.

One suggestion in this regard is that the suffering Son of Man is 'grounded in a concept that is common to both the Parables of Enoch and the Synoptics: identification of the savior figure with the oppressed and action on their behalf'.[40] But we have to be wary of reading the gospels back into 1 Enoch here. That the Son of Man represents the suffering saints in Daniel 7 does not need to imply that he also suffers: *representation does not necessarily entail participation*. The Similitudes, through interpreting Isaiah and Daniel, gives hope to its readers by promising to the righteous that the Son of Man

---

[39] On this theme see more recently H. Beers, *The Followers of Jesus as the 'Servant': Luke's Model from Isaiah for the Disciples in Luke-Acts* (LNTS 535; London: T&T Clark, 2015).

[40] Walck, 'The *Parables of Enoch* and the Synoptic Gospels', in *The Parables of Enoch*, 231–68, at 242.

will represent them and act on their behalf by displacing their sinful oppressors; Luke's Jesus claims that part of his salvific action as Daniel's Son of Man includes the Isaianic motif of direct identification with and *participation* in the experience and punishment of sinners. Thus, both Luke's Jesus and the Similitudes weave together the identities of the figures from Daniel 7 and Isaiah 53, but their readings of these texts and the soteriological actions of this composite figure starkly diverge within their own theological parameters. For the Similitudes, the Son of Man acts on behalf of the suffering righteous by overcoming their enemies – that is, by *not* being overcome by the exploitative kings and mighty. The hope of the righteous thus hangs on the essential asymmetry between their present experience and the experience of the Son of Man. He will be the one righteous individual who, when met with rejection, will experience no exploitation or defeat but rather dethrone those who perpetuate injustice in the land. For the suffering righteous, victory is found in the Son of Man's use and demonstration of his absolute power over those unjust kings. Jesus' participation in the judgement of sinners would actually appear disheartening to the author of the Similitudes, since this would mean that the Son of Man experiences the judgement which he is meant to enact upon others. Here the Similitudes' conversation with the gospels thus moves from a somewhat minor hermeneutical quibble into a deeper theological question regarding the nature of eschatological victory. What is the mode by which the Son of Man accomplishes eschatological redemption? From the perspective of the Similitudes, if the Son of Man is counted among the sinful, it unhinges the possibility of eschatological redemption, which is to be accomplished through the realization of the *antithesis* between the Son of Man and the condemned sinful kings doomed to be overthrown by him. In this respect, Luke's Jesus would appear to our Enochic author as coming dangerously close to uprooting the foundation of any and all eschatological hope.

Whom does the Son of Man save?

On the one hand, the Similitudes regularly characterizes moral deviants as 'sinners' (1 Enoch 38.3; 41.1; 45.2; 45.6; 46.4; 50.2; 53.2, 7; 56.8; 60.6; 62.2, 13) who will receive judgement directly from the Son of Man (69.27). On the other hand, the Son of Man has an explicit positive relationship with the righteous: he is 'a staff for the righteous' (48.4), preserves 'the lot of the righteous' (48.7), chooses the righteous out of Sheol (51.1–2), establishes peace for the righteous (71.17) and is revealed to the righteous (48.7). The Son of Man comes therefore to be 'the vindicator of their lives' (48.7) and accomplishes this by concomitantly displacing sinners and giving them into the hand of the righteous (38.5). The Similitudes presents a bipartite structuring of humanity made up of the sinners as the bearers of judgement and the righteous and the beneficiaries of salvation.

In Luke 19, Jesus runs into a rich (πλούσιος) chief tax collector (ἀρχιτελώνης) named Zacchaeus with whom he plans to reside (19.5), but this act is not welcomed by the others, who 'grumble' that 'he has gone in to be the guest of a man who is sinful (ἁμαρτωλός)' (19.7). In response to Zacchaeus' announcement that he will restore anyone whom he has defrauded in his tax-collecting position (19.8), Jesus rejoices at his repentance (19.9) and declares about himself that 'the Son of Man came to seek and to save the lost (τὸ ἀπολωλός)' (19.10; cf. 5.30).

As Walck reads Jesus' encounter with the tax collector Zacchaeus, he identifies a theological similarity between Luke's Jesus and the Similitudes' Son of Man: in the Similitudes, that the Son of Man sends out angels to 'gather the scattered righteous ones' expresses similar 'theological dynamics' to Luke's scene in which Jesus cares for 'those outside the bounds of the mainstream society'.[41] But identifying this parallel is only possible at a high level of abstraction which obfuscates the theological thrust of both texts. Classifying Zacchaeus as 'marginalized' obscures Luke's claim that he is a wealthy leading tax collector who manipulated his position of power to defraud and to steal from others (19.8). In the Similitudes, the kings and the mighty murder, disenfranchise, dispossess and consistently exploit the righteous and thus acquire 'ill-gotten gain' (63.10) and 'devour' what the righteous produce (53.2).[42] In a solemn turn of events, the confession of their sin is met by a God who refuses to heed their pleas for mercy and responds with eschatological rejection (63.1–12). In the justice-seeking eyes of the Similitudes, Zacchaeus would belong to these oppressors destined for condemnation, and thus for the Son of Man to 'rejoice' at the repentance of one of the 'mighty' who have exploited the people of God is therefore just a category error; his perpetuation of injustice should instead ensure his ultimate overthrowing by the Son of Man.

To press this further, Jesus' self-declaration that he has come for the 'the lost' (τὸ ἀπολωλός) responds to those who grumble about how he has joined the sinful Zacchaeus (ἁμαρτωλός) and thus signals that the 'lost' refers to *sinners* (cf. 5.30). Drawing a parallel between the two texts through the concept of the 'marginalized' overlooks both the fact that in the Similitudes the mission of the Son of Man is to vindicate the righteous *from* their oppressors – not just *qua* the marginalized but precisely *qua* the righteous – and that Luke's Son of Man inverts the function of the Similitudes' Son of Man. Jesus' self-announcement that he seeks the sinful lost presents a deep challenge to and even a critical inversion of the essential theological logic of the Similitudes, by claiming that he has come to save precisely those whom Enoch's Son of Man comes to destroy: ἁμαρτωλοί.

But for the Similitudes, Jesus' act towards Zacchaeus counts as neither just a hermeneutical difference nor a disagreement over the mode of divine victory: it is a fundamental rejection of divine justice. The divine act that characterizes God *as* God in the Similitudes is his promised instantiation of cosmic equilibrium in which sinners receive judgement and the righteous receive blessing, and the present theological discord – in which the unjust kings prosper at the expense of the righteous – places a question mark over (we could say) the Godness of God. The theodical impulse of the Similitudes is therefore to claim that the future event of cosmic and juridical

---

[41] Walck, 'The *Parables of Enoch* and the Synoptic Gospels', 260.
[42] There is a translational issue here regarding *ṣamawa* in 53.2. Daniel Olson takes *ḫāṭəʾān* as the subject of *yəṣāmewu*, which would therefore imply nothing about exploitation of the righteous (*Enoch: A New Translation* (North Richland Hills, TX: BIBAL, 2004), 27, 98–9). But I follow the suggestion of Nickelsburg and VanderKam that the subject is implicitly the righteous (1 Enoch 2, 196).

restabilizing protects the integrity and identity of God himself. From the Enochic perspective, a divine agent who comes to forgive the likes of Zacchaeus implicates God in a judicial scandal which only intensifies the problem that the Similitudes hopes to reverse and resolve. The 'Son of Man' is the very figure that the Similitudes retrieves to promise that God *will* resolve this present injustice, but it is all the more scandalous that Luke's Jesus utilizes the same 'Son of Man' to support the opposite contention – that through this figure God forgives *these* exploitative, sinful oppressors.

Alleged parallels

Charlesworth insightfully suggests that 'the concept "Son of Man" is attractively ambiguous': the eschatological material in Daniel 7 contains a high degree of semantic potential which can be realized and utilized in variegated ways depending on an interpreter's setting and theological imagination.[43] We have seen this phenomenon both in the Synoptics (at least Mark and Luke) and the Similitudes. While reading the same text, they at times interpret the somewhat ambiguous material of Daniel in divergent ways, and permit us, utilizing a dialogical method, to uncover the extent of the disagreement between them. The 'authority' in Daniel 7.14 is interpreted by the Similitudes as the Son of Man's ability to displace wicked rulers, but Mark interprets that same authority as Jesus' power to forgive. Whereas the correlation between the Son of Man and the people of God in Daniel does not imply suffering for the Similitudes, Luke's Jesus is portrayed as a Danielic and Isaianic figure who identifies with and participates in the suffering of sinners. The Son of Man's act of benefitting the people God in Daniel 7.13–14 is retrieved by the Similitudes to mean that he will vindicate the righteous over against their sinful oppressors, but Luke suggests that the Son of Man comes for those sinners.

As we saw above, in some cases scholars attempt to stretch the gospels and the Similitudes to manufacture parallels which, on second glance, are found wanting. The differences between the gospels and the Similitudes should not be downplayed by projecting the gospels' reading of Daniel into the Similitudes (e.g. stating that the gospels' reading must have been 'assumed' or obvious from the text of Daniel), and neither should we ignore these differences by abstracting the texts from the theological context within which they are embedded. In the rush to discover a precedent for early Christology, we need serious caution when looking for similarities between the New Testament and the Similitudes (and other texts, for that matter), lest we claim to have discovered parallels which are more our own constructs than anything else. And if the similarity between the Similitudes and the New Testament is in fact strikingly weaker than previously imagined, perhaps we should seriously scrutinize the asserted 'Enochic origins' of early Christology, since – to end where we began with the words of Samuel Sandmel – it is too often the case that 'we have not a true parallel, but only an alleged one'.[44]

---

[43] Charlesworth, 'Did Jesus Know', 202.
[44] Sandmel, 'Parallelomania', 3.

3

Peter and the Patriarch: Eschatological Perspectives from 1 Peter and 1 Enoch

Sofanit T. Abebe

The later Enoch traditions (i.e. 1 Enoch 91–108) identify the present age as the end-time marked by growing apostasy and the resumption of mythical evil. These visions of the end-time included the expectation that the righteous too would suffer in the tribulations of the last days. Within this eschatological framework, these traditions give prominent attention to the problem of evil and explore the notion of the oppressed as a paradigm for piety. As will be shown below, such themes and motifs are uniquely present in 1 Peter.

The similarity between 1 Enoch and 1 Peter has been noted as early as Friedrich Spitta's pioneering work in 1890, which first identified the eschatological context of 1 Peter 3.19 in Jewish literature.[1] A great number of Petrine scholars have since followed Spitta in identifying the eschatological material from 1 Enoch as a background. However, more nuance can be brought to the discussion through a thorough comparison that engages the Enochic traditions in conversations that extend beyond 1 Peter 3.18–22 and finds its basis in a close reading of the various texts that make up 1 Enoch. Also, given the prominence of the theme of suffering in both 1 Peter and 1 Enoch and its unique representation, arguably in both texts, as a necessary feature of the pious life, there is a need for a comparative analysis that would engage 1 Enoch in general and the Eschatological Admonition (1 Enoch 108) in particular on a par with a New Testament text that deals with the theme of suffering.[2] As John Elliott

---

[1] Friedrich Spitta, *Christi Predigt an die Geister (1 Petr. 3, 19ff.): Ein Beitrag zur Neutestamentlichen Theologie* (Göttingen: Vandenhoeck & Ruprecht, 1890); more recently, Chad Pierce has noted the 'Jewish apocalyptic' influence behind several features of 1 Peter, cf. Chad T. Pierce, 'Apocalypse and the Epistles of 1, 2 Peter and Jude', in *The Jewish Apocalyptic Tradition and the Shaping of New Testament Thought* (Minneapolis: Fortress Press, 2017), 307–25; see also Bo Reicke, *The Disobedient Spirits and Christian Baptism: A Study of 1 Peter III.19 and Its Context* (ASNU 13; Copenhagen: Munksgaard, 1946); William J. Dalton, *Christ's Proclamation to the Spirits: A Study of 1 Peter 3:18–4:6* (2nd ed.; AnBib 23; Rome: Pontifical Biblical Institute, 1989).

[2] In New Testament studies, 1 Enoch has not received sustained scholarly attention perhaps owing to the inaccessibility of its mostly Ethiopic recension. New Testament studies that do engage 1 Enoch in depth hardly extend beyond messianic themes from the gospel traditions and 1 Peter 3.18–22, 2 Peter 2.4–5, and Jude 6.14–15. For a limited exception, see for example, Loren T. Stuckenbruck and Gabriele Boccaccini, eds, *Enoch and the Synoptic Gospels: Reminiscences, Allusions, Intertextuality,*

notes,³ although 1 Peter is often stated as bearing close affinities to various traditions within 1 Enoch, there is need for an in-depth comparative analysis to warrant, for example, George Nickelsburg's interesting claim that '1 Enoch 108 was part of "Peter's" theological repertoire'.⁴

In the discussion below, after exploring expectations of the end in some Enochic traditions and 1 Peter, I will focus my comparative analysis in the neglected text of the Eschatological Admonition (hereafter, EA) and its striking similarity with 1 Peter. I will demonstrate that (1) differences notwithstanding, eschatological election in both the Apocalypse of Weeks (1 Enoch 93.1–10; 91.11–17) and 1 Peter is considered as both a generative act and one that is predicated upon faithful response, and that (2) in both the EA and 1 Peter, eschatological suffering functions as a paradigm for piety. This is expressed through common imageries of metallurgy and light/darkness so that exhortations in both texts serve as the call to remain unchanged, much like pure gold, or remain in the light of the new life the addressees have entered through divine election (through Christ in 1 Peter and Enochic revelation in 1 Enoch 108). This comparative reading will also indicate a potential background for 1 Peter's unique representation of suffering as a necessary feature of the eschatological age inaugurated by the Christ event.⁵

To this end, the discussion will focus on the nature and function of revelation and the temporal framework within which eschatology is expressed in selected passages from 1 Enoch and 1 Peter.⁶ Beginning with the Exhortation, I will highlight the more

---

SBLEJL 44 (Atlanta: SBL Press, 2016); Benjamin E. Reynolds and Loren T. Stuckenbruck, eds, *The Jewish Apocalyptic Tradition and the Shaping of New Testament Thought* (Minneapolis: Fortress Press, 2017); Loren T. Stuckenbruck, *The Myth of Rebellious Angels: Studies in Second Temple Judaism and New Testament Texts* (WUNT I/335; Tübingen: Mohr Siebeck, 2014); Mark D. Mathews, *Riches, Poverty, and the Faithful: Perspectives on Wealth in the Second Temple Period and the Apocalypse of John* (SNTSMS 154; Cambridge: Cambridge University Press, 2013); Harry Alan Hahne, *The Corruption and Redemption of Creation: Nature in Romans 8:19–22 and Jewish Apocalyptic Literature*, LNTS 336 (New York: T&T Clark, 2006).

3   John H. Elliott, *1 Peter: A New Translation with Introduction and Commentary*, AB 37B (New York: Doubleday, 2000), 637–710, at 914 lists more verbal and conceptual similarities than previously identified and notes that 'the author [of 1 Peter] is clearly familiar with concepts, terminology, traditions and perspectives evident in this diverse body of literature [represented by 1 Enoch]'. His focus remains on 1 Peter 3 and his discussion does not provide an analysis of the cited differences and similarities as this is beyond the scope of his commentary on 1 Peter.

4   George W. E. Nickelsburg, 1 Enoch: *A Commentary on the Book of* 1 Enoch, *Chapter 1–36; 81–108* (Hermeneia; Minneapolis: Fortress Press, 2001), 560.

5   Contra Kelly D. Liebengood, who identifies Zechariah 9–14 as the background to 1 Peter's theology of suffering, I consider the Enochic tradition explored here (the Eschatological Admonition) and the Animal Apocalypse (not included in my brief analysis here) provide 'the most plausible explanation' for the shepherd and fiery trials imagery of 1 Peter, cf. eadem, *The Eschatology of 1 Peter: Considering the Influence of Zechariah 9–14* (SNTSMS 157; Cambridge: Cambridge University Press, 2014), 79.

6   Furthermore, a fruitful venue of comparison that is little utilized in scholarship on 1 Peter is its construction of time within the matrix of early Jewish apocalyptic eschatology and its significance within the context of oppression; see however David G. Horrell and Wei Hsien Wan, 'Christology, Eschatology and the Politics of Time in 1 Peter', *JSNT* 38 (2016): 263–76, who present the contest of power in 1 Peter's presentation of time, which is conceived in terms of God's salvific act in the past. A consideration of analogous Jewish resistance discourses, with a similar socio-political context of domination and religious persecution as 1 Peter, might further nuance Horrell and Wan's analysis of 1 Peter's resistance discourse through its Christological eschatology.

prominent eschatological expectations of some of these texts, before proceeding to compare them with 1 Peter.

Eschatological perspectives in 1 Enoch 91–108

Several Enochic authors employ apocalyptic topoi to interpret events in their own times. Often, earlier Enochic tradition, as represented by the Book of Watchers (1 Enoch 1–36) and the Astronomical Book (1 Enoch 72–82), informs the later interpretations of adverse circumstances the author and his addressees face, or the overall view of life and reality a given text represents. The repertoire of topoi concerned with the end-time in the later Enoch traditions is similarly associated with revelation by Enoch. I will discuss below three literary units from 1 Enoch and their depiction of the end-time.

The Exhortation (91.1–10, 18–19)

The Exhortation was likely composed by an Enochic editor sometime during the mid- to late second century BCE. It begins in a formal testamentary setting where Enoch summons his progeny to disclose the revelation he has received regarding future events (1 Enoch 91.1–3). The divine source of this revelation is identified in terms that portray Enoch as a prophet on whom 'a spirit is being poured out' (v. 1b). Employing *vaticinium ex eventu*, the Exhortation gives a description of the upsurge of evil followed by the instance of judgement that will rid the earth of all evil. This will again be followed by a proliferation of evil that will once again be quenched through another judgement, which is depicted as being greater in scope and efficacy.[7]

Temporality and eschatology

Within 1 Enoch, the Exhortation contains the first instance of a *transparent* use of the flood imagery as model for eschatological judgement.[8] In this sense, perhaps the final judgement in the Exhortation can be thought of as unfolding through stages, with the Great Flood being the first phase. At any rate, the author's dependence on the 'great judgment' of the past (1 Enoch 91.5) to describe the 'great judgment' of the eschatological future (v. 7) indicates an *Urzeit–Endzeit* analogy between these two events. In addition to the flood imagery, there is also an analogous relationship between events leading up to the first judgement and eschatological events leading up to end-time judgement.

---

[7] The close parallels between verse 5 and the primordial sins of the second week of the Apocalypse of Weeks, as well as linguistic links between the rest of the Exhortation and the punishment outlined in the seventh week, lend support to taking the verse as referring to primordial events. Furthermore, that the second period of judgement is a reference to eschatological events is evidenced, for example, by the formulaic opening 'in those days' in verse 8 as well as the widely attested eschatological theme of the destruction of idols in verse 9 (cf. T. Mos. 10:7; *Tob.* 14.6; Wis 14.11). See also Loren T. Stuckenbruck, 1 Enoch *91–108*, CEJL (Berlin, New York: Walter de Gruyter, 2007), 178–9.

[8] Stuckenbruck, 1 Enoch *91–108*, 156.

This temporal dimension of the Exhortation's eschatology has provided the author with a framework to imagine what the eschatological future will look like.

Loren Stuckenbruck highlights a further dimension to this framework of temporality. He notes that besides reinforcing eschatology, apocalyptic writings that depict a correspondence between *Urzeit* and *Endzeit* employ language about the *Urzeit* 'to provide a basis for being confident about such an outcome: God's definitive activity is not only a matter for the future; rather, it is God's invasive presence to defeat evil in the past (at the time of the Great Flood) that guarantees its annihilation in the future'.[9] The allusion to divine victory in the sacred past thus functions in the Exhortation to encourage readers to face adverse circumstances, knowing that evil and demonic forces are but defeated agents that await complete destruction (cf. 91.9).[10] Significantly, the author of the Exhortation thus places his readers in the eschatological tension between 'already' of evil's defeat and the 'not yet' of its manifest destruction.

Revealed wisdom and eschatology

In addition to providing an outline of the eschatological future based on the template of the sacred past, Enoch's revelation further incorporates ethical elements in the form of a two-ways instruction. In a testamentary setting, Enoch addresses his children:

> Listen, children of Enoch, to every word of your father, and pay close attention to my mouth, for I am testifying and speaking concerning you, beloved ones: Love uprightness and walk in it.
>
> 1 Enoch 91.3[11]

Before reiterating the revelation he has received, Enoch exhorts his progeny to pursue uprightness and to do so without 'a double heart' (v. 4). The fictive addressees are also warned against associating with those who have a 'double heart'. Such a description usually denotes sinners in the scriptural tradition (Prov 16.31; 17.23; Job 24.13; Ps 119.30; cf. Wis 5.6) but is used in 1 Enoch for the first time in 91.4.[12] Nickelsburg also argues that revealed wisdom in 1 Enoch constitutes the eschatological community of the elect by providing instructions through which the righteous are to remain on the right path even in the midst of persecution.[13] Grant Macaskill further elaborates the notion of revealed wisdom as an element of 1 Enoch's eschatology, arguing that possession of Enochic writings takes on eschatological significance so that the readers of these texts are the eschatological community of the elect who have been given salvific wisdom.

---

[9] Stuckenbruck, *Myth of Rebellious Angels*, 275.
[10] Judgement resulting in the destruction of idols rather than the punishment of those who commit idolatry is without precise parallel in the Enochic corpus, cf. Stuckenbruck, 1 Enoch *91–108*, 156.
[11] Stuckenbruck, 1 Enoch *91–108*, 162.
[12] See further Nickelsburg, 1 Enoch *1*, 411; Stuckenbruck, 1 Enoch *91–108*, 165–6.
[13] George W. E. Nickelsburg, 'The Nature and Function of Revelation in 1 Enoch, Jubilees, and Some Qumranic Documents', in *Pseudepigraphic Perspectives: The Apocrypha and Pseudepigrapha in Light of the Dead Sea Scrolls* (STDJ 31; ed. Esther G. Chazon, Michael E. Stone, and with the collaboration of Avital Pinnick; Leiden: Brill, 1999), 91–119, at 98–9.

Despite the difficult text-critical problems associated with 1 Enoch 91.10, it is clear that in stating 'the righteous one will arise from his sleep, and wisdom will arise and be given to them', wisdom plays a pivotal role in the eschatology of the Exhortation (for close parallels see 92.3 and 93.10).[14] This is further clarified in 91.18 and 91.19, which provide closing exhortations for Enoch's progeny to choose the way of righteousness over the way of violence and unrighteousness. This two-ways instruction also includes an emphatic description of the punishment that awaits sinners in verses 6–9.[15] In addition to verses 1–9, the final two verses contain further two-ways instruction in the form of traditional wisdom such as that found in Proverbs 1–8 (cf. 1 Enoch 91.18–19).[16] The key difference lies in the fact that wisdom here can only be gleaned by revelation and therefore takes on eschatological significance, unlike the sapiential tradition which depicts wisdom as being immanent in creation.

Eschatological salvation

In the Exhortation, salvation rests squarely on possession of Enochic instruction regarding the ways of righteousness and sin. The salvific significance of the wisdom Enoch reveals is further evidenced by the emphasis in 1 Enoch 91.18 that it is Enoch who is disclosing the contents of the revelation he received. If the temple is in view in 91.9, then the description of its destruction by fire in the eschatological future suggests that as far as the Exhortation is concerned, eschatological salvation – that is, inclusion in the eschatological community of the elect – is now associated with Enochic revelation instead of the Jerusalem temple.[17]

Furthermore, taken together, the temporal framework of the Exhortation's eschatology and the role ascribed to revealed wisdom indicate that salvation or institution as the exclusive community of the righteous has been inaugurated. As Nickelsburg notes, in 1 Enoch revelations take the form of fictive prophecy, which 'although allegedly received in primordial antiquity, are promulgated in a present that stands on the threshold of the end time. Functionally, they are eschatological revelation ... Definitive deliverance will take place soon.'[18] This further constitutes 'inaugurated eschatology' with both realized (here the disclosing of salvific revelation) and future elements (such as events in vv. 8–9).

---

[14] Cf. Nickelsburg, 'The Nature and Function of Revelation', 181.
[15] Nickelsburg, 1 Enoch 1, 415.
[16] Nickelsburg, 1 Enoch 1, 335–7. On the relationship between wisdom and apocalyptic, see for instance John J. Collins, 'Wisdom, Apocalypticism and Generic Compatibility', in *In Search of Wisdom: Essays in Memory of John G. Gammie* (ed. L. G Perdue, B. B. Scott and W. J. Wiseman; Louisville: Westminster John Knox Press, 1993), 165–85; Daniel K. Falk, Florentino Garcia Martinez and Eileen M. Schuller, eds, *Sapiential, Liturgical and Poetical Texts from Qumran: Proceedings of the Third Meeting of the International Organization for Qumran Studies, Oslo 1998* (STDJ 35; Leiden: Brill, 2000); Charlotte Hempel, Armin Lange and Hermann Lichtenberger, eds, *The Wisdom Texts from Qumran and the Development of Sapiential Thought* (BETL 159; Leuven: Peeters, 2002); F. García Martínez, ed., *Wisdom and Apocalypticism in the Dead Sea Scrolls and in the Biblical Tradition* (BETL 168; Leuven: Peeters, 2003).
[17] For a discussion of verse 9's negative evaluation of the Second Temple, see Stuckenbruck, *1 Enoch 91–108*, 179.
[18] Nickelsburg, 1 Enoch 1, 42.

The Apocalypse of Weeks (93.1–10; 91.11–17)

Composed during the early part of the second century BCE, the Apocalypse of Weeks is a self-contained unit written by someone who has not authored other parts of 1 Enoch.[19] The Apocalypse presents history through a consistent pattern of ten 'weeks' within a sevenfold periodization and a final week 'without numbers' (91.17). One of the characteristic features of the Apocalypse is the innovative way it merges various biblical and early Enoch traditions to arrive at a unique presentation of history that represents arguably the first use of *vaticinia ex eventu* among historical Jewish apocalypses.[20] Its retelling of Israel's history culminates, in the wake of justice and judgement, in cosmic renewal and the turning of all humanity towards righteousness. Eschatology in the Apocalypse of Weeks is thus delineated through a retelling of history.

The revelation of wisdom, election and salvation

Passive constructions dominate the Apocalypse. These are found in descriptions of events that involve: 1) the disclosure of vision (93.2, 6, 10); 2) the selection of individuals (Noah, v. 4; Abraham, v. 5; Elijah, v. 8) or groups (the 'chosen', vv. 2, 10); and 3) the meting out of judgement (v. 14). The author's focus on the idea of election or divine choosing for predetermined purposes also finds expression in the passive construct of 91.11–13 that describes the agency of the remnant in eschatological judgement.

Enoch's opening speech in 93.2 is directed at 'the eternally chosen ones (בחדי עולמין)'. Having no precise parallel in the Enochic corpus, the designation *ḫəruyāna 'alam* indicates election lasting unto eternity.[21] However, according to 93.10, a further election takes place from among the elect of 93.2 to constitute the eschatological community of the elect based on revealed wisdom. Those who do not possess this salvific wisdom remain excluded. The wisdom given to the righteous also serves to empower the righteous to root out 'violence and deceit' and participate as agents in the first stages of eschatological judgement (91.11). This means that it is not as Israel (i.e. the plant of righteousness, 93.2) that Israel is saved; rather, salvation is envisaged in terms of divine choosing.[22] If in 93.10 the chosen ones from among the 'plant of righteousness' is read as a deliberate antithesis to the 'wicked generation' of 93.9, then it is possible that the

---

[19] So Stuckenbruck, *1 Enoch 91–108*, 49. For the argument that the Apocalypse was composed by the author of the Epistle, see for example Michael A. Knibb, 'The Apocalypse of Weeks and the Epistle of Enoch', in *Enoch and Qumran Origins: New Light on a Forgotten Connection* (ed. Gabriele Boccaccini; Grand Rapids: Eerdmans, 2005), 213–14. Even if the Apocalypse was composed by the author of the Epistle, its separate treatment in a literary analysis can be justified given its thematic coherence within its present literary setting in 1 Enoch.

[20] James C. VanderKam, 'Studies in the Apocalypse of Weeks (1 Enoch 93:1–10; 91:11–17)', *CBQ* 46 (1984): 511–23.

[21] Nickelsburg, 1 Enoch 1, 434, 442: 'the chosen of eternity'; Matthew Black, *The Book of Enoch or 1 Enoch: A New English Edition with Commentary and Textual Notes* (SVTP 7; Leiden: Brill, 1985), 85: 'the eternal elect'; for a literal translation that renders the designation as 'the chosen of the world' indicating the sphere from which they have been selected, see Michael A. Knibb, *The Ethiopic Book of Enoch: A New Edition in Light of the Aramaic Dead Sea Fragments*, 2 vols (Oxford: Clarendon Press, 1978), 2.223. The argument forwarded in this section is not dependent upon the temporal translation of the noun *'alām*.

[22] Stuckenbruck, 1 Enoch 91–108, 118.

chosen are chosen for being upright. But this would prove difficult in light of 93.8, which indicates pervasive sin and apostasy ('all those who live in the sixth week will become blind'). However, if we are to read 93.10 against the backdrop of the selection of Israel as 'the plant of righteousness' in week three (93.5), which is a more plausible reading, then it is possible that the means by which election occurs is through divine choice alone.[23]

However, it is important to note that the author's emphasis lies in identifying his readers as the eschatological community of the righteous who are constituted by the revealing of Enoch's wisdom. Human responsibility is also important to the author, as it was 'blindness' and the lack of wisdom that caused the scattering of the 'plant of the righteousness' to begin with (93.8, week six). Moreover, each of the text's paradigms for the elect were noted for their faithfulness: Enoch, Noah, Abraham and Elijah. Thus, while election in the Apocalypse is a generative act that functions independently of uprightness, it is also the case that improper response is depicted as having serious consequence.[24] As we shall see below, it is within this context that the exhortational component of the Apocalypse finds its significance.

Eschatological tribulation

The writer of the Apocalypse expects a final period of tribulation before the dawn of eschatological salvation. This is evidenced by the description of events in week seven (the author's own time): 1) the rising of a climactic evil generation (93.9); 2) election and the giving of salvific wisdom to the elect (93.10); and 3) the agency of the elect in the first phase of eschatological judgement (91.11). This is then followed by a description of eschatological blessing including the complete destruction of evil, the rebuilding of the temple and the appearance of a new heaven (91.12–17). Furthermore, the combination of 'violence (חמסא)' and 'deceit (שקרא)' in the seventh week, having its counterpart in the second week (cf. 93.4; 91.11), suggests that whatever present reality the terms might indicate, their recurrence shows the author's expectation that the eschatological future will include a final period of intense tribulation that resembles antediluvian wickedness.

---

[23] For a different reading that sees the righteous being chosen instead of the act of election bestowing the status of righteousness, see Logan Williams, 'Disjunction in Paul: Apocalyptic or Christomorphic? Comparing the Apocalypse of Weeks with Galatians', *NTS* 64 (2018): 64–80. Stuckenbruck accepts the possibility that both views might be at play in the text, with the author wishing to retain the tension between divine election on the one hand and human responsibility on the other, Stuckenbruck, *1 Enoch 91–108*, 118. This would fit well in light of the foregoing Exhortation that places an emphasis on human responsibility while at the same time recognizing the continued effect of events in the *Urzeit*, which, albeit weakened, still await complete eradication in the eschatological future. Although Williams is right to note the lack of substantial evidence in Klaus Koch's proposal that the Apocalypse is about the clash between cosmic forces, evil and demonic forces are still within the purview of the Apocalypse given 91.15, which imagines the eschatological future as bringing the destruction of the watchers before sin and evil is to be completely removed (91.17). This reading finds further support in the temporal dimension of the Apocalypse's eschatology that employs an *Urzeit-Endzeit* analogy: depicting the present and the future from the perspective of the mythical past allows the author to attribute rampant sin and apostasy *in part* to demonic forces.

[24] Stuckenbruck, *1 Enoch 91–108*, 118, 123–4.

Following this time of suffering, the righteous are given salvific wisdom and are empowered to execute judgement. Thus, it seems that eschatological tribulation here functions to inaugurate the first phase of the final judgement much in the same way that the intense suffering in primordial times resulted in the Great Flood. As in the Exhortation, the transient nature of evil is brought out in the author's further use of *Urzeit* language to describe events in his own time as well as in the eschatological future.

Final judgement

Language pertaining to divine judgement first appears in the description for week two where reference is made to the 'first end' (93.4). This reference indicates the parallel the author saw between the Great Flood and the final judgement in the eschatological future (cf. 91.5–9; 106– 107). Events in this week are described using the key terms of 'deceit' and 'violence', which will reappear in 91.11, indicating the eschatological events anticipated by the description of week two.[25]

The end comes with a final judgement that is expected to occur in stages. In recalling the sacred past, it can be said that for the author, the flood and the defeat of evil it implies is in a way the first phase of the final judgement. The use of *Urzeit* language to imagine events in the eschatological future suggests that the flood was not simply a past event – in recollecting it and employing it as a model, the author is indicating its lasting effect and significance for the present and the future. If the flood can thus be understood as the first phase of final judgement, then the second phase is depicted as involving the agency of the righteous to execute judgement against the wicked (91.11–12). The third stage is a cosmic scale judgement over the whole world (91.14) and the fourth and final stage of eschatological judgement is the judgement of demonic beings (91.14–15).[26]

Finally, the author's portrayal of events leading up to and including judgement through the flood as the first of many to come also indicates a basic understanding of history as following a predetermined pattern. The 'first end' occurs following a period of rampant 'deceit' and 'violence', just as the second would follow the rise of a climactic evil generation and the resumption of mythical evil on an even greater scale (93.9). Significantly, whatever historical events might be alluded to in the Apocalypse, the suffering of the righteous under mythical evil in week seven seems to function to inaugurate the final judgement.

---

[25] Stuckenbruck, 1 Enoch *91–108*, 130.
[26] The author seems keen to draw a distinction between the oppressors of weeks seven and eight on the one hand (91.11–12), and on the other the 'wicked' of week nine whose deeds will be destroyed (91.14). Given the influence of the Book of Watchers on the Apocalypse and thematic links within its wider literary context, it is likely that the Apocalypse here includes demonic powers as perpetrators of wicked deeds that mark the end-time (cf. 1 Enoch 10:16, 100.6 and 105.1); cf. Stuckenbruck, 1 Enoch *91–108*, 141; idem, 'A Place for Socio-Political Oppressors at the End of History? Eschatological Perspectives from 1 Enoch', in *Reactions to Empire: Sacred Texts in Their Socio-Political Contexts*, WUNT II/372 (ed. John Anthony Dunne and Dan Batovici; Tübingen: Mohr Siebeck, 2014), 1–22, at 11, 14–18.

Ethical exhortation

The Apocalypse's ethical thrust lies in its emphasis on depicting the present as the time of inaugurated eschatology. In common with other Enochic writings, the Enochic revelation the readers receive through this text functions to constitute them as the eschatological community of the righteous. The Apoclaypse further nuances the Enochic emphasis on the eschatological aspect of revelation by placing the inaugural event in the giving of wisdom. The Apocalypse's temporal framework thus places the readers in the already/not-yet of the eschatological future, which is further reinforced through depicting the present as the initial phase of eschatological judgement. This serves the purpose of providing comfort and encouragement, as Lars Hartman has noted.[27] Moreover, an inaugurated eschatology serves to provide a profound theological framework for understanding readers' identity as the elect and navigating through the present time of apostasy and sin.

The Apocalypse's hortatory agenda finds expression in the temporal duality the Apocalypse presents. As Anathea Portier-Young notes, 'the transience and finitude of temporal powers affirms God's governance of time and the outworking of God's plan in history and gives hope for a transformed future'.[28] Through structuring its eschatological anticipation on the template of the past, the Apocalypse assures the reader of God's control over the ordering of both time and space. Within this framework of historical salvation, the righteous, who are now victims of 'violence' and 'deceit', will soon be delivered and given control (91.11–12).

However, this message of hope is not entirely futuristic, as Portier-Young argues; as we have seen above, the author emphasizes the transformation of the present. This is achieved by the writer's convergence of *Urzeit* and *Endzeit*, which signifies the remarkable claim that the mythical evil that marks the period the addressees find themselves in is an already defeated force.[29]

The readers' description as the chosen and the righteous, as well as the presentation of history through alternating periods of righteousness and wickedness, also functions as implicit paraenesis that can be understood as an admonition against emulating the wicked and the apostate. Such an ethical purpose is also served by the notion of election. Despite being a generative act that has resulted in the choosing of Abraham and his progeny, the inappropriate response of the chosen has resulted in their 'scattering' (93.8).[30] In this sense, the ethical exhortation of the Apocalypse operates

---

[27] Lars Hartman, 'The Functions of Some So-Called Apocalyptic Timetables', *NTS* 22 (1975): 1–14, at 11–12.

[28] Anathea E. Portier-Young sees the Apocalypse as a resistance discourse against hegemony (*Apocalypse Against Empire: Theologies of Resistance in Early Judaism* (Grand Rapids: Eerdmans, 2014), 27). But given the Apocalypse's eschatological horizon, I am not convinced that designations for the righteous are technical terms reflecting a sectarian self-understanding on the part of the author and his group. Moreover, 1 Enoch 5.9, which lies in the background of this text, affirms such a reading. As Stuckenbruck notes, the Apocalypse 'does not suggest that the writer is concerned with a group that is categorically closed' (*1 Enoch 91–108*, 75; see also idem, 'Socio-Political Oppressors', 11–18).

[29] Stuckenbruck, *Myth of Rebellious Angels*, 240–56.

[30] As James VanderKam notes, 'the entire chosen race is scattered, not just a part of it' ('The Exile in Jewish Apocalyptic Literature', in *Exile: Old Testament, Jewish, and Christian Conceptions* (JSJSup 56; Leiden: Brill, 1997), 89–109, at 95).

within an 'inaugurated eschatology' that serves to comfort and encourage the righteous while at the same time exhorting them to live in light of eschatological blessing.

The Eschatological Admonition (108.1-15)

The EA was appended to the Enochic collection probably during the latter part of the first century CE. This editorial appendix appears in the form of a further revelatory disclosure made by Enoch to his son Methuselah (1 Enoch 108.1). The content of revelation presented in the EA comprises ethical instructions and descriptions of the eschatological future.

A chosen Enochic community receives hidden wisdom regarding future events (vv. 6-15). This is expressed by employing language and motifs from the sacred past. The author adopts *Urzeit* language to describe the fate that awaits his community's human persecutors with a unique appropriation for such punishment in the immediate afterlife. In the opposition between the readers and their oppressors, the author's emphasis remains on revelation regarding eschatological judgement and ensuing punishment and reward. In essence, then, the author employs revelation as a response to his addressees' real or perceived persecution.[31] He also employs the motif of Enochic revelation to constitute and inform their identity as the eschatological community of the chosen.[32]

Containing implicit exhortation, such characterizations serve a theological purpose: the readers are to recognize their identity in them and strive to uphold their faith commitment in hope of vindication. More profoundly, these designations indicate the status of the addressees as members of the eschatological community of remnants. By evoking the 'prophets' (the word's first and only appearance in 1 Enoch) and casting his addresses in remnant language, the author takes a radical stance to suffering and states that it is a necessary 'testing' by God to ascertain purity and fidelity, as well as an assurance of salvation and reward for those who will persevere (v. 9).

The author also makes recourse to the themes of sin, punishment and rewards in earlier Enochic literature and the prophetic tradition to establish the claim that God's saving acts are *consistent* across history. The writer implicitly admonishes his readers to persevere not only in hope of future vindication but also in the knowledge that their enemies, whose sins and punishments are like that of the fallen angels, are already defeated and excluded from the community of God's chosen and that their deliverance is already manifesting itself through their suffering and institution as the chosen recipients of God's revelations through Enoch.

---

[31] This is in line with Nickelsburg's observations regarding the nature and function of revelation in the Book of Luminaries (1 Enoch 72-82), the Animal Vision (1 Enoch 85-90) and the Epistle of Enoch (1 Enoch 92-105) and its importance for constituting and shaping an Enochic community. Nickelsburg's study of the theme in 1 Enoch, Jubilees and some Qumran texts (the Damascus Document, the Community Rule, the Hodayot, the Habakkuk Pesher) hints at but does not fully explore the possibility that revelation also functions as a response to suffering by distinguishing the community of the chosen from out-groups; cf. Nickelsburg, 'The Nature and Function of Revelation', 91-119.

[32] John J. Collins, *Apocalypse, Prophecy, and Pseudepigraphy: On Jewish Apocalyptic Literature* (Grand Rapids: Eerdmans, 2015).

In this sense, the author places his readers in the period of eschatological tension between the already of evil's defeat and the not-yet of its manifestation. Suffering in the EA is thus closely tied to the advent of Enochic revelation and necessitates the revelation of hidden knowledge regarding the future which is also effective in the here and now.

In sum, visions of the end in the three distinct literary units we have discussed above can be said to converge in the expectation that the end is a time of the resumption of mythical evil, whose complete destruction is still awaited. To varying degrees and with differing levels of clarity, all three texts portray the end-time suffering of the righteous as an eschatological event that is tied to the advent of Enochic revelation and the inauguration of the final stages of end-time judgement.

Eschatology in 1 Peter

First, Peter 1.3–12 is an important pericope that gives a glimpse of the letter's eschatological expectation. Already in 1.3, the author announces that God has 'begotten us again to a living hope' (ἀναγεννήσας ἡμᾶς εἰς ἐλπίδα ζῶσαν), thus identifying the inauguration of the beginning of the end in Christ's resurrection from the dead (see also 1.23). Despite the readers' suffering, 'the joyous salvation of the future' already marks the lives of the addressees (1.6–9).[33] As we will see in greater detail below, 1 Peter's eschatological focus is also brought out in the temporal framework of 1.10–12, which again depicts the present as the time of the long-awaited eschatological future.[34] Significantly, the Christ event and the reality of his appearance is a pivotal point in time that already marks the present as the end-time (1.20).[35] The breaking of the eschatological future into the present can be glimpsed from the judgement language of 4.5, which describes God as ἑτοίμως to judge the living and the dead.

Furthermore, at key points in the epistle, the author employs Christ's innocent suffering, death and subsequent glory as the interpretative framework to address his readers' persecution (cf. 2.19–25; 3.18–22; 4.1–2, 12–19; 5.8–11). This address takes the form of identifying the sufferers as the eschatological people of God whose suffering is described using metallurgical imagery: τὸ δοκίμιον ὑμῶν τῆς πίστεως (1.7). As Mark Dubis notes, δοκίμιον is a metallurgical term which should be understood as a neuter substantival adjective that refers to what 'emerges authenticated from the testing that the recipients are enduring (i.e. their faith, as the genitive πίστεως clarifies)'.[36]

---

[33] Horrell and Wan see a contest for power in 1 Peter's presentation of time, which they rightly note is conceived in terms of God's salvific actions in the past ('The Politics of Time in 1 Peter', 267).

[34] Contra Marvin Pate and Douglas W. Kennard, who take the eschatology of 1 Peter to be entirely futurist (*Deliverance Now and Not Yet: The New Testament and the Great Tribulation* (StBibLit 54; New York: Peter Lang, 2003), 352–77).

[35] J. De Waal Dryden, *Theology and Ethics in 1 Peter: Paraenetic Strategies for Christian Character Formation* (WUNT II/209; Tübingen: Mohr Siebeck, 2006), 65.

[36] Mark Dubis, *1 Peter: A Handbook on the Greek Text*, Baylor Handbook on the Greek New Testament (Waco: Baylor University Press, 2010), 12.

Additionally, following the metaphor of metallurgy that results in refinement upon repeated testing by fire, the idea of repeated testing to achieve a more refined faith is indicated by the 'various' trials the addressees undergo (1.7). In describing the right response to suffering, therefore, the author admonishes his addressees to remain upright and not be surprised by the πύρωσις they experience, as this 'fire' is meant to test and refine their faith (4.12).

When this ethical admonition is read in light of the letter's eschatological framework, it is then plausible to assume that the author saw the present age as a time of increased evil and apostasy, as did other Jewish writers in the Second Temple period.[37] The repeated testing and refinement of the readers' faith would enable them to overcome this time of eschatological temptation (cf. 1.17; 2.11–12, 19–20; 3.6, 10–17; 4.1–3, 12–19; 5.8–9, 12).[38]

Eschatology in 1 Enoch and 1 Peter: A comparison

If one is to take the overall eschatological perspective of both writings as a point of departure, there are several largely unexplored parallels and contrasts that appear between 1 Enoch 91–108 and 1 Peter.[39]

For example, 'A time of testing/trial (πειρασμός)'[40] or in the terminology of 1 Enoch 'a day of tribulation (יום צרה or 'əlata mənədābe)'[41] is a feature of the eschatologies of both 1 Peter and 1 Enoch. Within the context of religious persecution, both 1 Peter and 1 Enoch 108 portray suffering as: 1) social/cultural estrangement (1 Pet 1.1; 2.11 and 1 Enoch 108.7, 10); 2) verbal and physical abuse (1 Pet 2.12, 16; 3.12–17; 4.14, 16; cf. 1 Enoch 108.10); 3) unjust treatment (1 Pet 2.20–21; 3.14, 16; 4.1, 13, 16, 19 and 1 Enoch 108.3, 6); and (4) occurring as a result of piety (1 Pet 1.13–18; 3.1–6; 4.2–4; 5.10 and 1 Enoch 108.8, 10, 12).

Both first-century CE documents employ fiery images to portray suffering as meted out by God for the testing of faith (1 Pet 1.7 and 1 Enoch 108.9)[42] and incorporate the motif of sufferers' eschatological vindication (1 Pet 1.13; 4.13; 5.4, 6 and 1 Enoch 108.7, 10–13). Their authors' response to the diverse trials of both groups of addresses can be understood in terms of this fire imagery. Exhortations in both texts should thus be understood as the call to remain unchanged, much like pure gold or silver which remains unaffected by fire.

---

[37] See for example 1 Enoch 91.4–7; 93.8–9; 106.18–107.1; 4 Ezra 5; 6.24; 14.16–18.
[38] Mark Dubis, *Messianic Woes in First Peter: Suffering and Eschatology in 1 Peter 4:12–19* (StBibLit 33; New York: Peter Lang, 2002), 134–9.
[39] Although 1 Peter is not an apocalypse, it contains apocalyptic motifs, as has been noted by, for example, Dubis, *Messianic Woes*, 38–43; Pate and Kennard, *Deliverance*, 352–77. For a critique of one aspect of 1 Peter's apocalyptic character as reflected in 4.17, cf. Leonhard Goppelt, *A Commentary on 1 Peter*, trans. John E. Alsup (ed. Ferdinand Hahn; Grand Rapids: Eerdmans, 1993), 330.
[40] 1 Peter 4.12
[41] 1 Enoch 96.2; 98.10, 13; cf. 1 Enoch 45.2; 55.3; 63.8; 103.7
[42] Metallurgic imagery in 1 Enoch 108.9 is not as explicit as 1 Peter 1.7 and 4.12; nevertheless, the 'testing' of the readers is stated as having its objective in their 'purity', thereby signifying an allusion to this widespread use of metallurgic testing-refining imagery in Second Temple Jewish texts.

Furthermore, employing the metaphor of light and darkness, both authors perceive their communities as being the enlightened who have been called from darkness to light (1 Enoch 108.11; 1 Pet 2.9). Both authors thus see their addressees as constituting the eschatological community of God's elect who have been endowed with salvific revelation (as do the authors of the Apocalypse and the Exhortation, as shown above). While in 1 Enoch 108 eschatological significance attributed to revelation rests on the teachings of Enoch and the hidden wisdom he reveals, in 1 Peter it is the person and work of Christ that has constituted the addressees as the eschatological community of God's elect (1 Pet 1.3–5, 14–21).

Another point of comparison is how the prophetic tradition of scripture functions for both authors. Both 1 Enoch 108.6 and 1 Peter 1.10 refer to 'the prophets' in terms that identify the prophetic writing of scripture as divine revelation.[43] Several points can be made regarding this common reference. First, 1 Peter identifies this origin in the πνεῦμα Χριστοῦ (1.11) and takes the prophets as consciously relating a predictive prophecy concerning God's elect in the eschatological future (1.12). The author of 1 Peter identifies this community of the elect with his addressees and ascribes to his group exclusive interpretative correctness.

This understanding indicates that scripture in 1 Peter is taken as plainly referring to the addressees. In 1 Enoch 108.6 the prophets similarly receive revealed knowledge, the content of which seems to be about future divine action on earth concerning the righteous, which are here identified as the author's own groups (cf. v. 7). The Enochic author's ultimate concern is the fate of the righteous and the reference to prophets appears within the context of angelic explanation about the punishment that awaits the wicked who are charged with altering prophetic revelation. This indicates that for the author of 1 Enoch 108, correct interpretation of the prophets lies in the exclusive domain of his own group, which are identified as the eschatological community of God's elect (cf. 108.6, 8–10).

Second, the citation of prophets in both 1 Enoch 108.6 and 1 Peter 1.10 is immediately followed by a reference to angels:

And he said to me, this place you see in here [are] the spirits of sinners and those who are idle and those who do sin and those who alter all the things God did through the mouth of <u>the prophets</u> (about) what will happen upon the earth. For writings and inscriptions about them were found to be upon heaven, so that <u>angels</u>

---

[43] The referent of προφῆται in 1.10 is the focus of a number of discussions among 1 Peter scholars. The majority view is that Old Testament prophets are in view, while others, most notably Duane Warden and James Dunn. have followed E. G. Selwyn in arguing that 1.10–12 describes the ministry of Christian prophets who searched the scriptures for the benefit of Jewish and Gentile believers; cf. E. G. Selwyn, *The First Epistle of St. Peter: The Greek Text with Introduction, Notes and Essays* (London: MacMillan, 1946), 259–68; James D. G. Dunn, *Christology in the Making: A New Testament Inquiry into the Origins of the Doctrine of the Incarnation* (Philadelphia: Westminster Press, 1980), 159; Duane Warde, 'The Prophets of 1 Peter 1:10–12', *ResQ* 31 (1989): 1–12, at 5–6, 11, bases his argument on the absence of the article before προφῆται in verse 10 and the use of the second person plural in 1.10 instead of the first person plural as in 1.3 and elsewhere. For convincing arguments against this reading, see for example J. N. D. Kelly, *A Commentary on the Epistles of Peter and Jude*, Thornapple Commentaries (Grand Rapids: Baker, 1969), 58–9; J. Ramsey Michaels, *1 Peter*, WBC 49 (Waco: Word Books, 1988), 41–8; Paul J. Achtemeier, 1 Peter (Minneapolis: Augsburg Fortress, 1996), 108–9.

may read them and know what will befall sinners and the spirits of the lowly and those who afflicted their body and were compensated by God and those who were humiliated by evil men.

1 Enoch 108.6–7

Concerning this salvation, <u>the prophets</u> who prophesied about the grace that was to be yours searched and inquired carefully, inquiring what person or time the Spirit of Christ in them was indicating when he predicted the sufferings of Christ and the subsequent glories. It was revealed to them that they were serving not themselves but you, in the things that have now been announced to you through those who preached the good news to you by the Holy Spirit sent from heaven, things into which <u>angels</u> long to look.

1 Pet 1.10–12

In 1 Enoch 108.7a, 'the Enochic writer is recording what the angel tells him about what angels know about the future from heavenly books'.[44] The specific content of angelic knowledge is thus what awaits humanity in the immediate afterlife, that is, an already-existent eschatological blessing for the righteous which has not yet been revealed. Although heavenly inscriptions are alien notions to 1 Peter, the angels of 1 Peter are also cognizant of human fate and, moreover, they rejoice over the eschatological blessing of the righteous in and through the Christ event. According to 1 Peter 1.4, there is an 'inheritance kept in heaven', which is further described in 1.5 as 'salvation ready to be revealed'. In this sense, although the readers are delivered from the present evil age, they have eschatological blessing awaiting them, since evil's complete destruction is in the eschatological future. Thus, both 1 Enoch 108 and 1 Peter can be understood as highlighting the concept of already existing but not yet revealed eschatological blessings.[45]

Third, and finally, the reference to the prophets appears within the temporal framework of 1 Peter's inaugurated eschatology. The aspect of time evident in 1 Peter 1.12 can be understood in terms of (1) a sacred past that included prophetic revelation about future events that precluded the participation of these prophets and (2) a present that is marked by an eschatological tension. Thus, in 1 Peter 1.10–12, the author depicts the prophets and his addressees as standing in different 'time zones' (cf. νῦν in v. 12). For 1 Peter, the eschatological divide between the prophets and the addressees finds its origin in the Christ event. As we have seen above, 1 Enoch's Exhortation and Apocalypse as well as the EA are also marked by the tension between the already and not-yet of evil's defeat in the eschatological future.

The revelation of the Apocalypse is comprised of ethics and eschatology and includes, to a lesser extent, a cosmological perspective. One of its end-time expectations is the building of the eschatological temple. However, before the eschatological temple

---

[44] Stuckenbruck, 1 Enoch *91–108*, 713.
[45] Dubis cites 1 Enoch 48.7; 2 Bar. 4.5; 52.6–7; and 4 Ezra 12.32; 13.26 as conceptual parallels to 1 Peter 1.4–5 (*Messianic Woes*, 44).

can be built, the elect must be chosen and given salvific wisdom. Thus, election and salvation precede the building of the eschatological temple. This contrasts with the idea of the eschatological temple in 1 Peter that takes the Christ event as the inauguration of eschatology and the democratization of the temple so that the righteous themselves are the 'new' temple. Despite this difference, however, the notion of divine election occurs in both as an event that precedes the building of the eschatological temple.

In sum, significant differences notwithstanding, the eschatological perspectives of the Enochic texts find in 1 Peter an intensified and more nuanced counterpart that finds its point of departure in the Christ event.

4

Has Christian Tradition Influenced the Ge'ez and Greek Versions of 1 Enoch?*

Loren T. Stuckenbruck

It is well known that the earliest 'complete' manuscript witnesses for what has become known as 1 Enoch date to some thousand years after it was translated from Greek into Ge'ez. It is not without reason, therefore, that some scholars have in principle been inclined to question whether one can so easily speak of a Ge'ez version that provides us with access to this ancient collection of texts composed during a four-hundred-year span of time in the Second Temple period. With such a gap in time between the manuscripts and initial composition and early translation, can we be confident that parts of that tradition, which are not extant in any other ancient materials (especially the Aramaic fragments from the Dead Sea Scrolls), are anything other than 'Christian'? Certain momentum for such a view is not simply furnished by those few who have held part or much of 1 Enoch to have been composed by Christian circles.[1] Indeed, the notion of a Christian Ethiopic Enoch dovetails in with 'new philological' approaches that prioritize the study manuscripts as artefacts that should be read synchronically – i.e. in relation to what they reveal about their own material, social and theological contexts – rather than as witnesses to some ancient text from which they and the scribes that produced them were far removed.[2] Related to yet distinct from this way of analysing manuscripts has been the argument, held by an increasing number of scholars, that many so-called 'pseudepigraphal' writings,[3]

---

* I am grateful to funding through the Deutsche Forschungsgemeinschaft (Project DFG STU 649/1-1) which has supported research in this contribution.
[1] See esp. J. T. Milik, *The Books of Enoch: Aramaic Fragments from Qumrân Cave 4* (Oxford: Clarendon, 1976), 78, 94–6, argued a third-century CE date for the Book of Parables (chapters 37–71), largely on the basis of the importance given to 'the Son of Man' in the work, something Milik understood as reminiscent of the New Testament Gospels. For a further important contribution in this direction, see Folker Siegert, *Einleitung in die hellenistisch-jüdische Literatur* (Berlin: de Gruyter, 2015), 190–6 and 208–16.
[2] For an excellent overview of this approach, see Hugo Lundhaug and Liv Ingeborg Lied, 'Studying Snapshots: On Manuscript Culture, Textual Fluidity, and New Philology', in *Snapshots of Evolving Traditions* (TUGAL 175; ed. Hugo Lundhaug and Liv Ingebord Lied; Berlin: Walter de Gruyter, 2017), 1–19.
[3] On the problematic use of this term, see Loren T. Stuckenbruck, '"Apocrypha" and "Pseudepigrapha"', in *Early Judaism: A Comprehensive Overview* (ed. John J. Collins and Daniel C. Harlow; Grand Rapids: Eerdmans, 2012), 179–203.

previously thought to be originally Jewish but overladen and edited in Christian circles, are in fact products of Christian authors that, as such, draw here and there on Jewish traditions.[4]

There is, then, a plausibility structure in the context of contemporary scholarship that makes it worth asking questions concerning the religious character and provenance of the text traditions in 1 Enoch. In particular, apart from the numerous fragments from at least twelve manuscripts relating to 1 Enoch among the Dead Sea Scrolls (4Q201–4Q212 plus, possibly 1Q19 and 1Q19bis) that meaningfully cover barely more than 5 per cent of text found in the later Ethiopic tradition, the remaining materials, which preserve significant portions of otherwise unattested text, were *all* copied in various Christian contexts. This is certainly the case with the meagre amounts of text in the Syriac (to chapter 6),[5] Coptic (to chapter 93),[6] and Latin (to chapters 19, 99 and 106)[7] witnesses, but, in terms of the extent, even more so of the Greek[8] and of course the Ge'ez, the latter of which contains more of the text than any of the other versions. In the following discussion, I would like to focus on the question of whether or not, in a sampling of instances, the Greek and Ge'ez traditions betray 'Christian influence'. It is hoped that the cases subjected to analysis illustrate some of the variety of problems interpreters face when determining the religious framing within which some of the texts available to us were produced. The study below is structured around the textual sequence in the Ge'ez tradition.

---

[4] See e.g. Robert A. Kraft, 'The Pseudepigrapha in Christianity', *Tracing the Thread: Studies in the Vitality of the Jewish Pseudepigrapha* (EJL 6; ed. John C. Reeves; Atlanta: Scholars Press, 1994), 55–86; Harm Wouter Hollander and Marinus de Jonge, *The Testaments of the Twelve Patriarchs. A Commentary*, SVTP 6 (Leiden: Brill, 1997); Ross Shepard Kraemer, *When Aseneth Met Joseph: A Late Antique Tale of the Biblical Patriarch and His Egyptian Wife* (Oxford: Clarendon, 1998); Dale C. Allison, *Testament of Abraham*, CEJL (Berlin: Walter de Gruyter, 2003); James R. Davila, '(How) Can We Tell if a Greek Apocryphon or Pseudepigraphon Has Been Translated from Hebrew or Aramaic?', *JSP* 15 (2005): 3–61 and *The Provenance of the Pseudepigrapha: Jewish, Christian, or Other?* (JSJSup 105; Leiden: Brill, 2005). In relation to the much-debated Testaments of the Twelve Patriarchs, see David de Silva, who brings important considerations to bear on the matter in the more traditional direction: 'The *Testaments of the Twelve Patriarchs* as Witnesses to Pre-Christian Judaism: A Reassessment', *JSP* 23 (2013): 21–68.

[5] Sebastian P. Brock, 'A Fragment of Enoch in Syriac', *JTS* 19 (1968): 626–31.

[6] Sergio Donadoni, 'Un frammento della versione copta del 'Libro di Enoch'', *AcOr* 25 (1960): 197–202 (1 Enoch 93b–4a, 5ab and 93:6c–7a, 8cd).

[7] In addition to the citations in Pseudo-Cyprian, *Ad novatianum* 16.5 (1 Enoch 1.8–9; chapters 16–17) and Tertullian, *De idololatria* 4,3.22–38 (1 Enoch 99.6–7; cf. also 19.1), see the Latin text to 1 Enoch 106 published initially by M. R. James, *Apocrypha Anecdota. A Collection of Thirteen Apocryphal Books and Fragments* (TS II/3; Cambridge: Cambridge University Press, 1893), 146–50, 186.

[8] For an edition, although in need of reworking, cf. Matthew Black, *Apocalypses Henochi Graece* (Leiden: Brill, 1970), who assembles the fragmentary materials corresponding to 1 Enoch 1.1–32.6a; 19.3–21.9; and 94.7–107.3. On the further Greek materials, see M. Gitlbauer, 'Die Überreste griechischer Tachygraphie im Codex Vaticanus Graecus 1809', Fascicle 1, Denkschriften der Kaiserlichen Akademie der Wissenschaften philosophisch-historischen Klasse 28.2 (Vienna: Gerold, 1878), 16, 32, 55–7 and 92–3 (on 1 Enoch 89.42–49) and Randal Chesnutt, 'Oxyrhynchus Papyrus 2069 and the Compositional History of 1 Enoch', *JBL* 129 (2010): 485–505 (on 1 Enoch 77.7–78:1, 8; 85:10–86.2; 87.1–3).

Enoch 1.1: 'And the righteous will be saved'

The text in question occurs right at the beginning of the Book of Watchers. With the exceptions of Michael A. Knibb and Siegbert Uhlig's translations,[9] the phrase 'and the righteous will be saved' is included in all modern translations, presumably as belonging to the earliest recoverable text for 1 Enoch.[10] The phrase is preserved in the Greek Codex Panopolitanus: καὶ σωθήσονται δίκαιοι; however, no single witness among the Ge'ez manuscripts contains this text. The difference is best illustrated in the following synoptic comparison with Nickelsburg's translation:

Nickelsburg[11]	Translation (Eth.)
The words of the blessing with which Enoch blessed the righteous chosen who will be present on the day of tribulation, to remove all the enemies[12] *and the righteous will be saved.*[13]	The words of the blessing with which Enoch[14] blessed the elect and righteous[15] ones who will be present on the day of affliction for removing[16] all the wicked[17] ones

The negligible Aramaic evidence from 4Q201 (a manuscript dated to the first half of the second century BCE) offers little help in evaluating the final phrase of the verse. Here as elsewhere, Nickelsburg's translation, which is unambiguously eclectic, operates on the principle of producing a translation based on sifting through all the available

---

[9] Michael A. Knibb, *The Ethiopic Book of Enoch* (2 vols; Oxford: Clarendon, 1978), 2.57 and Siegbert Uhlig, *Das äthiopische Henochbuch* (JSHRZ V/6; Gütersloh: Mohn, 1984), 507.

[10] See e.g. the translations of Daniel Olson (*Enoch: A New Translation* (North Richland Hills, TX: BIBAL, 2004), 27), and George W. E. Nickelsburg (e.g. 1 Enoch 1 (Hermeneia; Minneapolis: Fortress, 2001), 137–8), as well as the reconstruction of the missing Aramaic by J. T. Milik in *The Books of Enoch* (Oxford: Clarendon, 1976), 142. This text-critical decision seems to have been influenced by the unexplained judgement of R. H. Charles, *The Ethiopic Version of the Book of Enoch* (Oxford: Clarendon, 1906), 3: 'Though E [the Ethiopic] omits, the clause may be genuine'.

[11] See Nickelsburg and VanderKam, 1 Enoch: *The Hermeneia Translation* (Minneapolis: Augsburg Fortress, 2012), 19–20.

[12] Cod. Pan. ἐξᾶραι τοὺς ἐχθρούς.

[13] The italicized follows Grk. Pan., for which there is otherwise no evidence.

[14] The textual notes on this text below are, however, incomplete, nevertheless representative and provide an overview of issues relating to the verse as a whole: the various readings include *qāla barakat zahenok, qāla barakat henok, zahenok qāla barakat, zahenok* ('of Enoch') *zahenok nabiy* ('of Enoch the prophet'); the manuscript EMML 8400 reads *zahenok nabiy* ('of Enoch the prophet') above the text as the title and *qāla barakat* ('the word of the blessing') at the beginning of the text. For a comparison of 1 Enoch 1 in its entirety as basis for considerations here and below, see Loren T. Stuckenbruck, '1 Enoch 1: A Comparison of Two Translations', *New Vistas on Early Judaism and Christianity* (Jewish and Christian Texts 22; ed. Lorenzo DiTomaso and Gerbern S. Oegema; London: Bloomsbury T&T Clark, 2016), 25–40.

[15] The manuscript EMML 8347 inverts the sequence: *ṣadəqāna waḫəruyāna* ('the righteous and the elect'); cf. Grk. Cod. Pan. ἐλέκτους δικαίους. Aram. in 4Q201 1 i 1 has 'elec[t. . .', which is reconcilable with either the majority Eth. I+II or Grk.

[16] Eth. *la'asasəlo*.

[17] Variant readings here include *kʷəllu rasiyān* ('all the wicked ones'); *kʷəllu/kʷəllo 'əkuyān warasiyān, kʷəllu 'əkuyān warasiyāna,* and *kʷəllu 'əkuyāna warasiyāna*.

evidence among the versions. At this point, he opts to follow the Greek text, presenting it as the most ancient recoverable tradition; in turn, it is this form of the text for which he provides commentary.[18] For example, the inclusion of the Greek reading in the translation makes it possible for Nickelsburg to observe an emphasis on 'the opposite fates' of the wicked and the righteous that can be anchored in antiquity. For parallels he refers to Deuteronomy 33.27 and 29, which, respectively, refer to God's having driven out 'the enemy (i.e. of Israel) before you' and to 'a people (who were) saved/delivered (נושע, σῳζόμενος) by YWHW'. In addition, Nickelsburg claims such a parallel for 1 Enoch 10.17 and 20, which refer to 'the righteous who *will* escape' (v. 17: Cod.Pan. ἐκφεύξονται, Eth. *yəgʷayyu*), before going on to state the divine command to the archangel Michael to 'remove (Cod.Pan. ἐξάλειψον, most Eth. I mss.*'aḥleqomu*) impurity that is done on the earth'. Beyond this, Nickelsburg is only able to appeal to 91.9 and 14, which refer in other language (v. 9: 'taking out', 'throwing out', 'destruction'; v. 14: 'going out') to the punishment of 'wrongdoing' (91.8) and 'the works of the wicked' (91.14).

None of the parallels adduced above offer enough of a linguistic match that lends plausibility to a reference to the 'righteous' being 'saved' as opposed to the 'removing' of the wicked at the beginning of the Book of Watchers. One could perhaps appeal to a more *contiguous* (and sequentially parallel) dual fate of these groups, one that is pronounced in the Epistle of Enoch (cf. 99.9–10), as well as to further references to the righteous or 'elect' being 'saved' in 1 Enoch (cf. 1 Enoch 48.7; 50.3; 51.2; 61.2; 106.15, 18 – here a reference, however typological, to Noah and his sons), although the concise opposition found in 1.1 does not occur. One might also appeal to the 'few' who will be 'saved' in 4 Ezra at 6.25 and 7.60 (cf. also and the 'people within my holy borders' in 13.48; on 9.13 see below), although again, the contrast between this fate and that of the wicked is apparent from the broader literary context of the work. The opposition created by the Greek in 1 Enoch 1.1 would have a parallel that is textually far less remote: in 1.7 the Geʻez tradition uniformly states that judgement will include the righteous ones. Here again, the difference between the Geʻez tradition and the Greek is reflected in the translations of Nickelsburg, and Olson as well, who prefer the omission in Codex Panopolitanus, over against those of Knibb and Uhlig, who follow the more difficult Ethiopic:

Nickelsburg	**Translation (Eth.)**
The earth will be wholly rent asunder,	And the earth will split[19]
and everything on the earth	and everything on the earth[20]
will perish,	will be destroyed,[21]

---

[18] Nickelsburg, 1 Enoch *1*, 21.
[19] In concert with the Greek text of Codex Panopolitanus ('will split') some Geʻez manuscripts have *watəśaṭaṭ* (or *watasāṭo*). The reading *watəśaṭam* ('will sink') is shared by others (with a few having *watāśaṭəm*).
[20] *kʷəllu zawəsta mədr* ('everything that is on the earth') is omitted in the manuscript EMML 8400 through homoeoteleuton.
[21] *yəthagʷal* is shared by some manuscripts here; other readings include *yəthāgwal*, *yəthāgwal*, *wayəthagwal* (the result of the last reading is 'and the earth and everything that is on the earth will sink, *and* it will be destroyed').

and there will be judgement upon all.	and there will be judgement upon all,[22] *even upon all the the righteous ones.*[23]

The Greek version here distinguishes between judgement on the ungodly (cf. 1.9) and the fate of the righteous, with whom God will make peace (1.8); moreover, it omits any notion that the judgement will be concerned with the righteous as well. As seen in the above synopsis, the older Ethiopic 'recension'[24] preserves the more difficult text.

Reading the traditions from 1.1 and 1.7 together in their discrete forms, we can infer the following picture. According to the Geʿez, the opening of 1 Enoch emphasizes that the 'day of tribulation' is such because it relates to the wicked, not the righteous. When it comes to the latter part of the chapter, the text goes on to explain that the judgement on 'all' (v. 7) really means 'all', i.e. it is a comprehensive event that includes the righteous, before explaining in 1.8 that the righteous will come through this judgement unscathed. While it is possible that the Geʿez has added the phrase 'even upon all the righteous ones', the addition at least makes clear how the comprehensiveness of the judgement is being understood. For 1.1, this means that 'the day' is one of 'tribulation' to be described as such only for the wicked. With respect to the Greek, however, a somewhat different emphasis results. In 1.1, the 'day of tribulation' is one that affects the righteous as well and it is from this that they will be saved. Then, in 1.7–8, it follows that the judgement – here seen more in terms of result (as in 1.9) rather than as a general event – relates to the wicked only. It seems to me that the Greek (for 1.1) and the Geʿez (for 1.7) ultimately preserve a similar emphasis, although it is placed differently. In contrast to 1.1, it is thus the shorter Greek version that in 1.7 may be more original. As for 1.1, the *plus* 'and the righteous will be saved' intrudes as a resumptive clause to the earlier part of the verse. As suggested above, although in the immediate sense the Greek construes 'the day of tribulation' as a time of danger for the righteous as well, the addition collides with the implicit agency the 'elect righteous ones' will enjoy in the removal of the enemy (Eth. 'evil and wicked ones'). The *plus* also adds narrative to a verse that until that point otherwise simply functions as a heading for the work that follows. This, in turn, suggests that the longer Greek text for 1.1 is secondary. 'And the righteous will be saved', if an addition, would have its closest parallel in later Jewish apocalyptic tradition (as e.g. 4 Ezra 9.13, both Syriac and Latin[25]), but, taken discretely, has a number of parallels in the New Testament. We note, for example, Matthew 10.22 and 24.13/Mark 13.13 (collective singular, 'the one who remains until the end will be saved'), while the longer, secondary ending to the Gospel of Mark at 16.16 states that 'the one who believes and is baptized will be saved, while

---

[22] Numerous manuscripts have $k^w\partial llu$ but some have $k^w\partial llomu$, 'all of them'.
[23] Add. 'even upon all the righteous ones': some manuscripts have *walāʾəla ṣādəkān k^{w}əllomu*; Tana 9 has *walak^{w}əllomu ṣādəkān*; EMML 8400 reads only *ṣādəkān* ('upon all, *even the righteous ones*').
[24] The term hast to be used advisedly, as there is not an 'Ethiopic I' recension in the same way as there is the standardizing 'Ethiopic II'.
[25] I have yet to check the Geʿez and Armenian traditions.

the one who is without faith will be condemned'. In John 10.9, the motif is given an explicitly Christological focus: 'I am the door, and whoever enters through me will be saved' (presumably from judgement). Two passages in Acts 2 mention eschatological salvation: while the quotation of Joel 2.32 in the Petrine speech at Acts 2.21 – 'everyone who calls upon the name of the Lord will be saved' (cf. also Romans 10.13) – it does not specifically state from what. Acts 2.40, however, has Peter say, 'be saved from this corrupt generation'. Again, with a Christological focus, Paul combines the notion of being 'made righteous' with being 'saved from wrath' (Rom 5.9; cf. also v. 10); and, drawing on language from Isaiah 10.22, Paul underscores God's faithfulness to Israel by stating that, despite many Jews' apparent lack of faithfulness, 'a remnant will be saved' (Rom 9.27). Together with the intrusive character of the phrase at the end of 1 Enoch 1.1 in the Greek Codex Panopolitanus, the abundance of such similar language in the New Testament, along with the existence of the early part of 1 Enoch *in Greek* during the late first to early second century CE,[26] lends strength to a hypothesis that 'and the righteous will be saved' is secondary (possibly an addition during Christian transmission). The Ge'ez tradition, on the other hand, betrays no such influence and derives from a lost Greek *Vorlage*.

Enoch 81.3–5: Allusions to Psalms or Romans 3–4

Commenting on a passage concerned with a divine commissioning of Enoch to return to earth and instruct his offspring, Nickelsburg has noted three parallels with the text of Romans 3 and 4, stating these 'should be noted and studied more carefully'.[27] The parallels, which are only cursorily mentioned by Nickelsburg, can be described as follows:

1. 1 Enoch 81.3: 'And then I blessed the Great God, the eternal King of Glory because he made all the works of the world, and I praised *God for his forbearance* (wasabāḥku 'əgzi'a bat'ətəstu), and I cried concerning the children of Adam'. Romans 3.25: 'he (God) did this to show his righteousness, because in his divine *forbearance* he *had passed over the sins* previously committed' (NRSV).
2. 1 Enoch 81.4: 'And then I said, "*Blessed is the man* who dies righteous and pious, and about whom *no* book of *iniquity has been written*, and (against whom) the day of judgement will not be found"'. Romans 4.7–8: 'Blessed are those whose sins are forgiven and whose sins are covered. / Blessed is *the man to whom the Lord will not reckon sin*' (citing Ps 31.1–2 LXX).
3. 1 Enoch 81.5: 'and he said to me, "Make known everything to Methuselah your son, and show all your children that *no flesh is righteous before God*, for he has created them"'. Romans 3.10–11: 'As it is written: "*there is no one righteous*, not even one; there is no one who has understanding, there is no one who seeks God"'; see

---

[26] Cf. the quotation of 1 Enoch 1.9 in Jude 15.
[27] Nickelsburg, 1 Enoch *1*, 341.

also especially Romans 3.20: 'through the works of the law *no flesh is justified before him*' (citing Ps LXX 142.2, 'for no life is justified before you (ὅτι οὐ δικαιωθήσεται ἐνώπιόν σου πᾶς ζῶν').

I comment on each of these instances in turn, although offer no conclusion until having finished with notes on all three. In the first instance, it is striking that the notion of God's forbearance or patience occurs relatively rarely, as it most often describes a commendable human trait (cf. e.g. 1QS iv 3; 4Q421 1 ii 14/4Q420 1 ii 2; Sir 16.13; Bar 4.25; 1 Macc 8.4; 2 En. 50.2; 62.1; 2 Cor 6.6; 12.12; Gal 5.22; Eph 4.2; Col 3.12; 1 Tim 1.16; 2 Tim 4.2; Heb 6.2; Jas 5.10). As a motif associated with God, however, it occurs in at least several texts from the Dead Sea:

1QH^a iv 29 – as part of a praise declaration of God's 'righteous deeds' and 'patience';
4Q301 3.4 – God is 'glorified' in his patience; and
4Q382 104.9 – God's patience is linked with God's 'greatness in all forgiveness' (although the reading of the last term is very uncertain).

Indeed, when it comes to Romans, the theme of God's patience, whether expressed through the term μακροθυμία or ἀνοχή, occurs several times, that is, not only in Romans 3.25, but also in 2.4 and 9.22. In noting the uncertainty of the reading 'forgiveness' in 4Q382 104, we may observe that in two of the texts in Romans, the emphasis lies on God holding back from punishing those who have engaged in wrongdoing (Rom 3.25; 9.22). In the latter passage, Paul mentions, within a lengthy rhetorical question (9.22–24), God's endurance 'with patience' the 'objects of wrath made for destruction', in order to have mercy on Gentiles as well as on Jews (v. 24). In chapter 3, Paul underscores the comprehensive significance of God's activity through Jesus in the 'now time' by declaring that sins previously committed were overlooked (i.e. went unpunished) due to God's forbearance. In both these texts, Paul implicitly draws attention to this aspect of God's character under the assumption that it is categorically commendable and will be regarded that way by the text's readers and hearers. This admiration of divine forbearance in the face of contemporary wrongdoing is comparable, seen in the context of 1 Enoch 81.3: Enoch's praise of God's patience is contrasted with the destitute situation of humanity at large (here, 'the children of Adam'), about which the seer laments.

In the second instance, the parallel to Romans 4.7–8 is at first glance rather vague. There are, nevertheless, two points worth considering. First, the makarism pronounced upon a 'man' is a formulation that is common enough. In the Enochic text, the blessedness is directed at one who 'dies' in a righteous and pious state. While in very general terms there is a correlation to Romans 4.8 (the man to whom the Lord will not reckon sin), which in turn draws exactly on the Greek text tradition to Psalm 31.2a, the correspondence is at best only one of general sense. It would be misleading, on such a basis alone, to posit a link between Romans 4 and 1 Enoch 81.4 in terms of a unilateral direction of influence from one to the other. Second, and more significant, the last part of 1 Enoch 81.4 is difficult textually: Nickelsburg and Knibb both render the text as follows: 'and against whom no guilt will be found (reading *wa'iyətrakab gegāya lā'əlehu*).²⁸ The translation is based on the standardizing recension, which in turn is found in only one of the earlier manuscripts (Petermann II Nachtrag 29 in Berlin, and a corrector to Abbadianus 35);²⁹ it posits a corruption in the longer recension from the verb, which is also attested in the perfect, plus the following word (*'itarakəba lā'əlehu*),³⁰ while following the future sense based on the context. The reconstruction is forced. The most widely attested reading among the older manuscript tradition has instead: 'and (against whom) the day of judgement will not be found [i.e. take place]'.³¹ Text-critically, the older recension is to be preferred, and in this form the relation to Romans 4 is verbally remote. The standardizing version, however, is much closer, not only to Romans 4.8a but also to Psalm 31.2a. This suggests that the wording of the text was later adjusted to accommodate these well-known traditions, although it is impossible to say which of the biblical texts, whether Romans or the Psalm, would have wielded the influence.

The third instance is worth noting and may stand on its own. The Enochic text specifies that the patriarch is told to pass on to his progeny that 'no flesh is righteous before God' and somehow explains this statement by adding that God created them (that is, those who are not righteous). Closest to this text is the phrase in Romans 3.20, 'no flesh is justified before him (God)'. On the other hand, 1 Enoch 81.5 likewise approximates Psalm 143.2, which states that 'because no life is righteous before God' (Hebrew), with the only difference in the Greek being the second person pronoun 'you' in place of God. However, as Nickelsburg notes,³² the Enoch text uses 'no flesh instead of 'no life' (although both literally with 'all' plus the negative particle), and the word order differs at the end, with 1 Enoch, just like Romans 3.20, having 'before God' at the end while the Psalm places 'no ... all life' at the end. While the possibility that Paul, whether directly or (as would be more likely) indirectly, knows of tradition emanating from 1 Enoch, cannot be dismissed out of hand, the convergence of the wording of 1 Enoch 81.5 and Romans 3.20 over against that of Psalm 142.2 is suggestive. In a text tradition preserved here in a large number of very late manuscripts, it is on balance possible that the wording has been influenced by a subtle accommodation to the Pauline text. That Paul is not drawing on the Enochic tradition is nonetheless clear, since as Psalm 142 the verb 'justified' is in the passive voice, while in the former the verb simply carries the stative sense, 'is righteous (*yəṣadeq*)'.

It is precisely the last of the three possibilities that, in retrospect, makes it possible to question at all whether the Pauline influence is already felt in 1 Enoch 81.3 and 81.4. As tempting as such a conclusion would be, my answer is a guarded 'no'. Instead, it is the happenstance that motifs reminiscent of, but not dependent on Pauline tradition, which may themselves have been composed prior to the first century CE, are sufficiently close that in the next instance, which is even closer to Paul than the previous two, the text ends up being shaped in the standardizing recension along the lines of Romans 3.20. (Such a tendency to 'Paulinize' (or, alternatively, to reflect the wording of

---

²⁸ Nickelsburg, 1 Enoch 1, 333; Knibb, *The Ethiopic Book of Enoch*, 2.187.
²⁹ For now, see Charles, *The Ethiopic Version of the Book of Enoch*, 154n22 and 154n23.
³⁰ So the explanation of Nickelsburg, 1 Enoch 1, 334.
³¹ So Uhlig, *Das altäthiopische Henochbuch*, 666 and Olson, *Enoch: A New Translation*, 175.
³² Nickelsburg, 1 Enoch 1, 341.

Psalm 31) can perhaps already be seen in the standardizing recension of the Geʻez tradition in 1 Enoch 81.4b). As Paul is not drawing on 1 Enoch (but instead reflects Psalm LXX 142), the greater likelihood is that the text of Romans 3.20 has interfered with Enochic transmission in 1 Enoch 81.5.

Enoch 94.2 and the 'cross'

Near the opening of the Epistle of Enoch, the patriarch offers initial instructions to his sons (cf. 92.1–5; 94.1–5), before launching into a series of oracles against the wicked and words of consolation and assurance to the righteous in the main part of the work (94.6–104.8). The text of concern here is that of 1 Enoch 94.2, for which the best reconstructable text may be translated as follows:[33]

> And to notable men from a generation the ways of wrongdoing and death will be revealed, and they will be distant from them and will not follow them.

In the text as it stands, the 'notable men (*sabʾ ʾəmurān*)' refers to the righteous who in the future (from the vantage point of the fictive author) will be given special revelation or insight (similar to the Apocalypse of Weeks at 1 Enoch 93.10) into what constitutes iniquity. The 'ways of iniquity', which are contrasted with 'the ways of righteousness' in 94.1, are elaborated by the next expression 'and death'. EMML 6281, a seventeenth-century manuscript belonging to the earlier recension, inserts 'the cross' prior to the reference to death: 'the ways of wrongdoing, the cross, and death (*fənāwāt gəfā masqəl wamota*'. The addition is clearly a Christian interpolation that has nothing to do with the earliest recoverable text tradition. The meaning of the text shifts in focus as a result. The text now includes the crucifixion (of Jesus) as something predicted by the patriarch and connects it to wrongdoing; moreover, the expression 'death' is now linked to what, from the Christian perspective, is *the* death, whose significance will be revealed to the righteous, who will not be held responsible for what happened to Jesus. EMML 6281 thus preserves a subtle and rare, yet real Christian polemic against those (Jews?) whose actions are thought to have resulted in Jesus' crucifixion. The possible background in Ethiopian tradition for this textual insertion should be further studied.

Enoch 105.1–2: The conclusion to the Epistle of Enoch

In contrast to the Geʻez text tradition, the last two verses of the Epistle of Enoch are missing in the Greek Chester Beatty Papyrus, leading J. T. Milik to regard the passage, as it stands in Geʻez, as a 'Christian interpolation'.[34] Well before the publication of the Greek, Charles had indeed argued such, by appealing to the positive use of 'children

---

[33] See Loren T. Stuckenbruck, *1 Enoch 91–108* (CEJL; Berlin: Walter de Gruyter, 2007), 243, 251–2.
[34] Milik, *The Books of Enoch*, 207–8. Milik thus omits any part of 105.1–2 from his reconstruction of the Aramaic, here for 4Q204 (4QEnᶜ).

of the earth' (contrast 1 Enoch 100.6 and 101.1) and to an apparent reference to '[t]he Messiah' (otherwise absent in the Epistle). Does this indicate that the text does not go back to the original work? On the other hand, it is the Ge'ez text tradition that consistently renders the text, which may be translated:

> In those days, says the Lord, they will summon and give testimony to the children of the earth from their wisdom. Show (it) to them, for you are their leaders and the rewards upon the whole earth. / For I and my son will join ourselves with them forever on the ways of righteousness during their lives. And you will have peace. Rejoice O sons of righteousness!

That a text tradition following the end of 1 Enoch 104 did exist during the Second Temple period is clear from the meagre number of words visible in the Aramaic text to 4Q204 (4QEn^c).[35] From the Aramaic, the following words, in the sequence in which they appear, can be read: (a) 'among the children of [the] earth[...' (4Q204 5 i 21, beginning of the line); (b) 'y]ou will be [' (4Q204 5 i 22); and (c) 'y]ours is all [' (4Q204 5 i 23), with possibly 'peace' to be reconstructed after it.[36]

Although one is assured that 105.1–2 – that is, text following chapter 104 – originally belonged to the Epistle, the visible Aramaic text does not fit without difficulty into what is preserved in the Ge'ez tradition. Aramaic reading (a) does have an equivalent in 105.1 (children of the earth). Reading (b) could be assigned to the phrase immediately following ('you are ...'), although, if the Ethiopic text relates to the Aramaic at all, the gap of text in the latter between (a) and (b) implies that the former is missing some (now lost) text. Reading (c) could relate to pronouncement of peace near the end of 105.2, although, as noted above, the word 'all' before 'peace' would have little precedent. These correspondences are enough to discount Milik's doubt that 105.1–2, even in the Ge'ez, is simply a Christian addition. However, it seems equally clear that the extant Aramaic of 4Q204 has not found its way to the Ge'ez tradition unscathed. Although the Ge'ez to 105.1 can, despite a structural difference, be linked to the early Aramaic text, such is much more difficult to establish for 105.2. Thus, while '105.1–2 existed in a pre-Christian Jewish version (4QEnc)', it does not do so in the same form preserved in Ge'ez.[37]

Coming at the end of the Epistle, 1 Enoch 105.1–2 offers a number of interpretative problems that cannot be addressed here, namely, how it functions within the frame of the Epistle and whether, as part of the frame, it is source-critically distinct from the main body of the work.[38] Here, it suffices to focus on the conspicuous text of 105.2: 'For I and my son will join ourselves with them forever on the ways of righteousness during their lives'. The 'ways of righteousness', of course, resonates with the same phrase found in both the Exhortation of 1 Enoch at 91.18–19, the Apocalypse of Weeks to 91.14 (so the Eth.; the Aram. reads with the sing. 'way'), and the Epistle itself at 92.3 and 94.1. The

---

[35] For the readings, see Milik, *The Books of Enoch*, 206–8.
[36] Cf. Stuckenbruck, 1 Enoch *91–108*, 591. I note, however, that 'all' before 'peace' would be unusual.
[37] Stuckenbruck, 1 Enoch *91–108*, 595.
[38] I have discussed these issues in 1 Enoch *91–108*, 191–2 and 211–15.

phrase 'I and my son', however, is surprising, even though in the context of the original Epistle, it would have referred to Enoch and his son Methuselah (cf. 92.1, esp. as in the Aram. to 4Q212 [4QEn^g] 1 ii 22; cf. also 94.1, 3). This is plausible within Jewish tradition itself, and it is possible that the same holds for the phrase 'we will join ourselves with them forever on the ways of righteousness'. It is nevertheless surprising to find the Enochic text including Methuselah in the return to earth. Thus August Dillmann, attempting to reconcile the text's content with ancient Jewish tradition, maintained that it is concerned with God and the Messiah and argued that this interpretation is made plausible by the Epistle's appearance after the messianic references in the Book of Parables that come earlier in the Book of Enoch (1 Enoch 48.10; 52.4; cf. also 65.5; 69.29).[39] Such a connection is possible, but not if one is thinking about the original context of the Epistle, which was composed centuries before the Parables and initially, and certainly in the Greek tradition, likely copied separately. In addition, in the Parables 'my son' is not so much 'the Son of Man' of the Parables or even Methuselah, who is never mentioned there, but rather the figure of Noah (1 Enoch 65.11). Thus, rather than deriving the text's interpretation from another part of 1 Enoch, I think it is possible that it has been shaped in a way that fits with Christian tradition, whether its precise content owes to editorial work at the level of Ge'ez transmission or goes back to a non-extant Greek *Vorlage*. The fit with Christian tradition is reflected rather transparently in a marginal note to the text found in the sixteenth-century manuscript from Hayq Estifanos, EMML 2080, which, commenting on 'I and my son', states: 'the Father and the Son, or Enoch and Methuselah (*'ab wawaləd 'awu henok wamātusālā*)'. At this level, that is, the transmission of the text in the Ethiopian context, a literary connection with the Parables would be possible to imagine on the part of the comment (not to mention to Christian tradition more generally). Remote from a Second Temple context, in which 'Father' as a title for God, together with a Messiah 'son', never occurs together,[40] the text may, in its present form, have cast the Enoch–Methuselah paradigm in language that echoes Christian tradition, while openly declaring the text's meaning in this way. While at the very least one can acknowledge that the text could be understood in Christian terms, it is further possible that the interpretative context influenced the unusual phrasing of the verse, which I do not think goes back to the Aramaic tradition.

Conclusion

The analysis above highlights the importance of several methodological considerations in respect of the study of the relation of the transmission of 1 Enoch to Christian tradition: 1) the need to distinguish between 'original' or 'early' Jewish tradition(s), on the one hand, and the 'emerging' text as it was being received in Christian circles, who copied and edited the text in Greek and Ge'ez, on the other; 2) the need to distinguish

---

[39] August Dillmann, *Das Buch Henoch* (Leipzig: Fr. Chr. Wilh. Vogel, 1853), 325.
[40] Apart from writings of the New Testament (cf. e.g. Mk 1.11 pars. Mt 3.17, Lk 3.22; Mt 12.18b; 17.5; Heb 5.5; 2 Pet 2.17).

between text-criticism within the Ge'ez itself and text-criticism that more broadly (and eclectically) attempts to recover a non-Christian Jewish text tradition from the Second Temple period; 3) the need to distinguish between the form of the text in itself (which may be early or late) and the interpretations copyists brought to it (which do not interfere with the text); and, finally, 4) the need to distinguish between literary study and scribal accretions that over time furnished the tradition with particular wording.

These issues and the complexity they represent for studying 1 Enoch suggest that, to an amazing degree, the Ge'ez text tradition resisted the temptation to interfere openly with the received text – this despite the obvious Christian interpretations in which the text was enveloped. At the same time, it is not surprising if here and there, a long process of transmission has shaped wording of the text that results in echoes of Christian tradition, whether they relate to the New Testament or later developments. Possible instances of this have been explored, including the possibility of Christian influence at the stage of Greek transmission not preserved in the Ge'ez. Thus, interpreters of *Maṣḥafa Henok* who seek an ancient tradition that can be read as a participant in Second Temple Judaism should never entirely dislodge themselves from the context in which the manuscripts conveying *most* of its text were copied.

5

Non-Human Animals in the Primeval History of Jubilees

James R. Hamrick

A rich array of beings populates the cosmos of Jubilees, including God, various angels and spirits, non-human animals, humans, and the offspring of spiritual beings and humans. Scholarship has unfortunately neglected the portrayal and role of non-human animals in this and other early Jewish and Christian works, focusing instead on theology, angelology and anthropology. Here I explore non-human animals in the primeval history of Jubilees, paying particular attention to the portrayal of animals as moral agents whose natures and behaviour were subject to change in history. This chapter is partly an attempt to experiment with different ways of engaging Ethiopic Jubilees.

My approach consists of three major steps. First, I begin by examining a specific theme in Jubilees in its own right. The theme has been selected without any regard to its relevance for understanding the New Testament, but rather because it is interesting and useful in our understanding of Jubilees as a work with its own independent historical, literary and theological value. This is an intentional decision, made in part to avoid a 'pillaging' approach that seeks to extract only what is useful as background for understanding the New Testament or other texts, or an approach that allows New Testament interests to unduly shape the conversation. As a second step, I turn to the New Testament, attempting to bring some of these texts into creative conversation with Jubilees. Finally, I offer some comments on the Ethiopian reception of Jubilees and the potential contemporary ethical relevance of our theme. Throughout my treatment I avoid discussion of Ethiopic Jubilees' redaction of Genesis. Redaction-critical approaches that focus on Ethiopic Jubilees as 'rewritten' scripture are important, but it is also possible to take cues from literary and canonical criticism and engage with Ethiopic Jubilees as a finished literary work. I also engage with the Ethiopic text, making use of VanderKam's critical Ethiopic text, rather than relying on the heavily reconstructed Hebrew fragments from Qumran.

Jubilees

Taxonomy of creation

In discussing a theme such as 'animals' or 'non-human animals', we must be cautious about forcing our etic categories onto ancient texts. Already a discussion of 'non-human animals' creates a binary between humans and all other life forms that we would today categorize as animals and implies that there really is something special about humans, or something in common between all non-human species, that allows us to discuss them as two distinct groups. We cannot assume that such divisions, which might seem natural to us, were shared by ancient authors. I attempt here a very basic emic overview of the cosmos and its creatures as presented in the primeval history of Jubilees.

The creation narrative of Genesis 1.1–2.3 offered a taxonomy of creation that later authors could interpret, appropriate and develop, in order to express their understandings of the created order. A first step in understanding the theology, angelology, anthropology, zoology, botany, or astronomy of Jubilees is an analysis of its own retelling of the seven days of creation. Jubilees enumerates its taxonomy of creation, offering both a daily count and a final tally (22) of the works (*gǝbr*) or kinds (*tǝwlǝdd*; *zamad*) that God made in the first six days. Divided by day, these are:

Day 1: heavens, earth, waters, spirits, depths, darkness, light, dawn, evening (seven works)[1]
Day 2: firmament (one work)
Day 3: dry land, bodies of water, plants, and the Garden of Eden (four works)[2]
Day 4: sun, moon, stars (three works)
Day 5: sea monsters, fish, birds (three kinds)
Day 6: land animals, cattle, everything that moves on the earth, humans (four kinds)

Identifying emic categories for the works of creation is not a simple task, in part because there are some difficulties reconciling the lists given with the daily tallies. Fortunately, the category with which we are concerned – *flesh* – is somewhat clearer. All of those life forms that we would classify as animals, including humans, seem to belong to this larger group, which is further subdivided into seven sub-groups, with at least some of these sub-groups consisting of a range of species:

<u>Fifth day creatures (the deeps, sea, and air)</u>
The great sea monsters (*'anābǝrt 'abayt*)

---

[1] How exactly we come to a total of seven works from the lengthy list is not clear. One possibility is heavens, earth, waters, spirits, depths, darkness/light, dawn/evening. Noting the difficulty, van Ruiten suggests heavens, earth, waters, spirits, depths, darkness and light (J. van Ruiten, *Primaeval History Interpreted: the Rewriting of Genesis 1-11 in the Book of Jubilees* (Leiden: Brill, 2000), 23).

[2] We face again potential difficulty reconciling the list of created works with the total given by Jubilees. We have opted for VanderKam's suggestion. James C. VanderKam, 'Genesis 1 in Jubilees 2', *DSD* 1 (1994): 300–21, at 310–11.

All that moves in the waters, i.e. fish (kwəllu zayəthawwas wəsta māyāt 'āśāt)
All that flies, i.e. birds (kwəllu zayəsarrər 'a'wāfa)

Sixth day creatures (land)
Animals of the earth ('arāwīta mədr)
Cattle ('ənsəsā)
All that moves upon the earth (kwəllu zayəthawwas diba mədr)
Humans (sab')

This category is introduced on the fifth day, with the author identifying monsters of the watery deeps as the first work 'of flesh (zaśəgā)', which VanderKam translates as 'animate beings'. Later, in the flood narrative, this term will be more explicitly fleshed out (5.2):

All animate beings [flesh] corrupted their way – (every one of them) from people to cattle, animals, birds, and everything that moves about on the ground (wakwəllu zaśəgā 'amāsanat fənotā 'əmsab' 'əska 'ənsəsā wa'əska 'arāwit wa'əska 'a'wāf wa'əska kwəllu zayānsosu wəsta mədr).[3]

Here humans, cattle, beasts, birds, and everything that walks on the earth (yānsosu wəsta, here in contrast to yəthawwas diba in the creation narrative) are all categorized as fleshly, zaśəgā. Sea creatures are excluded in the list in 5.2, although this exclusion is likely due to the difficulty of sea creatures being destroyed by a flood. Since sea monsters were classified as zaśəgā and all other subsequent created works were fleshly, it seems safe to assume that fish also belong to the category, although they are not explicitly labelled in this way. The primary domains of fleshly creatures are the deeps, the waters, the sky, and the land.

No clean/unclean distinction between animals is introduced at this point. Given its larger tendency to root Mosaic legislation in the ancestral period and primeval times, we might have expected Jubilees to retroject the Mosaic distinction between clean and unclean animals onto the creation narrative, or at least maintain it in the flood narrative. Perhaps this would have created tension with the idea of the Garden of Eden as a sacred site.

Humans belong to the same category of beings as the non-human animals, flesh. Jubilees is uninterested in making significant ontological distinctions between humans and the other animals, and actually omits the *imago dei* (it does appear later in 6.8). The work maintains, however, the authority of humans over the rest of the creation and does set them apart as the 'concluding creation' with the phrase wa'əmdəḫra kwəllu ('after all this') in 2.14.[4] Just as there are various species or kinds among the non-human animals, so there are variations among humans. Humans are gendered, and the distinction between Israel and the nations, or the elect and the non-elect, appears

---

[3] All English translations are from VanderKam.
[4] VanderKam, 'Genesis 1', 314.

already in the creation narrative. The latter is one of Jubilees' most significant embellishments of the Genesis account. While the humans belong to the category flesh, there is also a sense that humans are a liminal species, straddling the border between the animal world and the spiritual world. At least some spirits are portrayed anthropomorphically and are capable of being circumcised (15.27), marrying, and procreating with humans (4.15). Among humans the nations lean in the beastly or earthly direction, as they do not cover their nakedness (3.31), and Israel leans in the spiritual or heavenly direction, sharing angelic practices such as circumcision (2.30–31) and sabbath observance (15.26–27).

In Adam's naming of the animals, which lasts five days (3.1–2), the following categories are presented:

Day 1: animals (*'arāwit*)
Day 2: cattle (*'ənsəsā*)
Day 3: birds (*'a'wāfa*)
Day 4: all that moves upon the earth (*kwəllu zayəthawas diba mədr*)
Day 5: all that moves in the water (*kwəllu zayəthawwas wəsta māy*)

It is not made clear whether the sea monster is also named on the fifth day or not. These five categories are further subdivided into their respective (unspecified) kinds (*zamadomu*) and forms (*'amsālomu*).

A separate study would be required exploring the cosmology and metaphysics of Jubilees. One question that such a study would address is the corporeality of spirits such as the Watchers and the spirits of fleshly creatures. On the one side, spiritual beings are created circumcised and can procreate with human women (15.27; 5.1). On the other side, flesh – presumably including non-human animals – also contains spirit, as we see in 10.3, where Noah addresses God as the God of the spirits which are in all flesh (*zawəsta kwəllu zaśəgā*).[5]

Animals as nuisance

Adam and Eve worked in the Garden of Eden seven years before their expulsion (3.15, 17). Part of their task was to protect the garden from birds, beasts and cattle (3.16):

He would guard the garden against birds, animals, and cattle (*waya'aqqəb ganata 'əm'a'wāf wa'əm'arāwit wa'əmənsəsā*)

It is not specified exactly what this meant, but it is likely that it involved protecting the plants from destruction or consumption. Later, during the thirty-fifth jubilee, Mastema, the leader of evil spirits, sent ravens to disrupt the agricultural efforts of humans. The ravens ate the seeds from the fields and the fruit from the orchards, which required humans to protect the seed (*yə'qab zar'a*, 11.18) in order to survive. Abram manages to

---

[5] Cf. Num 16.22, 27.16. More parallels are offered by John C. Endres, 'Prayer of Noah: Jubilees 10.3–6', in *Prayer from Alexander to Constantine: A Critical Anthology* (ed. Mark Kiley; London: Routledge, 1997), 53–8.

become famous for scaring the ravens away (11.19–23), and later invents the first seed drill to protect the seeds (11.23–24). In this later account, humans are continuing the work that began in the Garden of Eden: protecting crops and produce. Jubilees' presentation of the garden is thus not entirely idyllic. While there is no indication that the animals harm and eat each other, animals and humans have at times an adversarial relationship.

Talking animals

In Jubilees, both spirits and fleshly creatures, including non-human animals, were created with the ability to speak, and were at one time capable of communicating with each other. Spirits teach and mediate truth to humans, and in the Garden of Eden animals were capable of interspecies communication. While some later traditions would come to see the talking serpent in Genesis 3.1–4 as the Devil, or as the Devil speaking through a literal serpent, in its original context and in some ancient interpretations of the text the serpent was simply a crafty animal who happened to speak with humans. One of the interesting features of the Genesis narrative is that no special attention is drawn to the fact that the serpent converses with Eve. For later interpreters, however, this raises several questions. How did they communicate? Was the serpent the only animal who could speak? Are serpents and any other animals still capable of speech? In its narration of the expulsion from the Garden of Eden, Jubilees offers an answer to some of these questions (3.28–29):

> On that day the mouths of all the animals, the cattle, the birds, everything that walks and everything that moves about were made incapable of speaking because all of them used to converse with one another in one language and one tongue. He dismissed from the Garden of Eden all the animate beings that were in the Garden of Eden. All animate beings were dispersed – each by its kind and each by its nature – into the place(s) which had been created for them.[6]

According to Jubilees, the serpent was by no means special. Before the expulsion from the garden, all creatures, or at least the creatures of the land and air, were capable of speaking with each other, and presumably with humans. The talking serpent was not a dummy for a satanic ventriloquist act, as some early Christian writers supposed, but reflected a primeval situation in which communication between species was normal – a situation that the expulsion from the garden changed.

The echoes of the Tower of Babel story are strong here: just as human language would later be divided and humans would be dispersed throughout the earth, so here the ability of humans and non-human animals to communicate ceases and all creatures are dispersed to the various places created for them. Jubilees does not address the issue

---

[6] *Wabayəʾəti ʾəlat tafaṣṣama ʾafa kwəllu ʾarāwit wazaʾənsəsā wazaʾaʿwāf wazayānsosu wazayəṯḥawwas ʾəmnabib ʾəsma kwəllomu yətnāgaru zəntu məsla zəntu kanfara ʾaḥada waləsāna ʾaḥada. wafannawa ʾəmganata ʿedom kwəllo zaśəgā zahallo wəsta ganata ʿedom watazarwu kwəllu zaśəgā baba zamadomu wababa feṭrātomu wəsta makān zatafaṭra lomu.*

of ongoing intra-species communication, but the parallels with the Babel story might suggest that some form of language or communication continued among the individual species.

Here we see a fundamental post-creation transformation in created beings. Within Jubilees, this transformation occurs *within history*. Its carefully structured chronological scheme does not allow us to make any meaningful qualitative distinction between a distant, primordial time, and normal, earthly history. The continual existence of the Garden of Eden on earth (4.23–26; 8.16, 19, 21) also prevents us from locating these early historical events in a mythical realm. The closing of the mouths of animals is a dateable historical event that occurred within this world, a point to which we will return below.

While this loss of speech continues until our day, the author of Jubilees may have considered it as something reversible. The expression that the animals' mouths were closed likely reflects influence from the story of Balaam's donkey, the other example of a talking animal in the Torah. Numbers 22.8 tells us that YHWH 'opened the mouth of the donkey', who then proceeded to speak to Balaam. The author of Jubilees perhaps reasoned that if the mouth of the donkey could be opened, and in the Garden of Eden there was at least one example of a talking animal, then maybe at some point the mouths of animals had been *closed*. The Balaam episode is thus a temporary reversal of a divine action carried out at the time of the expulsion from the garden.

The fact that animals had speech and that the serpent was able to carry on a conversation with Eve raises the question of how the author of Jubilees conceived of animal rationality. Within the Greek philosophical tradition, the existence and nature of animal language was discussed, and was connected to the larger debate about animal rationality – a discussion which continues today. Whether or not non-human animals are moral agents, a theme which we will look at below, was also debated within this context. For Aristotle and the Stoics, non-human animals did not possess rationality and had primarily utilitarian value. Some Platonists and others argued that they were rational beings with the ability to learn, make decisions, exhibit virtues and vices, and communicate.[7]

Jubilees exhibits awareness of and engagement with larger Hellenistic scientific and literary traditions, making it possible that the author was aware of such widespread and enduring philosophical debates.[8] We also cannot assume this, and there are no strong indications in the text that the author was trying to enter this debate. We can say, however, that the work's philosophically attuned ancient readers would have quite easily linked traditions about animal speech and portrayals of animals as moral agents

---

[7] See the extensive discussions in Ingvild Sælid Gilhus, *Animals, Gods and Humans: Changing Attitudes to Animals in Greek, Roman and Early Christian Ideas* (London: Routledge, 2006), 37–63, and Richard Sorabji, *Animal Minds and Human Morals: The Origins of the Western Debate* (London: Duckworth, 2001).

[8] Cana Werman '*Jubilees* in the Hellenistic Context', in *Heavenly Tablets: Interpretation, Identity and Tradition in Ancient Judaism* (JSJSup 119; ed. Lynn LiDonnici and Andrea Lieber; Leiden: Brill, 2007), 133–58. James R. Hamrick, 'No Faithful Oaths: A Comparison of Esau's Speech in *Jubilees* 37:18–23 with Achilles' Speech in *Iliad* 22.260–272' (MA thesis, Trinity Western University, 2014).

to this larger discourse, likely with a tendency to associate Jubilees with the anti-Stoic position.

New natures and the moral responsibility of animals

Along with Jubilees' creation narrative, its flood narrative provides us some of the most significant insights into the work's understanding of the non-human animal creation. At least two significant themes emerge: non-human animals as creatures who can stray from their divinely ordained paths (morally responsible agents), and non-human animals as recipients of new natures following the flood.

According to Genesis and Jubilees, God destroyed nearly all living land creatures with the flood (Gen 6.7, 13, 17; Jub 5.4, 20). What was the reason for this act of biocide? In its narration of the antediluvian period, Jubilees emphasizes the culpability of all flesh, specifying humans, cattle, animals, birds, and everything that moves on the earth (5.2, 3). The earth itself was corrupt and each fleshly creature had corrupted its way (*wakwəllu zaśəgā 'amāsanat fenotā*) and ordinance (*śər'ātā*). This included violence (*'amaḍā*) and eating each other. This may be the beginning of predation. As elaborated in a discussion of Noah's post-diluvian commandments to his descendants, there was a chain reaction of sin: first the Watchers intermingled with human women, then their children began eating and killing each other and humans (7.21–22). Humans then began to act unjustly and violently (7.22–24). Finally, the animals, birds, and those creatures that move and walk upon the earth also strayed (7.24).

The universal scope of the flood was justified by the universal failure of God's creation to remain on their prescribed paths. This indicates something that some in the antique, medieval and modern worlds are hesitant to accept: non-human animals are in some sense moral agents. While we must be careful about what moral philosophical terms and categories we apply to the text, we can at a bare minimum say: in addition to their individual habitats, each species has expected behaviours that can be violated, resulting in divine judgement. While humans are singled out for their evil thought life, there is an overall sense that humans and non-human animals were in the same boat.

While only Noah did not transgress and only the salvation of Noah is stressed (5.19), non-human animals were also subject to deliverance (*fannawa 'əmwəstetā 'arāwita waa'wāfa wazayəthawwas*: '(He) sent out from (the ark) the animals, birds, and whatever moves about', 5.32). Their redemption included not only passage on the ark, but also the gift of a new and righteous nature (5.12):[9]

> He made a new and righteous nature for all his creatures so that they would not sin with their whole nature until eternity. Everyone will be righteous – each according to his kind – for all time.[10]

---

[9] This verse was extensively discussed in an Oberseminar led by Professor Loren Stuckenbruck at the LMU München, and my treatment of this verse has been influenced by these discussions.
[10] *wagabra lakwəllu gəbru fəṭrata ḥadās waṣādqta kama 'iya'abbəsu bakwəllu fəṭratomu 'əska la'ālam. Wayəṣaddeq kwəllu baba təzmədu kwəllo mawā'əla.*

This is a new creative act that takes place at the time of the deluge. The recipients are *each* of God's works, which could include not only the human creation, but also the non-human creation and theoretically the fifteen other works that God made in the first week of the universe. Each of these works, however broad the envisioned scope, received a *new* and *righteous* nature. The purpose of this is that they do not transgress with their entire being, as they had before the flood. The consequence is that each will be righteous according to its species or type for all time.

It was difficult for Charles to accept that this dramatic act had already occurred at the time of the flood: 'But with the subsequent corruption of all the descendants of Noah till the time of Abraham and the universal apostasy of the Gentiles according to our author, such a statement is practically inconceivable'.[11] He thought the perfect form of the verb in the Geʽez (*gabra*) must be an error that occurred when Jubilees was translated from Hebrew into Greek.[12] Most other interpreters, however, accept the Geʽez as it stands, finding no difficulty with Jubilees' presentation of a 'non-eschatological' eschatological act.[13] We can understand God's activity here as a recalibration of a straying creation, which had lost its equilibrium when the Watchers caused a chain reaction by straying from the natural, ordained order of things. This did not mean that the new creation (1.29; 4.26) had already occurred, or that transgression would disappear, only that God's creation would not stray so thoroughly as it had before the flood.

Non-human animals are thus agents capable of incurring divine displeasure and judgement by straying from their paths, and also the recipients of new, righteous natures.

Eating and sacrificing

Animal sacrifice and the permissible consumption of animals is an important aspect of the post-diluvian relationship between humans and non-human animals. After disembarking from the ark, Noah builds an altar and offers animal sacrifices (6.1–3), which atones for the sins of the earth and is accepted as pleasing by God. God then gives Noah and his descendants authority over the creation (6.5) and gives humans all physical, non-human categories of life, with the exception of sea monsters, as food (6.6):

> I have now given you all the animals, all the cattle, everything that flies, everything that moves about on the earth, the fish in the waters, and everything for food. Like the green herbs I have given you everything to eat.[14]

---

[11] R. H. Charles, *The Book of Jubilees* (London: Adam and Charles Black, 1902), 44.

[12] Charles, *The Book of Jubilees*, 44–5.

[13] Gene L. Davenport, *The Eschatology of the Book of Jubilees* (Leiden: Brill, 1971), 38–49; James C. VanderKam, 'The Angel Story in the Book of Jubilees', in *Pseudepigraphic Perspectives: The Apocrypha and Pseudepigrapha in Light of the Dead Sea Scrolls* (STDJ 31; ed. E. G. Chazon and M. E. Stone; Leiden: Brill, 1999), 151–70, at 161–2. Berger and VanderKam maintain the perfect in their translations.

[14] *nāhu wahabkukəmu kwəllo ʾarāwita wakwəllo zayəsarrər wakwəllo zayəthawwas wəsta mədr wawəsta māyāt ʾaśāta wakwəllo lasisit kama ḥamla śāʿr wahabkukəmu kwəllo teblə'u.*

No distinction is made here between clean and unclean animals. The only restriction – and it is one that is very strongly stressed – is not to eat fleshly creatures with their blood (6.7):

> But you are not to eat animate beings [flesh] with their spirit – with the blood (because the vital force of all animate beings [flesh] is in the blood) so that your blood with your vital forces may not be required from the hand of any man. From the hand of each one I will require the blood of man.[15]

Here the blood and the spirit of fleshly creatures are explicitly connected with each other. One might have understood Genesis 9.4 as equating spirit (or life) and blood. Jubilees provides an additional statement that makes the connection clearer: the spirit of all fleshly creatures is *in* the blood.

The principle of not eating blood is so important for Jubilees that Noah and his living descendants swear an eternal oath that they will abstain from blood (6.10-14). The oath involves abstention from eating the blood of all flesh (6.10), but it is animals (*'arāwit 'arwe*) cattle (*'ənsəsā*) and birds (*'a'wāf*) that are specified (6.12).

The abstention from blood is again stressed by Noah in the twenty-eighth jubilee, when he speaks with his sons and grandsons. He tells them how they ought to conduct themselves (7.20-21) and reminds them of how failure to act rightly led to the flood. Noah is concerned, as he has noticed that his descendants, under the influence of demons, have begun to stray. He fears that after his death his descendants will shed human blood and begin consuming the blood of animals. This latter fear, which was already the subject of an oath taken by all of humanity, is developed again at length in 7.28-33. Absolutely no blood from animals, cattle and flying creatures is to be consumed (7.30), and the blood that is poured out is to be covered (7.31). Eating meat with blood is the equivalent of eating the spirit or life of other beings (*'itəblə'əwwā lanafs məsla śəgā*, 7.32). This prohibition has a divine source (7.31), and violation of it will result in judgement and destruction in this life and the next (7.29).

The prohibition comes up yet again in 21.6, as Abraham gives his testament to Isaac. Here again animals (*'arwe*), cattle (*'ənsəsā*) and birds (*'of zayəsarrər wəsta samāy*) are specified.

Summary

For Jubilees, the fifth and sixth days of creation included the creation of *flesh*, a larger category which consists of what we would designate as human and non-human animals, as well as the sea monsters. Flesh is further divided into larger families (sea monsters, fish, birds, beasts of the earth, cattle, all that moves upon the earth, and humans), and these in turn have internal variation and speciation. Habitat (deeps, waters, air, land), movement (swimming, flying, moving on land), and relation to

---

[15] *wabāḥtu śəgā zaməsla manfasu məsla dam 'itəblə'u 'əsma nafsa kwəllu zaśəgā wəsta dam wə'ətu kama 'iyətḥaśśaś daməkəmu wəsta nafsātikəmu 'əmwəsta 'əda kwəllu sab' 'əm'əda kwəllu 'aḥaśəśo ladama sab'.*

humanity (beasts of the earth = wild; cattle = domestic) seem to be principles that guide the taxonomy.

While humans belong to this larger category and are not presented as being metaphysically different from the other animals, they do have a relationship of authority to the rest of creation. The anthropomorphic presentation of spirits, particularly their ability to be circumcised and marry humans, may establish humans as a liminal species, which shares properties with the animals but also with spiritual or angelic beings. This is particularly the case for Israel, which is presented as a people chosen from the time of creation to exclusively participate in practices such as the Sabbath that are practised by the angels. The nations, on the other hand, are portrayed as being animal-like in their practices of public nudity.

Creatures of flesh are endowed with *spirit*. Fleshly creatures are also capable of undergoing dramatic transformations at key points within the course of earthly space and time. In Eden, all animals were capable of speaking across species boundaries and shared a common language, until in a Babelesque scenario their mouths were closed and they were scattered to their various habitats. When situated within ancient philosophical discourse, this raises questions about the ongoing linguistic abilities of animals and the nature of animal rationality.

Two other significant transformations occurred before and after the flood. Preceding and precipitating the flood was the straying of *all flesh*, specifically birds, humans and non-human land creatures. Non-human animals are presented as having what we might term moral responsibility. Each species has particular behaviours that are expected of it – a specific path – and it is possible for them to depart from the way and receive divine judgement as a result. The non-human animals were not collateral victims in the flood, they were deserving recipients of divine judgement. A second transformation occurs after the flood, as God gives all of his creatures a new/renewed nature. We have here, following a significant divine action, a fundamental and universal internal transformation of created beings within earthly space and time, new creation within the confines of the first creation. We can even date when this happened: in the twenty-seventh jubilee.

As already mentioned, humans are given authority over non-human animals. Other aspects of human/animal relations are: animals as nuisance to human agriculture; animals as clothing for humans; animals as food and sacrificial victims (after the flood). Sacrificial animals play a role not only in the cleansing and restoration of humans, but of the entire earth. In human/animal relations, Jubilees prioritizes the Noahide command to abstain from the consumption of blood. Unlike the sabbath, this is a commandment that is binding for all humans and is sealed with an oath taken by Noah and all of his living descendants.

New Testament connections

We can now attempt to bring the above overview of non-human animals in Jubilees into creative conversation with early Christian texts. Three areas will be briefly considered: irrational animals in 2 Peter and Jude; new natures, new creation; and Noahide laws.

Irrational animals in 2 Peter

In the overlapping sections from 2 Peter and Jude, we find a simile which compares opponents to irrational animals (ἄλογα ζῷα):

> But these people slander whatever they do not understand, and they are destroyed by those things that, like irrational animals, they know by instinct.
>
> Jude 10[16]

> These people, however, are like irrational animals, mere creatures of instinct, born to be caught and killed. They slander what they do not understand, and when those creatures are destroyed they also will be destroyed.
>
> 2 Pet 2.12[17]

In both versions, we find the phrase 'irrational animals' (ἄλογα ζῷα), the concept of nature or instinct (φυσικῶς, φυσικά), and a comparison of the text's opponents in some way with the irrational animals. They can be likened to irrational animals in their way of knowing, their behaviour and their destiny. In 2 Peter 2.12, the instinctual creatures are presented as being born for capture and destruction. I mentioned above the ancient debate over animal rationality. The phrase ἄλογα ζῷα is laden with meaning and would have functioned as a hyperlink to this much larger philosophical discourse that spanned centuries in the ancient Greek-speaking world. The use of this phrase could be understood as an indication that the authors of 2 Peter and Jude were participating in this discourse and weighing in on an ongoing debate. If so, these authors sided with the Stoics, assuming the irrationality of non-human animals and employing that assumption in a pointed rhetorical attack on their opponents.

One of the ways that we can engage in comparative work with ancient texts and bring a work like Jubilees into conversation with other early Christian writings is to move past genetically oriented comparative approaches that focus on influence and dependence, and attempt to situate the texts within larger discourses in the ancient world. In some cases, a text may be very explicitly and intentionally entering this discourse, in other cases more indirectly or unintentionally. Such an approach can help us pose questions to the texts that arise out its ancient context, offer us fresh perspectives, and help us better understand and imagine how the texts were read and received by their earliest readers.

In this case, we can attempt to situate both Jubilees and 2 Peter/Jude within the broader ancient discourse about animal rationality. Through its use of a key phrase from these debates, 2 Peter/Jude could have been read by the philosophically attuned reader as taking a side in these ancient debates, adopting the position that non-human animals are irrational. Jubilees, in its portrayal of non-human animals as beings who

---

[16] οὗτοι δὲ ὅσα μὲν οὐκ οἴδασιν βλασφημοῦσιν, ὅσα δὲ φυσικῶς ὡς τὰ ἄλογα ζῷα ἐπίστανται, ἐν τούτοις φθείρονται. Translations of New Testament texts here and below are from the NRSV.
[17] οὗτοι δὲ ὡς ἄλογα ζῷα γεγεννημένα φυσικὰ εἰς ἅλωσιν καὶ φθορὰν ἐν οἷς ἀγνοοῦσιν βλασφημοῦντες ἐν τῇ φθορᾷ αὐτῶν καὶ φθαρήσονται.

were at least at one time capable of speech and its portrayal of them as moral agents, can be read as taking another position within this larger discourse. When we move on to contemporary ethical engagement with these texts, Jubilees can provide a counterweight to texts such as 2 Peter 2.12 and Jude 10.

New natures, new creation

Jubilees provides a vision of fleshly creatures, human and non-human, who can undergo significant transformation within the course of earthly history. They can lose speech. They can become so corrupt in thought and deed that the only solution is complete destruction. And they can receive the divine gift of new natures. This makes Jubilees a fascinating conversation partner for many texts and themes in the New Testament, especially those that deal with how early Christians understood the impact of the Christ-event on their own lives and world. Key elements from Jubilees that we would need to keep in mind in such comparative work are:

1. The new creative act occurs as a dateable event within the course of earthly history, at a time when a dramatic corruption of the creation called for dramatic divine intervention.
2. The new creative act is universal, not just for humans, and not just for one segment of humanity.
3. The new creative act affects the natures of the creatures, and has impacts on their behaviour.
4. It is still possible to transgress and be judged (5.13–16).
5. One segment of humanity, Israel, has special provisions for dealing with transgression (5.17–18).

One text that suggests itself for comparison is 2 Corinthians 5.17, where Paul speaks of a 'new creation':

> So if anyone is in Christ, there is a new creation: everything old has passed away; see, everything has become new!
>
> NRSV[18]

The terminology here echoes particularly nicely with the Ge'ez of Jubilees 5.12 (*fəṭrata ḥaddās*), where the word *fəṭrat* can mean both 'nature' and 'creation'. While the Pauline literature is laden with future, unrealized eschatological expectations, in this case Paul emphasizes a new creative act that has already occurred and means the passing of the old and the arrival of the new. Like Jubilees, new creation is not only a future expectation, but something that has occurred within the context of earthly history.

One of the questions that arise as we bring this text into conversation with Jubilees is the scope of this new creation. As Hubbard phrases it, the question in 2 Corinthians 5.17 is whether Paul is speaking cosmologically or anthropologically. Does he envision

---

[18] ὥστε εἴ τις ἐν Χριστῷ, καινὴ κτίσις· τὰ ἀρχαῖα παρῆλθεν, ἰδοὺ γέγονεν καινά.

the creation of a new cosmos, or is he focusing on some human individuals who are already new creatures?[19] As Hubbard argues, the τις in the protasis points us towards an anthropological interpretation of the new creation in the apodosis, the conditional construction does not fit well with a cosmological reading, and the phrase fits better with an anthropological understanding.[20] While Paul does hope for the redemption of the entire creation (Rom 8.19–22), in this context it is a narrow section of humanity – those 'in Christ' – who are the beneficiaries of a new creative act.

Both Paul and Jubilees await a future, new/renewed creation (Jub 1.29; 4.2.6; Rom 8.19–22), and both believe God has already acted (re)creatively in the course of human history. However, at least in this case, Jubilees offers a more universal vision than Paul. For Jubilees, all of God's works were given new and righteous natures after the flood, whereas for Paul, it is those (presumably humans) who are *in Christ*. Jubilees still has particularistic elements, as Israel is given a method for dealing with post-new-nature transgressions (Jub 5.17–18)[21], but in this comparison the work's realized eschatology is more universal than Paul's.[22]

Noahide laws

Within the worldview of Jubilees, every species has its habitat and its path or ordinances. The angels, the Watchers, birds, cattle, Gentiles and Israelites all have their place and their path. This general framework allows for a complex and particularized ethic, with varying expectations for varying species or groups, and with these expectations rooted both in the created order and in a series of covenants between God and the creation. Jubilees makes a distinction between those practices that are expected of or prohibited for all humans and those that are unique to Israel. The Sabbath and circumcision are Israelite practices that are also observed by the angels in heaven (2.30–31; 15.26). The abstention from eating the blood of animals, however, is considered a universal norm that was agreed to by the descendants of Noah following the flood. Jubilees provides us with an early example of so-called Noahide laws – those commandments given to Noah and his descendants which are therefore considered normative for all people. In later Jewish literature, such laws would be discussed, defined and numbered.[23] In addition to the prohibition of eating blood, Jubilees' Noah offers a series of commandments to his descendants (7.20), commandments that all of humanity will be expected to keep. This distinction between what is expected of physical descendants of Israel and what is expected of all humans played an important role in the early Christian movements and is a central theme in the New Testament. Jubilees provides a fascinating precedent for and example of this distinction.

---

[19] Moyer V. Hubbard, *New Creation in Paul's Letters and Thought* (SNTMS 119; Cambridge: Cambridge University Press, 2004), 179.
[20] Ibid.
[21] Cf. 10.12–14, where the binding of the majority of the evil spirits is something that benefits all humanity, but the anti-demonic medicines that are taught to Noah are passed down through Shem.
[22] It would also be interesting to compare universal (Jn 1.9; 12.32) and particular aspects of Johannine Christology with what we see in Jubilees.
[23] For a comparison of different versions of the Noahide commandments, see Craig Keener, *Acts 3* (Grand Rapids: Baker Academic, 2014), 2266.

An especially interesting conversation partner for Jubilees in this regard is the list of suggestions or commands for Gentile Christians offered by the decree of the Jerusalem council in Acts 15.20 (cf. 15.29). There are noteworthy textual variants for this list, but one version of its contents is:

> But we should write them to abstain only from things polluted by idols and from fornication and from whatever has been strangled and from blood.[24]

The prohibition of eating strangled meat may have been connected to the prohibition of eating meat with blood in it, as an animal slaughtered through strangulation would not necessarily be drained of its blood.[25] The command to abstain from blood may likewise be understood as a prohibition of eating flesh with blood (which could create a redundancy with the strangulation prohibition), but can also be understood as abstention from violence.[26]

There are two binaries or potentially false alternatives that sometimes appear in the literature, both of which can be challenged or qualified by bringing the Jerusalem decree into conversation with Jubilees. The first is the question of background. Why were these prohibitions chosen? One possible background is the so-called Noahide law tradition. According to this interpretation, the Jerusalem council considered it necessary for Gentile believers only to observe those commandments that had been given to Noah and were thus binding for all people. Jubilees, especially 7.20, is often cited as an example of this tradition. Another option is the laws for resident aliens in Leviticus, particularly chapter 17, an interpretation we see as early as Origen.[27] Jubilees demonstrates that this must not be an either/or scenario. The author has taken passages from Leviticus and integrated them into their post-flood narrative.[28] The Mosaic law is placed on the lips of Noah, and the Mosaic laws for the resident aliens are ultimately rooted in the covenant with Noah and his descendants. The Jerusalem decree may be drawing on the tradition of Noahide commandments, but reflects a tradition, like the one we encounter in Jubilees, which incorporated legislation from Leviticus into its understanding of these commandments.

A second binary that appears in the literature is ritual versus ethical readings and receptions of the decree. Should we understand the prohibition of blood as an ethical injunction (avoiding violence) or a ritual one (not consuming the blood of animals)? The Western text, with its omission of strangulation and its addition of the golden rule, is considered an ethical interpretation by some, for instance. This distinction between ethics and ritual is generally problematic when applied to much early Jewish and Christian literature. Ritual acts may reflect, regulate and reinforce how we relate to

---

[24] ἀλλ' ἐπιστεῖλαι αὐτοῖς τοῦ ἀπέχεσθαι τῶν ἀλισγημάτων τῶν εἰδώλων καὶ τῆς πορνείας καὶ τοῦ πνικτοῦ καὶ τοῦ αἵματος.
[25] C. K. Barrett, *A Critical and Exegetical Commentary on the Acts of the Apostles*, ICC (2 vols. London: Clark, 2010), 732.
[26] Barrett, 733. D (a witness to the Western text) lacks καὶ τοῦ πνικτοῦ and the Western text adds a version of the golden rule.
[27] Origen, *Commentary to Romans*, 2.13.
[28] Van Ruiten, *Primaeval History*, 242–4.

human and non-human beings, thus having an 'ethical' character, and both 'ethical' and 'ritual' laws can be seamlessly incorporated into the same codes in the Torah.

The command to abstain from blood is an example of how problematic this distinction can be. If 'blood' in the Jerusalem decree is taken to mean violence, then it is considered 'ethical'. If it is taken to refer to slaughter/eating practices, specifically the abstention from eating flesh with blood in it, then it is considered 'ritual'.[29] This is a false distinction that leads us to a false alternative. First, the blood prohibition in the Torah as well as in Jubilees, although it would have implications for ritual acts, can be considered ethical. Only an anthropocentric bias, which would limit ethical activity to the human realm, would allow us to classify the blood prohibition as purely or primarily ritual in nature. The primary reason to avoid blood given by Genesis, Leviticus, and strongly emphasized by Jubilees, is that the spirit or life of the animal is in its blood. The post-diluvian consumption of non-human animals is a new development that takes humanity away from its vegetarian origins and makes the killing of animals acceptable. However, the violence of humans against non-human animals is still regulated: they are not allowed to consume the spirit of the victim through the consumption of its blood. The ritual requirements for properly slaughtering an animal, which involve draining it of its blood, are ultimately the practical result of an ethic that seeks to limit or regulate violence against non-human animals.

An additional problem with the ritual/ethic distinction is that both Genesis and Jubilees closely tie the consumption of blood to other forms of violence. Jubilees 7.21–33 illustrates this well. After having rehearsed the antediluvian violence among the giants, humans and non-human animals (7.22–25), Noah combines the shedding of human blood and the consumption of the blood of flesh, extending the death penalty Genesis prescribed for murder to the consumption of blood as well.[30] Within Jubilees, there is essentially one prohibition of blood with two aspects (the consumption of blood and the violent spilling of blood) and one punishment (destruction).

Ethiopian reception and its implications

While written originally in Hebrew in a pre-Christian context, the work was welcomed and received in antiquity, the Middle Ages and modern times by a range of readers in

---

[29] Barrett, 735–6: 'It has often been maintained that when the Old Uncial text and the Western text are compared we find on the one hand a set of essentially ritual requirements: abstinence from sacrificial food, from fornication (which could be understood to mean forbidden marriages or sacral prostitution), from non-kosher food, and from food containing blood; and on the other hand an ethical code, requiring the rejection of idolatry (which, put positively, means adherence to the exclusive worship of the one true God), avoidance of all unchaste behaviour, avoidance of murder, and obedience to the fundamental moral law, expressed in the Golden Rule.' Barrett goes on to reject this as an oversimplification, claiming that there were both ethical and ritual elements in the decree.

[30] Cf. 1 Enoch 7.3–5, which mentions the giants eating humans and each other, transgressing against animals, and drinking blood. Ted Erho has recently edited and translated an Ethiopic fragment of *Jannes and Jambres*, which similarly portrays the giants eating earthly creatures and drinking blood: 'Where are Amān and Bārān, the giants who devoured men like locust<s> and wild animals and cattle and birds? They drank <blood> and despoiled the Orient ...' Ted M. Erho and W. Benjamin Henry, "The Ethiopic *Jannes and Jambres* and the Greek Original," Archiv für Papyrusforschung 65 (2019): 176-223, at 190.

multiple languages. Its most enduring reception has been in the Ethiopian Tewahedo Orthodox tradition, which has preserved the work in its entirety in a scribal tradition that continues until the present day. As it exists today, Jubilees is an Ethiopian Christian text. What does it mean to take this fact seriously?

First, it means that we should take the Geʿez language seriously, seeing it as an essential or first-rung primary source language for scholars who specialize in Second Temple Judaism or the early history of scriptural interpretation, and at least a second-rung language for those working more generally in New Testament/early Christian studies. This recognition of the language's importance could be demonstrated by the creation of more learning and reference materials, more introductory courses in Geʿez in universities, and the editing, publication and translation of the plethora of Geʿez texts that either have no editions or only severely outdated ones. Nestle-Aland is on its twenty-eighth edition, while some significant and fascinating texts await their very first.

Second, it means giving attention to the work's reception in the Ethiopian tradition. This may primarily include the study of interpretative and exegetical traditions (Tergwāmē, Andemta, homilies); text-critical work that gives attention not only to establishing the earliest recoverable Ethiopic text, but also to scribal practices and developments within the Ethiopic tradition; approaches in the spirit of manuscript philology; and taking the work's scriptural status in the Ethiopian and Eritrean Tewahedo Orthodox churches as a cue for constructive theological and ethical readings of the text. It is this final possibility that I would like to explore here, as I believe such approaches can broaden the interest in Ethiopic Jubilees and the Geʿez textual tradition more generally by demonstrating the significance of such texts for theologically oriented approaches to the New Testament and for contemporary theology and ethics.

Those works received by the churches and synagogues as scriptural continue to be sources for theological and ethical reflection today, with their influence extending beyond their religious communities into the secular and inter-religious spheres. However, the canons that one finds today in the dominant Jewish, Protestant and Roman Catholic Bibles do not contain all of the writings that played an important role in the formation of Judaism and Christianity or in their long histories. The very existence of Jubilees today is testimony to the fact that ancient, medieval and modern Jewish and Christian communities found the work useful. Jubilees was read, copied, translated and excerpted in Greek, Latin, Syriac and Geʿez. Avoiding questions of the historical and contemporary canonical status of the work, we can at least say that for a range of Jews and Christians in a range of time periods, this work – which claims itself to be divine revelation – has proven useful. The Ethiopian Tewahedo Orthodox tradition provides us with an example of an ancient and lively Christian tradition that continues to value and use Jubilees today. This historical and contemporary use and acceptance of the text can provide contemporary theologians and ethicists with an impetus for engaging Jubilees in their work.

This engagement can look diverse. Jubilees provides us with a conversation partner, a lens through which we can read and engage undisputed canonical works such as Genesis and Exodus. Its presentation and interpretation of sacred history may provide us with fresh readings and insights that help us break free of traditional interpretative assumptions. It can offer us insight into the many different ways that Torah could unfold in the Jewish tradition. It may serve as illuminating 'background' to undisputed canonical texts in the New Testament, but it may also introduce creative tensions, contrasts, or complements to these texts. In some cases, it may provide us with significant alternative understandings or may fill in thematic gaps in the New Testament witness. Apart from its contributions in relation to and in conversation with the canonical works of the Old and New Testaments, Jubilees also has its own independent voice and value.

Our discussion above did show that Jubilees is a useful 'background' source for reading some New Testament texts (the Jerusalem decree, for instance). But it also hopefully demonstrated that there are some cases where Jubilees is a productive conversation partner in constructive readings of these texts. While Paul's soteriology does include universal and cosmic elements, there are points where his vision of the already-realized benefits of the Christ-event are more limited and particular. Jubilees' vision of a diluvian gift of new and righteous natures for all of God's works can provoke us to develop realized soteriologies that are more cosmic in scope. Jubilees can prompt us to ask whether our 'not-yet' is more inclusive than our 'already'.

Jubilees also has something to say to contemporary ethical issues. The human community is faced with ethical challenges today related to environment, ecology and our fellow creatures. We are also living in an exciting time when scientific advances in fields such as neuroscience offer us more insights into the human and more-than-human creation – advances which we can learn from and grapple with. Jubilees' treatment of non-human animals is an example of its potential value for this contemporary ethical reflection. Two points that a treatment of non-human animals in Jubilees might focus on:

1. *Taxonomy*. In what ways do our methods of categorizing creatures and the creation reflect and affect our perception of the world, and how do they influence our interaction with the more-than-human creation? Jubilees offers a taxonomy that still privileges human beings, but places them within the same broader category, *flesh*, as the other animate beings.
2. *Animal rationality and moral responsibility*. To what extent are non-human animals conscious, thinking beings? To what extent are they able to make decisions, and to what extent can we consider them to be moral agents? Many give attention to our moral responsibility as humans towards our fellow creatures, but are they also moral agents? These are questions that were discussed in the ancient world, and continue to be discussed today by zoologists, philosophers and neuroscientists. How we answer these questions has an impact on how we relate to and understand the more-than-human creation, and how we understand ourselves.

Jubilees can be read as supporting some level of animal rationality and moral agency, which goes against the tradition of 2 Peter and Jude as well as much of the historical Christian philosophical and theological tradition. There was a vigorous ancient debate about these questions, and much of the church eventually took an approach that has had disastrous consequences for non-human animals. Yet Jubilees, a text read and preserved since antiquity, may offer us resources to revisit this debate, and to develop – in conversation with contemporary science and philosophy – new ethical understandings of non-human creatures. Taking cues from Jubilees and the Old Testament, we can construct an ethic that not only focuses on our moral responsibility towards animals – a good emphasis that can also contribute to the problem in its portrayal of non-human animals as passive agents – but also presents other animals as complex moral agents.

6

The Trial of Isaiah: On Alleged Jewish Backgrounds of the Ascension of Isaiah

Jan Dochhorn

For the majority of the slowly growing tribe of Ethiopicists, the first piece of literature to be read about the Ascension of Isaiah might be the entry in the monumental *Encyclopaedia Aethiopica*, written by Stefan Weninger in 2007.[1] In this piece, they will read that the Ascension of Isaiah mainly deals with the martyrdom of Isaiah (he was sawn asunder with a wooden saw under King Manasseh) and with his vision of the heavenly world (including Christ and the righteous ones). They will also read that this work is to be dated to the second century after Christ, was probably composed in Syria, and is preserved in several languages yet complete only in Geʿez. Concerning source criticism, they will be informed that traditional research[2] emphasized the composite character of the Ascension of Isaiah, whereas newer research[3] sees it as a unified composition. In the martyrdom section (chapters 1–5), Weninger supposes it to be a reworking of a Jewish source, perhaps a written one; here he takes up a theory that dominated the field until the 1970s, which is definitely older than the work of Norelli, whom Weninger references as holding a traditional position. Weninger's article further stresses that an Ethiopian perspective on the Ascension of Isaiah is still wanting; a study of the history of reception of the Ascension of Isaiah in Ethiopian culture remains a *desideratum* – although the result might be rather modest, given the fact that the Geʿez version of the Ascension of Isaiah is preserved in only a few manuscripts (eleven, mainly connected to the Book of Isaiah).

I can follow this view. I belong to the more recent camp of researchers, who see this work as a unified composition. I would also agree with Weninger that the Ascension of Isaiah was composed during the second century in Syria, although I generally regard this geographical term as a makeshift solution (with the word Syria mainly meaning 'we don't know'). However, this chapter does not attempt to argue for a more concrete localization.

Above that, I can, like Weninger, see that a gap needs to be filled in scholarship with regard to the impact of the Ascension of Isaiah on Ethiopian culture and how it was

---

[1] Stefan Weninger, 'Isaiah, Ascension of', *Encyclopaedia Aethiopica* 5.195–6.
[2] Norelli, 1995.
[3] Knight, 1996.

understood or transformed in this context. And I have not really anything to contribute here, apart from the peculiar fact that a new textual witness of the Ascension has emerged (EAP 357/1/1, accessible online),[4] which is a manuscript from the twentieth century presenting the text separately. Some decades ago, there must have been Ethiopians (or was it just one single Ethiopian?) who focused on this text – perhaps influenced by European research? I can also state that a list of names for the Devil, preserved in a manuscript from the British Library (Ms. add. 16221, fol. 55a),[5] contains at least two satanonyms (*Bərəyâl* and *Mamṭa'ankos*[6]) which recall the satanology of the Ascension (however, *Samāyal* and *Malkirā*, both very typical of the Ascension, are missing in this list). Concerning the name *Bərəyâl*, it needs to be stated that the Falasha too make use of it (both in Teezāza Sanbat and in Maṣḥafa Malāekt),[7] and that it appears in textual tradition of Dersāna Sanbat,[8] which according to some researchers was the source of the two works mentioned before. I am not completely convinced, however.[9] Does this satanological knowledge stem from the Ascension? *Bərəyâl* is the Vulgate reading of the Ethiopic version of the Ascension; only a minority of manuscripts has the reading *Bələyâr*[10] whereas the standard version of the Greek satanonym

---

[4] See https://eap.bl.uk/archive-file/EAP357-1-11.

[5] The text runs as follows: *'asmāta Sayṭān* (Names of Satan): *Refān, Belḫor, Diyābəlos, Səbəlonyos, 'Abdon, Apāyədon, Bərəyāl, Saṭānā'el, Teṭāri, Ləbā, Mamādis, Mamṭan'akos*. Cf. August Dillmann, *Catalogus Codicum Manuscriptorum qui in Museo Britannico Asservantur, Pars Tertia: Codices Aethiopicos Amplectens* (London, 1847), 59 (Manuscript No. 73).

[6] The name *Mamṭan'akos* recalls the alias of *Bərəyâl / Bələyâr* in Asc Isa 2.4 where the most recent edition reconstructs *Maṭanbəkus*; the manuscript F reads *Maṭanbəkos* which comes nearer to *mamṭan'ako*. Cf. Lorenzo Perrone, Ascensione di Isaia profeta: Versione etiopica', in *Ascensio Isaiae: Textus* (trans. Enrico Norelli, Corpus Christianorum, Series Apocryphorum 7; ed. Paolo Bettiolo et al.; Turnhout 1995, 1–129, esp. 49.

[7] In the printed edition of Halévy the name *Bərnâ'el* dominates, both in Teezāza Sanbat and in Maṣḥafa Malāekt, but also *Bərəyâl* occurs, cf. J. Halévy, *Tĕ'ĕzāza Sanbat (Commandement du Sabbat), accompagné de six autres écrits pseudo-épigraphiques admis par les Falachas ou Juifs d'Abyssinie* (Paris 1902), 1–40; 51–6 (for the name *Bərəyâl* cf. e.g. p. 52). In the manuscripts I have at hand the form *Bərəyâl* is generally used. I plan to produce an edition of Maṣḥafa Mlāəkt.

[8] Cf. the parallels to Maṣḥafa Malāekt in Dersāna Sanbat according to the manuscript EAP 286/1/117, foll. 19–24 (try the net or ask the author of this chapter). There still lacks a critical edition of Dərsāna Sanbat; I know about thirty-seven manuscripts cf. Jan Dochhorn, 'Menschenschöpfung und urzeitlicher Teufelsfall in Überlieferungen der Falascha: Der erste Teil von Teezâza Sanbat in der von Halévy veröffentlichten Version', in *The Other Side: Apocryphal Perspectives on Ancient Christian 'Orthodoxies'* (NTOA / SUNT 117; ed. Tobias Nicklas, Candida R. Moss and Joseph Verheyden; Göttingen: Vandenhoeck & Ruprecht, 2017), 193–224, especially 205, n.37.

[9] Cf. Steven Kaplan, 'Te'ezáza Sanbat: A Beta Israel Work Reconsidered', in *Gilgul. Essays on Transformation, Revolution and Permanence in the History of Religions Dedicated to R.J. Zwi Werblowsky* (ed. Shaul Shaked, David Shulman and Gedaljahu Stroumsa; Leiden: Brill, 1987), 107–24 and Denis Nosnitsin, 'Dərsanä Sänbät', *Encyclopaedia Aethiopica* 2.141–2.

[10] That *Bərəyâl* is read by the majority of manuscripts can be concluded from Perrone's apparatus to Asc Isa 1.8 (cf. note 4). There we learn that the witnesses ABEFGL read *Bərəyâl* (six from nine manuscripts used by Perrone). Perrone prefers the reading *Bələyār*. However, if one does not like to be convinced by the number of manuscripts supporting *Bərəyâl* (arguing by majority is not always wrong in textual criticism) one other detail may indicate that contra Perrone *Bərəyâl* is the better reading: It is also attested by G which according to Perrone (p. 4) strongly coincides with D, the Abbā Garimā manuscript (No. 2), which, as new research claims, with high probability goes back to late antiquity and is considerably older than all other witnesses (it is only a fragment, consisting of one page, fol. 307 in the Codex, cf. Weninger [n. 1]). Perrone does not use the Abbā Garimā manuscript (see p. 4) for reasons I do not understand.

*Βελιαλ < Βελιαλ in Ethiopia appeared to be *Belḥor/Belḥor/Belhor* (preserved both in Jub 1.20 and in 2 Cor 6.15).

Concerning the Jewish backgrounds of the martyrdom of Isaiah, it seems to me that the major trend in the few last decades of research on the Ascension consisted not so much in a shift from source criticism to 'unitarianism'[11] but rather in that the Ascension of Isaiah – and especially the account of his martyrdom – has been 'dejudaized'. For research until the 1970s, the main distinctive mark is that there had been reconstructed (erroneously, I would maintain) a Jewish core text narrating the martyrdom of Isaiah and providing Jewish background for New Testament studies (not least for Pauline angelology and satanology).[12] This Jewish source, I would state, no longer exists.

In this chapter I go a step further, restricting myself, however, to a case study that does not answer everything: I claim that even a specific moment of the martyrdom narrative in the Ascension which has clear Jewish parallels does not build upon Jewish tradition. Specifically, I mean the charges against Isaiah for which he is put to death. This motif also exists in a tradition that seems to be or is in fact Jewish, but did not, in my view, originate in Judaism. In what follows, I will first present and discuss this motif in the Ascension of Isaiah and explain it by Christian presuppositions. I will then treat the parallels which lead people to believe that this tradition could have been borrowed from Judaism, demonstrating that the sources either do not really derive from Judaism or that Jews have adopted their traditions from Christians. Finally, I will discuss the methodological impact of this study and briefly assess to what degree Judaism still needs to be regarded as a reference world of the Ascension of Isaiah.

This chapter is more concerned with pseudepigrapha studies, early Christian studies and research on ancient Judaism than with Ethiopian Christianity and Ethiopian

---

(note 10 cont.) It is also problematic that Perrone does not document deviant readings for the name *Bələyār* after Asc Isa 1.8. As a rule, manuscripts display the original forms of a name in later sections rather than in the beginning – due to the psychology of copying. At the beginning names are unconciously mistaken by the copyist; in later passages the copyists get used to them and no longer misspell them. I would be curious to know if this rule proves to be relevant for textual criticism in this case. Alternatively, I regard it as possible that the form *Bələyār* was introduced later into the tradition – not unconciously, but from Greek tradition, which would imply that we have variance in a tradition that goes back to late antiquity in which Greek tradition was still accessible for Ethiopians. Francis Watson claims similar processes for the transmission of the Ethiopian Gospel of Matthew, where we can observe that the recension B modifies older tradition (recension A, attested not least by an Abbâ Garimâ manuscript) according to Greek textual tradition. which could only take place in late antiquity; cf. Francis Watson in Judith S. McKenzie/Francis Watson, Michael Gervers, *The Garima Gospels. Early Illuminated Gospel Books from Ethiopia*, Manar Al Athar-Monographs 3 (Oxford, 2016).

[11] For a unitarian view of the Ascension, see Jonathan Knight, *The Ascension of Isaiah*, Guides to the Apocrypha and Pseudepigrapha 2 (Sheffield: Sheffield Academic, 1995); Anna-Maria Schwemer, 'Review of »Ascensio Isaiae. Text und Kommentar, ed. Enrico Norelli (Corpus Christianorum. Series Apocryphorum 7–8), Turnhout 1995', *Zeitschrift für Kirchengeschichte* 110 (1998): 398–402; Richard Bauckham, 'The Ascension of Isaiah: Genre, Unity and Date', in *The Fate of the Dead: Studies on the Jewish and Christian Apocalypses*, Supplements to Novum Testamentum 93 (Leiden: Brill 1998), 363–90; Jan Dochhorn, 'Die Ascensio Isaiae (JSHRZ II,1: Martyrium Jesajas)', in *Unterweisung in erzählender Form: Mit Beiträgen von J. Dochhorn, B. Ego, M. Meiser und O. Merk*, JSHRZ 5.1.2 (ed. G.S. Oegema; Gütersloh 2005), 1–48. Cf. also Vacher Burch, 'The Literary Unity of the Ascensio Isaiae', JTS 20 (1919), 17–23.

[12] Cf. Martin Dibelius, *Die Geisterwelt im Glauben des Paulus* (Göttingen: Vandenhoeck & Ruprecht, 1909) where material from the Ascension plays an important role for illustrating Pauline theology. In my view it rather illustrates reception history of Pauline thought than its presuppositions.

culture. It follows the tradition of taking an Ethiopian source as point of departure for exploring something that is older than Ethiopian Christianity. There is still good reason for this kind of research, although I fully appreciate the new achievements of Ethiopian studies proper.

The charges against Isaiah and his fellow prophets

Unlike the majority of texts that mention a martyrdom of Isaiah (throughout with the special notion that he was sawn in two),[13] the Ascension of Isaiah narrates the special circumstances of that martyrdom, not least that a trial preceded the martyrdom. This trial was instigated by a false prophet descended from a lineage of pseudoprophets who opposed Elijah and Micah in the northern kingdom (cf. Asc Isa 2.12–3.5); the name of this false prophet is Belchira or Bechira (the reconstruction of the original name still remains problematic). He reported Isaiah and the prophetic group led by him (consisting among others of Joel and Habakkuk) to King Manasseh, who took over the kingdom after the pious King Hezekiah and did not follow the good ways of his predecessor (his father). Belchira raised the following charges against the prophets and especially Isaiah:

1. Isaiah and his prophets announce the devastation of Jerusalem and the cities of Judah (3.6).
2. They foretell that Benjamin will be led into captivity (3.6).
3. Concerning King Manasseh, they prophesy that he will go (bound) with hooks and chains of iron (3.6).
4. They utter false prophecies concerning Israel and Judah (3.7).
5. Isaiah claims that he sees more than Moses. Moses has said that nobody can see God and survive, whereas Isaiah has said that he has seen God – stating boldly that he remains alive (3.8–9).
6. They are false prophets. Isaiah calls Jerusalem Sodom and declares the princes of Judah and Jerusalem people of Gomorrah (3.10).

We see that the whole group of prophets is under accusation. But Isaiah is in the focus. Two charges are related especially to him, namely that he claimed to have seen God and that he used the unflattering labels Sodom and Gomorrah for designating Jerusalem and the elite of the kingdom. These two charges are those which we also will encounter in the parallels discussed below; they will play a decisive role in this chapter. However, also the whole set is to be analysed. What can be stated about Belchira's accusations against the prophets and Isaiah?

Two things can be detected almost at first glance. First of all, these charges are basically true. Anybody who reads a bit in the Bible, in passages reporting prophecies of Isaiah and in stories which deal with Manasseh, will find that Isaiah and other

---

[13] For a (not comprehensive) list of such texts see Dochhorn, *Ascensio Isaiae* (n. 9), 12.

prophets have indeed said words resembling what Belchira reports. Prophets announced misfortune for Jerusalem and Judah in the days of Manasseh (2 Kgs 21.10-15), and Isaiah predicted the exile in the days of Hezekiah (2 Kgs 20.16-18; Isa 39.5-7). That Manasseh was bound with iron chains is not prophesied but narrated in 1 Chronicles 33.11; here the Ascension of Isaiah probably concludes from the event (as found in the Book of Chronicles) that there must have been a prophecy announcing the event and puts this into the mouth of Belchira. Isaiah also claimed that he has seen God (Isa 6.1), and it can be inferred from Ex 33.20 that Moses regards seeing God as impossible. What is missing in Isa 6.1, however, are the bold words ascribed to Isaiah: 'and look, I am alive' (Asc Isa 3.9 [eth]: *wanawā ḥəyāw 'ana*; Asc Isa [gr]: καὶ ἰδοὺ ζῶ). Also the designations Sodom and Gomorrah are used by Isaiah (Isa 1.10) – for Jerusalem and the elite of Judah, fully in accordance to what Belchira says. (Neither Isaiah 1.10 nor any other prophecy in the canonical book is dated to the days of Manasseh, but Belchira too does not date these prophecies – in his view, false prophecies.)

Something else can be observed as well: the charges of Belchira can be convincing, not only for any politician – even somebody who is a little more trustworthy than Manasseh – but also for a ruler who respects the religious rules of Judaism. This is especially true for one of the charges exclusively linked with Isaiah: that he has – in contrast to Moses – claimed to have seen God. Why are the pseudoprophet Belchira and King Manasseh (who will in fact be convinced by these charges and will put Isaiah to death) so keen to defend the primacy of Moses, and why are they concerned to rule out any claim that would cast doubt on the invisibility of God – indeed a central issue of Jewish theology and one of the reasons why the rabbis later tried to keep secret the Maaseh Bereshit and the Maaseh Merkavah? King Manasseh is known as an idolatrous king, at least from the biblical tradition. Interestingly enough, among the many bad things the Ascension of Isaiah tells about the rulership of Manasseh – for example, adherence to Samael and Beliar (in the Ethiopian text *Samāyal* and *Bəryāl*), iniquity, magic and several techniques of divination – idolatry is missing. Manasseh, as depicted by the Ascension of Isaiah, could in fact be just a Jewish king whose religious practice and politics are not what other Jews claiming to be authentic believers of the religion of the true God would expect. Manasseh looks like a Jewish ruler who persecutes other Jews – and this not because of charges wrongly ascribed to these people, but because of what these people really have stated.

It is clear in which logical framework such a constellation makes sense – and the clue is in the text itself. Isaiah announces his own martyrdom as that of a Christian. He will, as he states, 'inherit the heritage of the beloved one' (*wabarəstu lafequr 'ana 'ətwarras*; Asc Isa 1.13); the Beloved one is in the Ascension of Isaiah nobody other than Christ. And at the end he is sawn asunder 'with a saw of wood' (*bamośarta 'əḍ* Asc Isa 5.1) which is not a pruning saw but, according to Justin *Dial*. 120.5 (who accuses the Jews concerning Isaiah with the words ὃν πρίονι ξυλίνῳ ἐπρίσατε), a saw made of wood, thus recalling the death of Jesus on the cross. There is also a parallel in the Testimony of Truth (NHC IX.40.21–41.4) that asserts a typological relation between the saw cutting up Isaiah and the word of the cross separating Christians from the world (and day from night, male from female, and so on). Both Justin and the Nag Hammadi text may be traces of reception rather than parallels to the Ascension of Isaiah.[14]

The martyrdom of Isaiah is obviously something like bearing the cross – and it is this conceptual frame in which the trial and the charges against Isaiah narrated in the Ascension of Isaiah make sense: also in the trial of Jesus the accusations are in a special manner true. The accusation of the false witnesses according to which Jesus has predicted that he will tear down the temple and rebuild it within three days (Mt 26.61 par) is not contradicted by Jesus (Mt 26.63 par) and neither is an attempt made by the gospels to demonstrate that it is not covering the facts. To the contrary, both Mark and Matthew imply that what the false witnesses have said is fulfilled by Jesus' resurrection (cf. Mt 27.39-40 // Mk 15.29-32), thus presenting it as a special kind of prophecy. In the Gospel of John, the words of the false witnesses become words of Jesus (Jn 2.19). We can see the same structure in the martyrdom of Stephen, which is depicted by Luke along the lines of the passion of Jesus. The charge of Stephen's opponents that he polemicizes against the temple (Acts 6.13-14) is rather corroborated than contradicted by his own speech (which according to most exegetes is not historical). Thus, it is clear that if Jesus would have wished to be defended by an advocate, he should not have chosen the narrator(s) of the passion narrative(s); nor should Stephen have opted for Luke (or the author of Luke's source). Similarly, the narrator of the Ascension of Isaiah would not have been a good choice for Isaiah. All these Christian storytellers do not want to demonstrate that their heroes have been accused wrongly but that they have been accused for the truth, with the consequence that also the accusations represent – at least to a degree – the truth.

Taking this as the basic pattern, we can also state that there are considerable motif overlaps between the charges against Isaiah and the other Christian noble death stories mentioned above – and not least that these charges fit a Christian mindset. Isaiah claims to have seen God, and also in the passion narrative the visible God plays a role in what Jesus says in his trial: more open Merkavah-talk than in the (indirect) confession of Jesus to be the Messiah, the son of God (Mt 26.64) is hardly possible. And Stephen even claims to see God – and Christ standing beside him (Acts 7.55-56) – which is the immediate reason for his death (Acts 7.57-60). Above all, the text from which the claim of Isaiah reported in the Ascension of Isaiah is taken, the vision in Isaiah 6 turns out to be an important source for another Christian theologian (who might be contemporary with the Ascension of Isaiah), namely John. The Gospel of John states that Isaiah has seen the glory of God (τὴν δόξαν τοῦ θεοῦ; 12.41) which in the context (Jn 12.42-43) can be identified with Jesus himself. Here Isaiah 6 is understood in the sense that Isaiah has not seen God himself (which according to Johannine theology, in full agreement with Jewish tradition, is impossible; cf. e.g. Jn 1.18) but his glory, namely Jesus. In the heavenly vision of Isaiah reported in the Ascension of Isaiah 6-11, more than that happens: Isaiah is granted the power to see also the highest person of the Trinity (Asc Isa 9.39). Belchira is right in the charges he

---

[14] For more ancient Christian texts that may help to ensure the Christian provenance of the martyrdom story in the Ascension of Isaiah, see Antonio Acerbi, *Serra Lignea: Studi sulla fortuna della Ascensione di Isaia* (Roma: Editrice A.V.E. 1984), 69-102.

brings against Isaiah: the assertions of this prophet, at least as we know him from the Ascension of Isaiah, are anything but modest.

We can see also other parallels to Christian sources. The label Sodom used by the canonical Isaiah against Jerusalem and repeated in the Ascension of Isaiah is also taken up in the Revelation of John. The place where Jesus was crucified (a city which we recognize as Jerusalem) is given a 'spiritual' name in Rev 11.8, namely Sodom and Egypt. And we can observe that the martyrdom of Isaiah resembles the death of Jesus and the martyrdom of Stephen also in other aspects: the wooden saw as a reference to the cross has already been mentioned; here we can add that, like Stephen, Isaiah was 'in the spirit' during his martyrdom (Asc Isa 5.14: *'afuhu yətnāgar lamanfas qəddus* = 'his mouth conversed with the holy Spirit'; cf. Acts 7.55), confirming the trustworthiness of his message, like Stephen (Isa 6.9–10; cf. Acts 7).

Isaiah suffers like a Christian, and he is persecuted by Manasseh, who behaves like a Jewish authority. A situation is foreshadowed which is similar to what happened to Jesus and Stephen, who were both condemned to death by the Sanhedrin (whether this is historical or not). Like the first Christian noble death stories, the Ascension of Isaiah locates its noble death within a context that is marked by Jewish dominance (the passion narrative too attests Jewish dominance, at least in a cultural sense). How does such a constellation fit the biblical tradition of the idolatrous King Manasseh (cf. 2 Kgs 21.1–18)? In my view, the most probable solution is that the motif of the idolatrous king is not forgotten but remains in the background for the more Jewish portrait of this king in the Ascension of Isaiah. If we take both pictures together, the result might be: Judaism without Christ is basically equivalent to idolatry. This is stated in the Epistle to Diognetus, which presents Christianity as a third race in contrast to Jews and Pagans; like the Pagans, the Jews venerate God in their temple (Diogn 3). We read similar views on Judaism in the Kerygma of Peter.[15] And in the Revelation of John, the Synagogue of Satan (2.9; 3.9) and the throne of Satan (2.13), the one a Jewish entity and the other associated with Roman political power, obviously stand in parallel. Both oppose Christianity and at least in this regard they are identical. To my mind, this is what the Ascension of Isaiah too insinuates by describing the notorious idolater Manasseh as motivated by anti-heretical concerns that were specifically Jewish. (While Jewish cultural dominance may still be an issue in the context of the Ascension of Isaiah, we must be cautious about taking its narrative as mere projection from the present age of the author. This could result in some kind of historical allegorizing, not necessarily less fanciful than the traditional theological kind.)

Jewish backgrounds?

Charges against Isaiah that resemble those in the Ascension of Isaiah are attested in patristic and in Jewish sources. This raises the question of whether the Ascension of Isaiah has taken over extant traditions, possibly from Judaism. Fairly well documented

---

[15] *apud* Clement of Alexandria, *Stromateis* VI.5.40–41 [GCS *sine numero*; Stählin II.451–452]; Origen, Comm Joh XIII,17,104 [GCS 10; Preuschen 241].

is the accusation that he claimed to have seen God (in contrast to Moses). Without specifying its provenance, Origen reports a tradition that the crowd/nation (*populus*) sawed Isaiah in two on the basis of this accusation.[16] However, it is questionable if this tradition is independent from the Ascension of Isaiah. Origen most probably knows the Ascension of Isaiah; he refers to an apocryphal book of Isaiah when mentioning his martyrdom in *Epistula ad Africanum* 9.[17] In his view, this book was distorted by Jews in order to make it untrustworthy. Here we encounter a constellation we will see again: tradition recalling the Ascension of Isaiah is cited by a Christian author, and the same author elsewhere turns out to be familiar with the Ascension of Isaiah, which he regards as a Jewish book. The underlying assumption is probably that a book inhabiting the narrative world of the Old Testament must stem from the Jews. Origen likes such traditions: in his commentary on Matthew he defends apocryphal books mentioning martyrdoms of the prophets, not least the martyrdom of Isaiah, pointing to the fact that also New Testament writings cite apocryphal traditions.[18] We can conclude that Origen most probably knows what he has in common with the Ascension of Isaiah from the Ascension of Isaiah itself (maybe indirectly), which he regards as handed down – and interpolated – by Jews.

The next church father to be mentioned is Jerome. He reports that Isaiah was sawn in two because he used the terms Sodom and Gomorrah in a provocative way and because he claimed to have seen God. And he explicitly introduces this piece of information as a tradition narrated by the 'Hebrews' (*hebraei*).[19] Does he really present a Jewish tradition? He obviously thinks so, but elsewhere he cites a passage from a work he explicitly calls *Ascensio Isaiae*, which according to him is apocryphal and confuses women in Spain and Lusitania.[20] Obviously, he knew of the Ascension of Isaiah (and did not really like it). He may have taken his tradition directly from it – or he may have slightly transformed knowledge borrowed from Origen, on whom he often depends; the above-mentioned tradition of Origen about Isaiah's martyrdom occurs in a homily about Isaiah on which Jerome may have drawn for his own commentary. I would not regard Jerome as an independent witness to a Jewish tradition resembling what we know from the Ascension of Isaiah. The same can be stated about other references to the martyrdom of Isaiah which also recall the Ascension of Isaiah and are labelled by him as Jewish.[21]

A similar constellation can be observed in the works of Didymus of Alexandria, who clearly knows the Ascension of Isaiah.[22] He also narrates a version of the story of Isaiah's martyrdom that reports the two charges directed specifically against Isaiah as

---

[16] Homilies in Isaiam 1 (Lommatzsch 13.245f).
[17] MPG 11,64b/c.
[18] Comm Ser in Mt 28 (GCS 38).
[19] Comm Es 1.10 (MPL 24.33b).
[20] Comm Jes 64.4 (MPL 24.646bc).
[21] Comm Jes 15, on Isa 57.1–2 (MPL 24.567–568).
[22] Comm Gen in Tura Papyrus I, 13B 5 and Comm Eccl in Tura Papyrus VI,329,21–25.

we know them from the Ascension of Isaiah.[23] However, Didymus does not here mention the Ascension of Isaiah, and we find a motif well-known from Jewish tradition: Isaiah was put to death because he polemicized against an idol Manasseh had erected. This tradition is, in the Jewish sources, associated with the words that Isaiah directs against the temple in Isaiah 66.1 (cited also by Stephen in Acts 7).[24] I can imagine that Didymus took over Jewish knowledge here, but this does not pertain to the charges against Isaiah, which he rather borrowed from the Ascension – thus blending Jewish and Christian material. Material from the Ascension of Isaiah could obviously become more or less anonymous knowledge, and as knowledge it also underwent transformation.

We can detect such processes in a tradition preserved by Ambrose, who in his voluminous commentary on Psalm 118 reports a scene from Isaiah's martyrdom which clearly resembles Asc Isa 5 (and helps reconstructing the meaning of the text which is slightly obscure in the Ethiopian version) but on the other hand considerably differs from the Ascension of Isaiah.[25] Whereas in Asc Isa 5 Beliar talks to Isaiah while Isaiah is sawn in two, Ambrose narrates that the Devil spoke to a prophet, probably Isaiah, in the prison. Ambrose is, as we see, not sure if it really is Isaiah who was addressed by the Devil, and he labels his knowledge as anonymous tradition (using the word *fertur* = 'it is said' in order to introduce it).

In general, we have no good reason to conclude from the patristic sources that there existed a Jewish tradition about the charges against Isaiah. What about sources that indisputably are Jewish? First of all, we have a lot of texts mentioning that Isaiah was sawn in two under Manasseh. Many of them are Christian, and some are Jewish, not least the Life of Isaiah in the Lives of the Prophets (*Vita Prophetarum*) which – in the view of Anna Maria Schwemer – is Jewish and probably the oldest text ascribing to the prophet that cruel death.[26] However, what we find in the Life of Isaiah is only a short notice.[27] But we also have expanded versions of his martyrdom in Jewish sources. These generally report that Isaiah fled from Manasseh and was swallowed up by a tree, either a cedar or a carob tree, which was then sawn, causing Isaiah's death (Tosephta

---

[23] Tura Papyrus III 218.3–14, on Ps 34.15. For the reception of the Ascension of Isaiah by Didymus, cf. Dieter Lührmann, 'Alttestamentliche Pseudepigraphen bei Didymos von Alexandrien', ZAW 104 (1992): 231–49, esp. 233–9.

[24] Cf. Tosephta Targum to Isa 66.1 (in the margin of the Codex Reuchlinianus)[16] and a similar tradition in Pesiqta Rabbati 4. See Meir Friedmann (ed.), *Pesikta Rabbati. Midrasch für den Fest-Cyclus und die ausgezeichneten Sabbathe. Nebst einem Lexikon der vorkommenden griechischen und lateinischen Fremdworte von Moritz Güdemann* (Vienna, 1880), 14.

[25] § 12.32 (CSEL 62.270).

[26] Cf. Anna Maria Schwemer, *Studien zu den frühjüdischen Prophetenlegenden. Vitae Prophetarum, Band I: Die Viten der großen Propheten Jesaja, Jeremia, Ezechiel und Daniel. Einleitung, Übersetzung und Kommentare* (TSAJ 49; Tübingen. J. C. B. Mohr (Paul Siebeck): 1995), 91–158 (particularly pp. 102–15 about the martyrdom of Isaiah in the Vita Isaiae; Schwemer ponders the possibility that the special kind of martyrdom ascribed to Isaiah is based upon a historical event, namely an execution of 'Deutero-Isaiah' by the Persians on grounds of blasphemy as it might be reflected in Isa 53; sawing asunder was a punishment enacted by the Persians in such cases).

[27] Cf. Theodor Schermann (ed.), *Prophetarum Vitae Fabulosae, Indices Apostolorum Discipulorumque Domini Dorotheo, Epiphanio, Hippolyto aliisque Vindicata* (Leipzig: Teubner, 1907), who presents several versions of the *Vitae Prophetarum* (for the death of Isaiah in Vit Isa cf. pp. 8, 41, 60, 68, 104).

Targum to Isaiah, Jerusalem Talmud;[28] Babylonian Talmud Pesiqta Rabbati[29]); a shorter story about the death of Isaiah is to be found in Tosephta Targum to 2 Kings.[30]

In general these stories do not mention charges against Isaiah – with one exception that has the potential to persuade people that the charges against Isaiah have been invented by Jews, and not by the Christian author of the Ascension of Isaiah. Talmud Babli Jebamoth 49b not only narrates that Isaiah was killed after having been swallowed up by a cedar, but also reports a list of accusations against him. The first accusation mentioned is one that we also encounter in the Ascension of Isaiah: 1) in contrast to Moses, Isaiah claimed to have seen God. Two other accusations are not to be found in the Ascension of Isaiah: 2) Moses said, 'who is like our Lord whenever we call to him' (Deut 4.7) whereas Isaiah said 'Seek the Lord in case he can be found' (Isa 55.6); 3) Moses said 'I [God] will complete the days of your life' (Ex 23.26) whereas Isaiah said (to Hezekiah): 'I [God] will add to your life fifteen years' (2 Kgs 20.6). The logic of the accusations is to be reconstructed by the readers. The first one has already been discussed. According to the second, Isaiah seems – unlike Moses – to cast doubt on the assumption that God can always be addressed by prayer, whereas the third accusation apparently infers that Isaiah has a less deterministic view than Moses on how long a life can last. After reporting the charges against Isaiah, the rabbis find reasons for arguing that all three charges are wrong. This does not need to be discussed here; apparently here the tradition in the Talmud considerably differs from the Ascension of Isaiah, which is not at all interested in a juridical view on the case of Isaiah.

There exists an interesting parallel to the Talmud Babli tradition in a source transmitted by Christians: Pseudo-Jerome, *Quaestiones ad Paralipomena* cites in a comment to 2 Chron 33.16[31] first the two accusations we already know from the Ascension of Isaiah (i.e. that Isaiah calls Jerusalem Sodom and claims a vision of God) and then those two additional ones we also find in bJeb 49b. Pseudo-Jerome labels his knowledge as Hebrew tradition. Our author, according to Rhabanus Maurus not Jerome but 'a Jew who in modern times flourished in knowledge of the law' (*Hebrae[us] [qui]dam modernis temporibus in legis scientia floren[s]*)[32] has obviously taken over narrative material from the Talmud Babli itself or a lost Jewish text similar to the

---

[28] Cf. Tosephta Targum to Isaiah 66.1 (Codex Reuchlinianus), Pesiqta Rabbati 4; Talmud Jerushalmi, Sanhedrin, § 10.2, p. 28c, l. 38–43 according to the First Edition in Venice. Cf. Peter Schäfer / Hans-Jürgen Becker (ed.), *Synopse zum Talmud Yerushalmi, Band IV: Ordnung Neziqin; Ordnung Toharot: Nidda* (Tübingen: Mohr Siebeck. 1995), 203–4 (with the parallel in Ms. Leiden) and Gerd A. Wevers (trans.): *Sanhedrin. Gerichtshof*, Übersetzung des Talmud Yerushalmi IV/4 (Tübingen: Mohr Siebeck, 1981), 273 (there: 28c, 44–48).

[29] Talmud Babli Jebamoth 49b. Cf. Lazarus Goldschmidt (ed. / transl.), *Der Babylonische Talmud mit Einschluss der vollständigen Mišnah, Vierter Band: Jabmuth, Kethuboth, Nedarim* (Leipzig: Harrassowitz 1922), 168–9.

[30] Targum to 2 Kings 24.3 (again in the Codex Reuchlinianus). Cf. Alexander Sperber (ed.), *The Bible in Aramaic Based on Old Manuscripts and Printed Texts, Volume II: The Former Prophets According to Targum Jonathan. Second Impression* (Leiden: Brill, 1992), 327 (apparatus).

[31] MPL 23.1466.

[32] MPL 109.231. On Pseudo Jerome's commentary on Chronicles cf. Abraham Rahmer, *Ein lateinischer Commentar aus dem IX. Jahrhundert zu den Büchern der Chronik kritisch verglichen mit den jüdischen Quellen, Erster Theil* (Thorn: Justus Wallis, 1866); Louis Ginzberg, 'Die Haggada bei den Kirchenvätern, erster Theil: Die Haggada in den pseudo-hieronymianischen "Quaestiones"' (PhD Diss., Heidelberg/Amsterdam, 1899).

tradition in bJeb 49b. In every case he cannot exclusively depend on the Talmud as the first charges must stem from elsewhere. I would maintain that most probably Jerome (the authentic one) was the source for the first two charges who designates them as Hebrew tradition (cf. Jerome's Commentary on Isa 1.10), whereas the other ones come from the Talmud. Our author has blended two sources inspired by the fact that they overlap – and thought that in both cases he refers to Jewish tradition.

Actually, how Jewish are the sources we deal with here? The first one, Jerome, presents in fact Christian tradition which he regards as Jewish. The other one, bJeb 49b, is definitely Jewish. Yet is the material used in this source also of Jewish origin? What has happened in the prehistory of bJeb 49b?

I must state that I can no longer believe that bJeb 49b is to be regarded as a Jewish source which independently from the Ascension of Isaiah testifies that at least the charge against Isaiah based upon Isaiah 6.1 has been invented by Jews. We have to be aware that in the whole Jewish tradition it is exclusively the Talmud Babli, a comparably late source, that reports such a charge against Isaiah; the parallel tradition about Isaiah's martyrdom in the Jerushalmi (Sanhedrin, § 10.2) only tells of a martyrdom (which is clearly paralleled by other Jewish tradition and may have been created independently of the Ascension of Isaiah, based perhaps upon the tradition in the *Vitae Prophetarum*).

Another important consideration is that we have found good reasons why the Christian author of the Ascension of Isaiah could have invented the accusations against Isaiah and the prophets, especially those focusing directly on Isaiah and citing words from his canonical book (see §2). As a consequence, it makes sense to regard the Ascension of Isaiah as the point of departure of this tradition.

What then can be said about the tradition of Isaiah's martyrdom in the Babylonian Talmud? The Babylonian rabbis may have taken up tradition about the trial of Isaiah which stems from the Ascension of Isaiah without being aware of its originally Christian background. They obviously only came in contact with the charge based upon Isaiah 6.1. They combined this (probably oral) tradition with their martyrdom story (the prophet in the tree)[33] and added two other charges that function in the same manner as the one based upon Isaiah 6.1: Isaiah and Moses appear to contradict each other. They thereby created an exegetical debate, nice and a bit undramatic compared to the Ascension of Isaiah (which unfortunately lacks any humour – but not all circumstances enable one to see the world from a humorous perspective).

Epimetrum

In one sense, I do not like what I have done. There is a tendency in research, not least inspired by the excellent German scholar Peter Schäfer (now working in the USA), to

---

[33] The backgrounds of the martyrdom of Isaiah in the tree deserve its own investigation, cf. the material assembled and discussed by Kurt Galling, 'Jesaja-Adonis', *Orientalistische Literaturzeitung* 33 (1930): 98–102; M. Gaster/B. Heller, 'Beiträge zur vergleichenden Sagen- und Märchenkunde 7. Der Prophet Jesajah und der Baum. Jüdische Baumsagen', *Monatsschrift für Geschichte und Wissenschaft des Judentums* 80 (1936): 32–52.

turn around the tradition-historical relationship between Early Christianity and Jewish sources by claiming that much more Jewish material is influenced by Christianity than we originally believed. A tendency to date Jewish material later than in the older mainstream of research on Early Christianity and Judaism quite often accompanies this new view. I was originally inclined not to follow these steps, in every case not without protest. I remember also that, on mentioning the martyrdom of Isaiah at a conference and briefly referring to the rabbinic traditions, a colleague asked me if the rabbinic tradition can be regarded as depending on the Ascension. I reacted a bit angrily; I dislike new trends, especially when they are mentioned at conferences with the attitude of being fascinated by allegedly brand new things. But in the given case I do hold this position. Sometimes new strategies seem to work – which does not mean that they always do so (for example, I still cannot believe that the Son of Man traditions in 1 Enoch 37–72 are a Jewish reaction to Christianity, something that Schäfer claims as well).

We probably have to accept that reconstructing tradition history can result in quite different stories, depending on which tradition we are dealing with. In the present case, I would state that the author of the Ascension of Isaiah has taken over a Jewish tradition about Isaiah being sawn in two under King Manasseh – but no more. He transformed this tradition by identifying the saw as wooden, thus creating a Christological connotation. He added claims against Isaiah that tied Isaiah's martyrdom to the passion of Christ, and that are also in other regards rooted in a Christian mindset. Parallel to how Jews invented the story about the prophet swallowed up by a tree, he takes up the tradition about the prophet sawn in two by Manasseh as well. In addition to that, they narrated stories about Isaiah opposing Manasseh's idolatry (based on 2 Kings 21, 2 Chronicles 33, where anonymous prophets protest against the idolatrous king). Christians took up the tradition about the charges against Isaiah and regarded them as being Jewish (mixing up Old Testament parabiblical knowledge and Judaism). Didymus blended what he knew from the Ascension of Isaiah with knowledge about Isaiah's polemics against Manasseh's idolatry – perhaps integrating Jewish tradition. Probably a little later, Jews in Babylonia enlarged their martyrdom story by an (oral?) tradition dependent indirectly on the Ascension of Isaiah about the accusation based on Isaiah 6.1, and made a larger exegetical debate of it. A converted Jew combined this Jewish knowledge with other knowledge borrowed from Jerome, which Jerome presented as a Jewish tradition but in fact derived from the Christian Ascension of Isaiah.

This is, in short, the history of the traditions about Isaiah's martyrdom. The result in respect of the Ascension of Isaiah is that one more important motif can no longer be regarded as deriving from non-Christian Judaism. To what degree Judaism should still be identified as a background in the Ascension of Isaiah is a question that needs to be discussed elsewhere. Here one remark may suffice: with some degree of probability, the specific profile of Manasseh in the Ascension of Isaiah indicates that the dominating – and mostly threatening – cultural power in the world of its author may still have been a kind of Judaism that was in conflict with Christians (not least because of cultural affinity). This, however, may even more have instigated this author to tell a very Christian story about the prophet Isaiah.

7

The *Vorlage* of the Ethiopic Version of the *Epistula Apostolorum*: Greek or Arabic?

Darrell Hannah

The *Epistula Apostolorum* is a post-resurrection dialogue of the risen Christ with his eleven apostles in the period between Easter and the ascension. While post-resurrection dialogues were a favourite genre in gnostic circles, in this particular dialogue the risen Christ teaches his disciples orthodox or proto-orthodox doctrine. In particular, the author emphasizes the reality of Christ's bodily, even fleshly, incarnation, death and resurrection, and the future resurrection of believers 'in the flesh'. The *Epistula*'s author also stresses the oneness of God and the divinity of Christ, to such a degree that the result is a naïve Monarchianism. Scholars are agreed that the *Epistula* belongs to the second century; some would place it in the second half of that century, while others would date it mid-century or slightly earlier. With regard to provenance, in the past Egypt was the most often named location, while today it seems that scholarship tends to favour the arguments which point toward the Roman province of Asia, with a minority holding out for Syria. This fascinating text was not composed by a profound theologian. Nonetheless, it presents us with a window into a crucially important period, when Christian doctrine was in an embryonic process of formation and clarification.

The textual witnesses of the *Epistula Apostolorum*

The *Epistula Apostolorum* has been preserved partially in Coptic and Latin, and in its entirety in Classical Ethiopic or Geʻez. The earliest and, for much of the text, most important witness is found in a single fragmentary Coptic papyrus, in the Akhmimic dialect. This manuscript dates from the end of the fourth century or the beginning of the fifth. There is good reason to conclude that this small, single quire codex contained only the *Epistula* and was intended for personal use. Unfortunately, about 40 per cent of the manuscript's leaves have perished, or at least have not yet come to light. An instance of dittography, subsequently corrected by the original scribe, demonstrates that the codex is not the autograph of the Coptic version, but a copy of a previous Coptic *Vorlage*. General considerations, the transliteration of a large number of Greek technical theological terms and the Septuagint text of the third Psalm, cited entire in *Ep.Apost.* 19, makes it certain that the Coptic version is a translation of a Greek original.

Regarding the Latin witness, a palimpsest manuscript of the fifth or sixth century, now in Vienna but formerly at Bobbio (Cod. Pal. Vindobonensis 16), preserves on a single leaf portions of *Ep.Apost.* 12–13 and 17. The exemplar of this manuscript must have been defective, for the last, incomplete sentence of chapter 13 passes immediately, mid-sentence, into the opening line of the seventeenth chapter, omitting the final clause of chapter 13, the first few words of chapter 17 and all of the intervening material. This Latin manuscript originally contain both the *Epistula* and the Apocalypse of Thomas. On the whole, the Latin text stands closer to the Coptic than the Ethiopic, but a few agreements with the Ethiopic against the Coptic testify to the antiquity of the Ethiopic text at these points.[1] Finally, transliterated Greek technical words and general considerations again strongly suggest the Latin is a translation from a Greek *Vorlage*.

The preservation of the whole of the *Epistula Apostolorum* is due to its introduction into Christian Ethiopia. In the Ethiopian tradition the *Epistula Apostolorum* does not exist as a distinct text, but only as part of a larger work variously entitled *Kidān za-'Egzi'əna wa-Madḫānina 'Iyasus Krəstos* ('The Testament of our Lord and Saviour Jesus Christ') or *Nagar za-nagaromu 'Egzi'əna 'Iyasus Krəstos la-'aśśartu wa-kəl'etu 'ardā'ihu ba-Galilā* ('The Discourse which our Lord Jesus Christ spoke to the twelve disciples in Galilee').[2] The Ethiopian *Nagar ba-Galilā* consists of a short apocalyptic work, followed immediately by the much longer text of the *Epistula Apostolorum*, without any break between the two. The eleven chapters which make up this short apocalyptic work are heterogeneous and appear to have been culled from several sources – even from the *Epistula* itself.[3] In most, but not all, the manuscripts, the text of the *Nagar ba-Galilā* is immediately preceded by a church order from the second half of the fourth century or later, with the similar title of *Kidān za-'Egzi'əna wa-Madḫānina 'Iyasus Krəstos* ('The Testament of our Lord and Saviour Jesus Christ'). This work, not to be confused with the *Nagar ba-Galilā*, also exists in Syriac and Arabic, and is generally known in scholarship as the *Testamentum*

---

[1] For example, in chapter 13, both the Latin and the Ethiopic do not have the Coptic's cumbersome 'Now Michael is the commander-in-chief of the angels …', but rather preserve a smoother reading which merely identifies Michael as one of the four archangels. The Latin and Ethiopic attest a longer reading in chapter 17; the shorter text of the Coptic doubtless resulted from a transcriptional error occasioned by haplography. The Latin and the Ethiopic also agree that the risen Christ predicts his Parousia in terms of *years*, whereas in the Coptic he announces that his Parousia will be after 'after the hundred *part* and the twentieth *part* have been completed'. Finally, while the manuscript is difficult to read, it may support the Ethiopic's reading of a hundred and fifty (years), against the Coptic's a hundred and twenty (parts).

[2] The former is found in the majority of Mss and is used by Guerrier in his critical edition (see below). However, that latter appears in particularly early and important Mss and it is the designation I prefer.

[3] I.e. almost all of chapter 4 of the 'short apocalyptic work' parallels *Ep.Apost.* 34–35 and, indeed, are at times useful in correcting the text of *Ep.Apost.* 34–35. In addition, the end of the fourth chapter, the whole of the fifth and the second half of the sixth parallel material in *Testamentum Domini* i.9–11. For the *Testamentum Domini* see immediately below.

Domini.⁴ All the manuscripts of the *Epistula* which I have been able to consult make clear, by the use of symbols or different colour ink, that the *Nagar ba-Galilā* and the *Kidān* are to be regarded as two distinct works.⁵

The text of the *Nagar ba-Galilā* has been preserved in a number of manuscripts dating from the fourteenth/fifteenth to the twentieth centuries. It has been edited only once, in 1912, by L. Guerrier,⁶ who had only five manuscripts at his disposal, one of which he did not use. Since Guerrier's critical edition, ten more manuscripts have come to light. The fifteen manuscripts group themselves into, more or less, two families.⁷ Mss A, B, C, E, K, N, O, T belong to family 1, and M, P, L, S, Q, R, V to family 2.⁸ However, B shares many readings with family 2, while Q and R frequently agrees with family 1. C and N are manifestly closely related to one another, probably copied from a common ancestor. According to Buchholz,⁹ a similar relationship exists between A and T. Those who have studied the text, Wajnberg, Hills and Pérès, are agreed that family 1 generally contains a text superior to that of family 2. The manuscript I identify as E has not, to my knowledge, been studied by any scholar. Indeed, its existence was only announced in 1999, with the publication of the third volume of the catalogue of manuscripts from the Lake Tānā area.¹⁰ In my opinion, it is our best witness to the Ethiopic version.

For my forthcoming commentary on the *Epistula*, I have collated all the manuscripts of family 1, except T (photographs or microfilms of which I have been unable to locate), as well as MLS of family 2. During my work with the manuscripts, I have become convinced that codices EO are our best Ethiopic witnesses, followed closely by K. Codex E is the oldest manuscript of the *Nagar ba-Galilā* and O is possibly the next oldest, although this honour could go to A. There are times when EKO alone, or nearly alone, preserves the original reading. For example, in the first chapter, EKO alone retains the epistolary greeting 'we greet you'. Again, in the second chapter, EKO alone retains what must be the original order of the disciples: John, Peter, Thomas, Andrew...

---

⁴ I. E. Rahmani, *Testamentum Domini nostri Jesu Christi* (Mainz: Kirchheim, 1899). An English translation was prepared by J. Cooper and A. J. Maclean, *The Testament of our Lord: Translated into Engish from the Syriac with Introduction and Notes* (Edinburgh: T&T Clark, 1902). According to Rahmani, the Arabic version was translated from Coptic. Rahmani promised an edition and translation of the Arabic manuscript, but to my knowledge this was never published. For the Arabic version, see Rahmani, *Testamentum*, xii and C. Schmidt, *Gespräche Jesu mit seinen Jüngern nach der Auferstehung* (TU; Leipzig: Hinrich, 1919), 158–60. The Ethiopic version has been edited by R. Beylot, *Testamentum Domini Éthiopien: Édition et traduction* (Louvain: Éditions Peeters, 1984).

⁵ One occasionally encounters the claim that the first eleven chapters of the *Nagar ba-Galilā*, i.e. the non-*Epistula* chapters, are another version of *Testamentum Domini* i.2–14. So D. D. Buchholz, *Your Eyes will be Opened: A Study of the Greek (Ethiopic) Apocalypse of Peter* (SBLDS 97; Atlanta, GA: Scholars Press, 1988), 137–8 and A. Y. Collins, 'The Early Christian Apocalypses', *Semeia* 14 (=*Apocalypse: The Morphology of a Genre*) (1979), 77. This is an overstatement. As noted above, however, there is a relationship between *Nagar ba-Galilā* 4–6 and *Testamentum Domini* i.9–11.

⁶ L. Guerrier (with the assistance of S. Grébaut), *Le testament en galilée de notre-seigneur Jésus-Christ: Texte éthiopien, édité et traduit en Français*, in *PO* 11 (1912) 141–236 [1–96].

⁷ J. V. Hill, *Tradition and Composition in the* Epistula Apostolorum (Cambridge, MA: Harvard University Press, 1990), 7–8; J.-N. Pérès, *L'Épître des Apôtres et le Testament de notre Seigneur et notre Jésus-Christ* (Turnhout: Brepols), 57–8.

⁸ See the Appendix 1 below for these symbols.

⁹ Buchholz, *Your Eyes will be Opened*, 134–9.

¹⁰ V. Six, *Äthiopische Handschriften vom Ṭānāsee 3: Nebst einem Nachtrag zum Katalog der Äthiopische Handschriften deutscher Bibliotheken und Museen* (Stuttgart: Steiner Verlag, 1999), 233–7.

(cf. *Ep.Apost.* 11). All the other manuscripts reverse the order of Peter and Thomas. In chapter 15, these three manuscripts and, somewhat surprisingly, M include the detail that the angel who rescued the unnamed disciple (probably Peter) from prison was none other than Gabriel. In this EKMO are supported by the Coptic. Other examples could be multiplied.

A simplified stemma can be found in Appendix 2. From it the following conclusions follow. Family 1 preserves the better text, EO are our best witnesses of family 1, followed by K, and then CN and A(T). A reading supported by all the members of family 1, ABCEKNO(T), is usually, but not always, superior to a reading found only in MLS. Family 2 probably represents a text further debased than the text of family 1, but even the text of the latter does not preserve the pristine text of the Ethiopic translation of the *Epistula Apostolorum*. Already in our earliest manuscripts, EOA and, to a greater extent, B, the text has suffered in the course of transmission. Thus, caution is necessary: none of our Ethiopic manuscripts are particularly early and the text which they attest has probably suffered greatly from centuries of copying. Ethiopic scribes are often careless and the manuscripts with which we have to do are no exception. Even M, L and S alone may at times preserve the best reading,[11] and, regrettably, often the original reading is simply unattainable.

One further category of textual evidence should be mentioned. In addition to discrete manuscripts of the *Nagar ba-Galilā*, quotations of and allusions to the *Epistula* appear in some Ethiopian theological works. Although there may well be others, at least two works, the *Maṣḥafa Milād* ('Book of the Nativity') and the *Maṣḥafa Mesṭir Samāy wa-Mədr* ('Book of the Mysteries of Heaven and Earth'), cite our text. Both works belong to the literary activity associated with the reign of King Zarʾa Yaʿaqob (1434–68) and both have been critically edited.[12] Of the two, only *Maṣḥafa Milād* is textually significant.

The introduction of the *Epistula Apostolorum* into Ethiopia (or external evidence)

With these brief remarks on the *Epistula* and its textual witnesses, we can now turn to the interrelated questions of the age of the Ethiopic version and its immediate exemplar. The two are interrelated because there are, generally speaking, two periods in which Christian texts were translated into Ethiopic: the period of the evangelization of the ancient Kingdom of Aksum, that is, from the mid-fourth to the mid-seventh centuries, when translations would most likely have been made from Greek; and after

---

[11] Note, e.g., that in *Ep.Apost.* 11 BLM, supported by the Coptic, preserved what must be the original reading: the risen Christ found the disciples while they were *hiding*. All the others, influenced no doubt by the story of Jesus' appearance on the shores of the Sea of Galilee (Jn 21.3ff; *Gos.Pet.*14 [60]), has the risen Christ appearing to the disciples while they are *fishing*.

[12] K. Wendt (ed. and trans.), *Das Maṣḥafa Milād (Liber Nativitatis) und Maṣḥafa Sellāsē (Liber Trinitatis) des Kaisers Zarʾa Yāʿqob* (CSCO 221-2, 235-6; Leuven: Peeters, 1962, 1963) and J. Perruchon and I. Guidi, eds and trans., *Le Livre des mystères du ciel et de la terre*; and S. Grébaut (ed. and trans.), *Les trois derniers traités du Livre des mystères du ciel et de la terre* (PO 1.1 and 6.3; Paris: Firmin-Didot, 1903, 1911).

the so-called 'restoration of the Solomonic Dynasty' in c. 1270, when there was a renaissance of learning and literary activity. In the latter period, nearly all new translations were made from Arabic exemplars, which very often were translations, in turn, from Coptic. Thus, if it can be shown that the exemplar of the Ethiopic version of the *Epistula* was Greek, it would be certain that it entered Ethiopian tradition early – sometime during the late Aksumite period. And, vice versa, if it could be shown that the *Epistula* was translated early in the history of Christian Ethiopia, then it is most likely that the *Vorlage* used was Greek.[13] Consequently, the reverse is also true: evidence for an Arabic *Vorlage* would point to a later date for the translation into Ethiopic and, vice versa, evidence for a late date of translation would almost certainly mean an Arabic exemplar.

Greek was unquestionably the most important foreign language within the Aksumite Kingdom. It was the language of international trade and knowledge of it must have been widespread, for both Aksumite coins and inscriptions were often in Greek or included Greek alongside Ge'ez.[14] Furthermore, there is good linguistic reasons to suppose that the scriptures were translated into Ethiopic, in the main, from Greek – although some would urge that the translators also worked from Syriac.[15] However, when in the thirteenth and fourteenth centuries, after nearly six hundred years of cultural stagnation and relative isolation, Ethiopia experienced a literary and cultural renaissance, the international situation had changed completely. Then the most significant influence on the Ethiopian Church emanated from the Coptic Church in Egypt, and the *lingua franca* of the later was Arabic – although Coptic still retained its pre-eminence in the liturgy.[16]

Thus, what is needed is either external evidence for the time at which the *Epistula Apostolorum* entered Ethiopia or, failing that, internal evidence that points to translation from Greek, on the one hand, or Arabic (and/or Coptic), on the other. Not surprisingly, given how little we know about the origins of Christianity in Ethiopia and the processes by which Christian literature was translated into Ge'ez, there is no direct external evidence for the introduction of the *Epistula Apostolorum* into Ethiopia, neither in the Aksumite period nor after the 'Solomonic restoration'.[17] The most that can be said is

---

[13] Although, one cannot rule out Syriac altogether for this period. See below.
[14] Cf. e.g. S. Munro-Hay, *Aksum: An African Civilisation of Late Antiquity* (Edinburgh: University of Edinburgh Press, 1991), 10–13; E. Ullendorf, *The Ethiopians: An Introduction to Country and People*, 2nd ed., (London: OUP, 1965), 54–5; idem., *Ethiopia and the Bible* (Schweich Lectures; London: OUP, 1968), 41; H. G. Marcus, *A History of Ethiopia*, 2nd ed. (Berkeley: University of California Press, 2002), 6–7.
[15] So Ullendorf, *Ethiopia and the Bible*, 55–62. But note the criticisms of M. A. Knibb, *Translating the Bible: The Ethiopic Version of the Old Testament* (Schweich Lectures; Oxford: OUP, 1999), 1–46. Cf. also R. Zuurmond, *Novum Testamentum Aethiopice: The Synoptic Gospels. General Introduction – Edition of the Gospel of Mark* (Wiesbaden: Steiner Verlag, 1989), 90–133 and H. J. Polotsky, 'Aramaic, Syriac, and Ge'ez', *JSS* 9 (1964), 1–10. I find Knibb's, Zuurmond's and Polotsky's arguments that the Ethiopic version of the scriptures were in the main translated from the Greek, not Greek and Syriac, convincing.
[16] Cf. Ullendorf, *Ethiopia and the Bible*, 55–62; idem, *Ethiopians*, 66–71.
[17] The date of our earliest manuscript (cod. E), second half of the fourteenth to second half of the fifteenth century, leaves only about a century or a century and a half for the work to be translated from Arabic and, then, copied at least once. But that is ample.

that other non-canonical Christian works such as the Ascension of Isaiah, the Apocalypse of Peter and the Shepherd of Hermas entered Ethiopia in the earlier period, and must have been translated from the Greek. The same is true of Jewish works, such as Jubilees and 1 Enoch, which most likely had been transmitted by Christian missionaries. There is, then, no *a priori* reason to exclude the Aksumite period and Greek from our consideration.

The Ethiopic translation of the *Epistula Apostolorum* (or internal evidence)

Most recent investigations into, or at least pronouncements on, the question have opted for an Arabic *Vorlage*. Wajnberg argued that 'in view of the Coptic text' and the fact that the *Testamentum Domini* exists in Arabic, and that the two works always circulate together in Ethiopic, it is likely that the *Epistula Apostolorum* was translated into Ethiopic from an Arabic *Vorlage*.[18] Wajnberg's conjecture – for it is no more than that – has been repeated a number of times and would seem to have carried the day.[19] It is nonetheless scarcely compelling. In one detail, at any rate, we now know Wajnberg was in error: The *Testamentum Domini* did not always circulate with the *Nagar ba-Galilā*, as the discovery of codex E, our earliest Ethiopic manuscript, now demonstrates.

Guerrier's odd argument

Is there, then, evidence for a Greek *Vorlage*? Even before Wajnberg, Guerrier had pointed to an odd reading in Ms. B, near the beginning of chapter 31, and suggested that it could be evidence for a Greek exemplar. The majority of Mss here reads: *wa-kʷəllo gəbaru lotu ba-kama lakəmu gabarku 'ana* ('Do everything for him [i.e. the apostle Paul] that I have done for you'). Instead of the Ethiopic first person singular pronoun *'ana*, B inexplicably has *'əgo*, a meaningless term in Ge'ez, but which physically looks like *'ana* and which is a fair transcription of ἐγώ, the Greek first person singular pronoun! This *'əgo* looks like an unintentional transliteration, rather than a translation.[20] The infrequency of this reading is not necessarily an argument against its originality, for scribes would naturally have sought to correct the meaningless word and even for a scribe ignorant of Greek, *'ana* would be an obvious solution.

---

[18] Wajnberg in Schmidt, *Gespräche Jesu*, 18–19.
[19] E.g. M. Hornschuh, *Studien zur Epistula Apostolotum* (PTS 5; Berlin: De Gruyter, 1965), 1; H. Duensing, *Epistula Apostolorum* (KlT 152; Bon: Marcus and Weber, 1925), 3; G. Graf, *Geschichte der christlichen arabischen Literatur* (SeT 118; Vatican City: Biblioteca Apostolica Vaticana, 1944), I.241–2; J. Hartenstein, *Die Zweite Lehre: Erscheinungen des Auferstandenen als Rahmenerzählungen frühchristlicher Dialoge* (TU 146; Berlin: Akademie Verlag, 2000), 98; R. Cameron, *The Other Gospels: Non-Canonical Gospel Texts* (Louisville, KY: Westminster/John Knox Press, 1982), 131; H.-J. Klauck, *Apocryphal Gospels: An Introduction* (trans. B. McNeil; London: T&T Clark International, 2003), 152.
[20] For a modern, partial parallel, cf. C. A. Gieschen, *Angelomorphic Christology: Antecedents and Early Evidence* (AGAJU 42, Leiden: Brill, 1998), 37, where Gieschen gives a sizeable quote from Bousset in the original German, but inadvertently translates an 'und' into 'and'.

Nonetheless, this one possible 'translational' error, appearing in a single manuscript, is far from convincing and could well be nothing more than a transcriptional error unrelated to Greek.

Distance from the Ethiopic New Testament

One should bear in mind the general consideration that allusions to NT passages in the Ethiopic version of the *Epistula* stand at some distance from the Ethiopic translation of the NT, and that the latter does not appear to have greatly influenced the textual transmission of the *Epistula*. I discuss this at some length in my forthcoming commentary, but one or two especially clear examples should suffice to illustrate the phenomenon. In *Ep.Apost.* 5 we have an account of 'the Gerasene demoniac' (Mk 5.1–20; par. Mt 8.28–34; Lk 8.26–39). The Synoptic accounts all include the detail that the herd of swine perished in the sea, but Mark and Luke are decidedly more picturesque than Matthew in their description of this detail. Matthew relates that herd 'rushed down the steep bank into the sea *and died in the waters*' (καὶ ἀπέθανον ἐν τοῖς ὕδασιν; Mt 8.32), whereas Mark says 'they choked in the sea' (καὶ ἐπνίγοντο ἐν τῇ θαλάσσῃ; Mk 5.13) and Luke that the herd went 'into the lake and was drowned' (εἰς τὴν λίμνην καὶ ἀπεπνίγη; Lk 8.33). The *Epistula* knows this more gruesome detail, relating that the demon Legion 'entered into (a herd of) swine and submersed them in the sea *and they were choked*' (... *wa-taḥanqu*).[21] The Ethiopic verb *ḥanaqa* could render either Mark's πνίγω or Luke's ἀποπνίγω, but cannot be dependent on Matthew's more pedestrian account. Significantly, however, the Ethiopic recensions of Mark,[22] except for one of the latest, have all been influenced by Matthew at this point:

Eth^{ACabD}: *wa-mota ba-wəsta bāḥr* ('and it [the herd] died in the sea').[23]
Eth^{CcdM}: *wa-motu ba-wəsta bāḥr* (Cd om. *ba-*) ('and they died in the sea').
Eth^E: *wa-tasaṭemu wəsta bāḥr* ('and they were submerged in the sea').[24]

There is as yet no critical edition of the Gospel of Luke. However, the earliest reading we have of Luke 8.33 relates that the herd went *wəsta qalāy wa-mota* ('into the abyss

---

[21] So the majority of Mss. Ms. O has a redundant reading, which still nonetheless includes this detail: '... and they were choked and died (*wa-taḥanqu wa-motu*).'

[22] Zuurmond distinguishes five or six different recensions of the Synoptic Gospels in Ethiopic: A, B, C, D, E and M. Recension B only occurs in the Gospel of Matthew; the other Synoptic gospels have five recensions, A, C, D, E and M, while Matthew exists in all six. However, only recensions A and B have any claim to representing an ancient translation. The others represent revisions of the Old Ethiopic made on the basis of an Arabic version. I shall designate these Eth^A, Eth^B, etc. See Zuurmond, *Synoptic Gospels*, 48–89, 133.

[23] However, some Mss of Eth^A, including two of the earliest, Abbā Garimā 1 and 3, omit the entire phrase.

[24] Acc. to Zuurmond, *General Introduction*, 86–8, the E-recension is represented in the Gospel of Mark by a single manuscript of the eighteenth century. Moreover, the earliest manuscript of this recension, Ms. 218, which has an E-text in its text of Matthew, dates from the seventeenth century and originated in Jerusalem.

and died').[25] The Ethiopic recensions of Matthew 8.32 all (Eth^AB(C)DM) have the phrase *wa-motu (ba-)wəsta māy* ('and they died in the water'), except Eth^E, which reads instead *wa-boʾu wəsta māy* ('and they went into the water'). Thus, the Ethiopic versions of Mark and Luke must have been influenced by the text of Matthew, perhaps because the meaning of the Greek words πνίγω and ἀποπνίγω were unknown to the translator(s) of the gospels. But it is precisely the Markan or Lukan verb which is presupposed in *Ep.Apost.* 5.

Significantly, the early Coptic translators seemed to have had the same difficulty with πνίγω and ἀποπνίγω. The Sahidic of Mark 5.13 and Luke 8.33 both have the same harmonization as in the Ethiopic NT. According to Copt^sa in Mark, the swine rushed into the sea ⲁⲩⲱ ⲁⲩⲙⲟⲩ ϩⲛ ⲑⲁⲗⲁⲥⲥⲁ ('and died in the sea'), while in Luke the translation has the herd of swine going ⲉⲡⲉⲥⲏⲧ ⲉⲧⲗⲓⲙⲛⲏ ⲁⲩⲙⲟⲩ ('down to the lake [and] they died').[26] The later Bohairic corrects the Sahidic at this point, rendering both Mark's πνίγω and Luke's ἀποπνίγω with ⲱϫϩ ('to choke').[27]

That the translator of the Ethiopic version of the *Epistula* chose the verb *ḫanaqa* ('to choke, strangle'), rather than *mota* ('to die'), testifies to his independence from the Ethiopic NT, as well as from the earlier versions of the Coptic NT. However, because we cannot compare his work to the Coptic of *Ep.Apost.* 5 at this point, we can, consequently, derive nothing which directly relates to the question of his exemplar. Nonetheless, this autonomy from the Ethiopic NT suggests that he worked in an early period, before the influence of Ethiopic NT had become too great. And that, in turn, supports the hypothesis that the Ethiopic version of the *Epistula Apostolorum* was made directly from a Greek exemplar.

Another example occurs in chapter 41's parallel to a dominical saying recorded in the Gospel of Matthew:

> And we said to him, 'O Lord, did you not say (to us), "Do not call (anyone) on earth fathers – nor master, for one is your father and teacher, he who is in heaven."'

This is nearly a direct citation of Matthew 23.8–9 – perhaps the closest we come to a quotation of any NT passage in the *Epistula*. That being the case, it cannot be unimportant that none of the scribes of the *Epistula* sought to remove the *Epistula*'s striking additions ('nor master', 'and teacher') to the Matthean text. Comparison with the Coptic confirms that the Ethiopic manuscripts have preserved the original form of this passage. This general observation, which could be repeated in numerous other instances of allusion to NT passages, cannot in and of itself prove the case for a Greek

---

[25] Abba Garima 2 reads: '[the herd] went down that cliff into the abyss and died' (...*wa-wadqa ʾənta ṣadəf wəsta qalāy wa-mota*); EMML 6907 is similar: '[the herd] fell over a cliff into the abyss and died' (...*wa-ṣadəfa wəsta qalāy wa-mota*). Abba Garima 1 is illegible until the words '...and died' (...*wa-mota*), which are very clear. Abba Garima 3 is lacunose. Moreover, Eth^M agrees with Abba Garima 2. These four Mss Abba Garima 1, 2 and 3, and EMML 6907, are Zuurmond's principal witnesses for Eth^A in his editions of Matthew and Mark.

[26] Cf. Copt^sa of Mt 8.32: ⲁⲩⲙⲟⲩ ϩⲣⲁⲓ ϩⲛ ⲙ̄ⲙⲟⲟⲩ ('they died in the water').

[27] An equivalent of the Sahidic ⲱϭⲧ.

Vorlage, but is more explicable in an early period before the influence of the Ethiopic NT had become too great.

Transcription

The Ethiopic version of the *Epistula* also offers a number of words which look as if they were transcribed directly from Greek. Many of these are names, such as *Yoḥannəs* (John), *Tomās* (Thomas), *Peṭros* (Peter), *Filəpos* (Philip), *Mātewos* (Matthew), *Pilāṭos* (Pilate), *Mikā'el* (Michael), *Gabr'el* (Gabriel), etc. All of these follow Hellenistic orthographic conventions and would be spelled differently if they had been transcribed from Arabic. On the other hand, other words clearly follow Semitic orthographic conventions, such as *'Abrahām* (Abraham), *Yā'qob* (James [= Jacob]), *Yəhudā* (Judas [= Judah]), *Kefā* (Cephas) and *dinār* (denarius). Similar phenomena occur in the Ethiopic Bible: familiar Semitic names, for example, Jacob/James and Judah/Judas, are left in their Semitic form;[28] others are transcribed from the Greek and retain their Hellenistic apparel.[29]

There are, however, two transcriptions of Greek words in the *Epistula* which could well point to a Greek *Vorlage*. In chapter 17 we encounter a transliteration of Πεντηκοστή (Pentecost): *Panṭaqʷasṭe*. A transliteration of this from a Semitic language, and especially the Arabic, would look rather different. The term Pentecost in its Greek dress is, nonetheless, so pervasive in Ethiopic Christian documents that the transliteration of this particular word cannot be decisive. The occurrence of *Qarānyo* in chapter 9, on the other hand, is much more significant.[30] The Ethiopic translator has transcribed the Greek term in the nominative or accusative form: κρανίο(ν).[31] This particular form (*Qarānyo*) suggests a Greek *Vorlage* in which the final *nu* was suspended: κρανίο̄. Interestingly, in three of the four references to 'the place of the skull' in the NT, κρανίον is in the genitive (κρανίου; Mk 15.22; Mt 27.33; Jn 19.17). Luke, however, has the accusative: τὸν τόπον τὸν καλούμενον Κρανίον (23.33). Indeed, the phrase in the Ethiopic text of *Ep.Apost.* 9 looks like a precise citation of Luke 23.33: '(at) the place named/called *Qarānyo*'. Although there is a lacuna in the Coptic Ms., the latter also reads like a citation of Luke: ⲉⲛ ⲟⲩⲧⲟⲡⲟⲥ ⲉϩⲁⲣⲟⲩⲙⲟⲩⲧⲉ ⲁ[ⲣⲁϥ ⲕⲣⲁⲛⲓ]ⲟⲛ, 'in a place nam[ed (the) Sku]ll'. Here we have the Greek loan word for 'place' (τόπος), a Coptic verb which very naturally translates τὸν καλούμενον, and, after the lacuna, the accusative ending – on. On the other hand, the Arabic NT, as far as I have been able to ascertain, always *translates* the term for skull. The so-called Alexandrian Vulgate, two early Arabic manuscripts of Matthew and Mark, and the Arabic Diatessaron all use the

---

[28] Jan Dochhorn has pointed out to me that if the *Epistula* were translated from the Arabic, 'Jacob' would be *Yā'qub*, not *Yā'qob*. This may well be the case, but *Yā'qob* is so prevalent in Ethiopic that nothing can be concluded from the fact that at *Ep.Apost.* 27 all the manuscripts read *Yā'qob* and not *Yā'qub*.

[29] Cf. the discussion in Zuurmond, *Synoptic Gospels: General Introduction*, 92–106.

[30] The following argument has been considerably strengthened through criticisms and suggestions made by participants at the Durham conference. Once again, I am especially indebted to Jan Dochhorn.

[31] All the Mss agree in the spelling *Qarānyo*, except B which gives *Qarānyos*, as if the noun were second declension masculine (κρανίος), rather than second declension neuter (κρανίον).

Arabic term for a skull rather than transliterating κρανίον.³² It is, therefore, likely that a putative Arabic translation of the *Epistula* would also have translated κρανίον. Thus, here in this transliteration, we may well encounter a definite trace of the translator's Greek *Vorlage*.

This conclusion finds some support in the fact that the various recensions of the Ethiopic Gospels are far from uniform at this point and while *Qarānyo* appears in many, there are a number of other variants. The evidence is as follows:

Matthew 27.33: ... ὅ ἐστιν Κρανίου Τόπος λεγόμενος, ...
Eth^A: *za-yəbələwwo Qarānyos*³³
Eth^(2?)4: *wa-za-tərgʷāme-hu Qarānyo*³⁴
Eth^B: *za-ba-tərgʷāme-hu Qarānyu*³⁵
Eth^C: *za-ba-tərgʷāme-hu yəbələwwo Qarānyos*³⁶
Eth^D: *za-ba-tərgʷāme-hu dəmāḫ*³⁷
Eth^E: *za-ba-tərgʷāme-hu yəbələwwā Qarānyo*³⁸
Mark 15.22: ... ὅ ἐστιν μεθερμηνευόμενον Κρανίου Τόπος.
Eth^ACD: *za-ba tərgʷāme-hu yəbələwwo Qarānyo makān*³⁹
Eth^E: *za-ba tərgʷāme-hu Qarānyo*⁴⁰
Eth³¹: *za-ba tərgʷāme-hu yəbələwwo Qarānyos makān*⁴¹
Luke 23.33: ... ἐπὶ τὸν τόπον τὸν καλούμενον Κρανίον, ...⁴²
Eth¹: *bəḥera za-səmu Qarāno)*⁴³
Eth⁴: *bəḥera za-səmu Qarānos*⁴⁴
Eth²,³: These manuscripts are either lacunose or their leaves are disordered.

---

³² For the Alexandrian Vulgate, I consulted Walton's Polyglot. The two early manuscripts are Vatican Borg. Ar. 95 and Berlin Or. oct. 1108. See B. Levin, *Die Griechisch-Arabische Evangelien-Übersetzung: Vatican Borg. Ar. 95 und Berlin Or. oct. 1108* (Uppsala: Almqvist & Wiksells, 1938). For the Arabic Diatessaron, see A.-J. Marmardji, *Diatessaron de Tatien* (Beirut: Imprimerie Catholique, 1935).

³³ '... which is called *Qarānyos*.' This assumes κρανίος, as if the Greek word were masculine. This same error is found in *EpApost*. 9, codex B (see n. 31 above).

³⁴ '... and in translation *Qarānyo*.' Mss 2 and 4 (Abba Garima 3 and EMML 6907, respectively) are both witnesses to Eth^A. Ms. 2 agrees with the other witnesses to Eth^A in reading '...which is called' rather than '...which in translation'. Apparently, Zuurmond cannot be sure, from the notoriously difficult to read photographs of this Ms., whether *Qarānyo* has the final S.

³⁵ '... which in translation (is) *Qarānyu*.' In using the genitive κρανίου, the translator agrees precisely with the Greek text of Matthew.

³⁶ '... which in translation is called *Qarānyos*.' See n. 31 above.

³⁷ '... which in translation (is) skull.' *dəmāḫ* is Ge'ez for 'skull'. Zuurmond argues that this recension is the result of a revision based on an Arabic version of the Gospel, perhaps Tatian's *Diatessaron* in its Arabic dress. See Zuurmond, *Synoptic Gospels*, 82–5.

³⁸ '... which in translation is called *Qarānyo*.'

³⁹ '... which in translation is called the place *Qarānyo*.'

⁴⁰ '... which in translation is *Qarānyo*.'

⁴¹ '... which in translation is called the place *Qarānyos*.' According to Zuurmond (*Synoptic Gospels*, 77–8), Ms. 31 belongs to Eth^Cc, the sub-recension which is the 'most perfect conflation' of Eth^A and Eth^B.

⁴² As noted above, there is as yet no critical edition of the Gospel of Luke. I have consulted the four earliest Mss and the Majority text.

⁴³ '... (to) the place which is named/called *Qarānyo*.' Eth¹ is Abba Garima 1.

⁴⁴ '... (to) the place which is named/called *Qarānyos*.' Eth⁴ is EMML 6907.

Eth^M: *bəḥera za-səmu Qarāno*⁴⁵
John 19.17: ... εἰς τὸν λεγόμενον Κρανίου Τόπον, ...
Eth^A: *bəḥera za-səmu Qarāniyu*⁴⁶
Eth^(Ab Cbd E): *bəḥera za-səmu Qarānyo*⁴⁷
Eth³⁰⁰: *'əska ḫaba za-yəbələwwo dəmāḫ*⁴⁸

While *Qarāno* is the majority of reading, there are plenty of variants, which reduces the possibility that the translator of the *Epistula* was influenced by a uniform Ethiopic Gospel text. Moreover, it is to be noted that one Ethiopic recension demonstrably influenced by an Arabic version (Eth^D) replaced a form of *Qarānyo* with *dəmāḫ*, the Ethiopic word for 'skull', in the gospels of Matthew and John. The Arabic manuscripts behind this Ethiopic recension could not have had the transliterated Greek word for 'skull'. This strengthens the impression that if the Ethiopic *Epistula* had been translated from Arabic, it is unlikely to have included a transliteration of κρανίο(ν).

The supposition of a Greek *Vorlage* is the best explanation for *Qarānyo* in *Ep.Apost.* 9. There is, however, another explanation. Among the cluster of rock-hewn churches of Lalibela is 'a cross hewn from solid rock called Qeranio'.⁴⁹ Beneath this is found the 'tomb of Adam'. Ethiopian tradition makes much of the popular belief that Christ was crucified at the place where the skull of Adam was buried.⁵⁰ According to Ethiopic tradition, this cluster of churches were hewn from the rock in the thirteenth century, during the reign of King Lalibela, as a kind of Jerusalem within Ethiopia, to which pilgrimage could be made and thus rendering the arduous journey to Palestine superfluous.⁵¹ In fact, recent research suggests that the construction of Lalibela extended over a much longer period of time than the reign of their eponymous 'creator'. Some of the structures may be as much as half a millennium older than the thirteenth century, even if not originally excavated as churches. Others were added over the centuries, with the final monuments probably added during the thirteenth century. It may have been King Lalibela who transformed the site into a place of pilgrimage and bestowed on it the symbolism of a New Jerusalem after the fall of the Holy City to Salah-ad-Din in 1187.⁵² The Tomb of Adam, the church named Golgotha and the cross

---

⁴⁵ '... (to) the place which is named/called *Qarānyo*.' For Eth^M I have used the edition of T. Pell Platt, *Novum Testamentum Domini Nostri Jesu Christi Aethiopice* (London: British and Foreign Bible Society, 1830).
⁴⁶ '... (to) the place which is named/called *Qarāniyu*.' A genitive; cf. Mt 27.33 Eth^B (above).
⁴⁷ '... (to) the place which is named/called *Qarānyo*.'
⁴⁸ '... until [that place] which is called skull.' Cf. Mt 27.33 Eth^D (above). According to M. G. Wechsler (*Evangelium Iohannis Aethiopicum* [CSCO 617; SAeth 109; Leuven: Peeters, 2005] xxv–xxvi), Eth^D represents a revised text influenced by the Arabic 'Alexandrian Vulgate' and the Arabic Diatessaron.
⁴⁹ Sergew-Hable Sellassie, *Ancient and Medieval Ethiopian History to 1270* (Addis Ababa: United Printers, 1972), 272–3.
⁵⁰ The earliest extant source for this tradition is Origen, *Comm. Ser. Matt.* 126 (on Mt 27.33). It is repeated by numerous Fathers including Epiphanius (*Pan.* 46.5.1–8), who claims that was known to Tatian. It thus reaches back to the third century, and could be as old at the second.
⁵¹ Cf. e.g. Sergew-Hable Sellassie, *Ethiopian History*, 271–8.
⁵² For this hypothesis, see D. W. Phillipson, *Ancient Churches of Ethiopia: Fourth – Fourteenth Centuries* (London: Yale University Press, 2009), 123–81, esp. 177–81. Cf. also Phillipson's more succinct and earlier statement in his *Ancient Ethiopia. Aksum: Its Antecedents and Successors* (London: British

Qarānyo all three belong to this period. It could thus be argued that for a monument to be named *Qarānyo*, in precisely that form, at such an important religious site, suggests the significance of the term in Ethiopian piety. In addition, late religious Ethiopic texts, such as the *Book of the Mysteries of Heaven and Earth* and the *Zəna Lalibela*, also use the term, again in this same form *Qarānyo*.[53] In other words, could not the distinctive *Qarānyo* in the Ethiopic version of *Ep.Apost.* 9 have resulted from Ethiopian scribal activity which reflects the importance of the term in Ethiopian piety? If we answer in the affirmative, then there is no need to posit our translator working directly with the Greek text.

However, for this argument to be persuasive, the fourth/fifth-century Coptic manuscript would have to support a different reading. As it is, the preserved text, with the accusative ending -ον, looks too much like κρανίον for this to be judged likely. It is just as probable that an early Ethiopic translation of the *Epistula*, as well as the developing Gospel textual tradition, accounts for importance of the term *Qarānyo* in Ethiopian piety. The thirteenth-century monumental cross named *Qarānyo* and the appearance of the term in later religious texts would then depend on an Ethiopic translation of the *Epistula*, not the other way around.

Mistranslations

Three examples of mistranslations or possible mistranslations may also point toward a Greek *Vorlage*. In chapter 12, according to the Coptic, the risen Lord says to the Eleven: 'Ri[se a]nd I will reveal to you the things which are above the heavens, the things which [are i]n the heavens and your rest (ἀνάπαυσις), which is in the kingdom of heaven.' In the Ethiopic, this becomes: 'Stand up and I shall reveal to you what (shall be in) the heavens and what (shall be) above the heavens, and your resurrection which (shall be) in the kingdom of heaven.' Here clearly a translator or scribe has misread the Greek word for rest, ἀνάπαυσις, as if it were the word for resurrection, ἀνάστασις. The ease by which this error could have happened is especially clear when the two words are written in Greek uncials: ΑΝΑΠΑΥCΙC and ΑΝΑCΤΑCΙC. That exact error has apparently occurred in the Coptic manuscript of the Gospel of Thomas (NHC II.2) at logion 51, which reads ⲁⲛⲁⲡⲁⲩⲥⲓⲥ ('rest') in a context that demands ⲁⲛⲁⲥⲧⲁⲥⲓⲥ ('resurrection'). The ⲁⲛⲁⲡⲁⲩⲥⲓⲥ in logion 50 probably caused the scribe to misread ⲁⲛⲁⲥⲧⲁⲥⲓⲥ as if it were ⲁⲛⲁⲡⲁⲩⲥⲓⲥ. With regard to *Ep.Apost.* 12, however, the question is, was this error committed by the Ethiopic translator working directly from Greek, or did the Ethiopic translator merely repeat an error originally made in Greek (or Coptic) and taken over into the Arabic? That the Coptic manuscript of the *Epistula* reads ⲁⲛⲁⲡⲁⲩⲥⲓⲥ at this point does not necessarily rule out such a possibility, for the error

---

Museum Press, 1998), 133–6. Cf. also N. Finneran, '(Town of) Lalibäla' and M. Heldman 'Churches of Lalibäla,' both in S. Uhlig et al., eds, *Encyclopedia Aethiopica*, Vol. 3 (He–N) (Wiesbaden: Harrassowitz, 2007), 482–9.

[53] For the *Book of the Mysteries of Heaven and Earth*, see *PO* 6 (1911), 429; the *Zena Lalibela* is cited by Sergew-Hable Sellassie, *Ethiopian History*, 276. Both these texts are late. According to M.-L. Derat, '(King) Lalibäla,' in *Enc.Aeth.*, III.479, the *Zena Lalibela* may well be later than the fifteenth century.

could have occurred after our Coptic manuscript was copied or at least independent of that manuscript. We have in our Coptic and Ethiopic witnesses evidence for the misreading of the Greek word ἀνάπαυσις, but we cannot be sure, by this one variant alone, at what stage the error was made.

At *Ep.Apost.* 29 there is a substantial disagreement between our two textual witnesses. The Ethiopic has the disciples ask the risen Christ: 'O Lord, will there be another doctrine *and disaster*?' The final word, *ḥəmāme*, could be rendered either by 'disaster,' 'affliction,' 'misery' or 'envy,' 'jealousy.'[54] The Coptic, on the other hand, reads: 'O Lord, then will there exist teaching from others, *besides what you have told us*?' (ⲡⲁϫⲉⲛ ⲇⲉ [ⲛⲉϥ] ϫⲉⲡϫⲁⲉⲓⲥ ⲙⲏ ⲟⲩⲛ̄ [ⲣ̄ⲛ̄ⲥ]ⲃⲟⲩ ⲁⲛ ⲛ̄ⲕⲉ[ⲕⲉⲩⲉ ⲛⲁ]ⲣϣⲱⲡⲉ ⲛ̄ⲡⲃⲗ̄ ⲛ̄ⲛⲉⲧⲁ[ⲕ]ϫⲟⲟⲩⲉ ⲛⲉⲛ?) The latter makes more sense and better fits the context. The Ethiopic would seem to be in error. It is possible that this error occurred at the level of the Greek text, with the original φθέγγομαι ('to speak, to utter, to proclaim') being confused for φθείρω ('to destroy, ruin, corrupt') or φθονέω ('to envy'). While φθέγγομαι may not be the most obvious Greek verb for teaching, it is used with this meaning at Acts 4.18.[55] Of course, if this is on the right track, then two scribal errors must be presumed: the first confused ἐφθεγξῶ ('you told us') for ἔφθειρας ('you corrupted, destroyed, ruined') or ἐφθόνησας ('you envied'), which was then 'corrected' to the substantive φθορά ('corruption, destruction') or φθόνος ('envy, jealousy').

Another, more significant, mistranslation occurs in the 'annunciation' scene of chapter 14. The risen Christ states that when he appeared to Mary 'in the form of the archangel Gabriel', according to the Coptic, Mary's 'heart accepted me, she believed and she formed me and I went into her womb and became flesh' (ⲁ ⲡⲥϩⲏⲧ ϣⲁⲡⲧ ⲁⲣⲁⲥ, ⲁⲥⲣ̄ⲡⲓⲥⲧⲉⲩⲉ ⲁⲥⲣ̄ⲡ[ⲗⲁ]ⲁⲥⲥⲉ ⲛ̄ⲙⲁⲓ̈ ⲁⲓ̈ⲃⲱⲕ ⲁϩⲟⲩⲛ ⲁϩⲏⲧⲥ ⲁⲓⲣϣⲱⲡⲉ ⲛ̄ⲥⲁⲣⲝ̄).[56] The verb for 'formed' is the Greek loan word πλάσσω. The Ethiopic is similar, but differs at just this word. It relates that Mary's 'heart accepted, she believed *and laughed* and I, the Word, entered into her and became flesh'. Wajnberg argued that the Coptic text, from which the putative Arabic translation was made, and which in turn served as the *Vorlage* of the Ethiopic, must have here mistakenly read ⲅⲉⲗⲁⲥⲥⲉ for ⲡⲗⲁⲥⲥⲉ.[57] This is unlikely. It is much more plausible to assume that the Ethiopic preserves the original reading, and ⲡⲗⲁⲥⲥⲉ is the Coptic translator's, or a later Coptic scribe's, transcriptional error or correction for ⲅⲉⲗⲁⲥⲥⲉ. Two considerations suggest this. First, a parallel in *Sib.Or.* 8.456–472,[58] which may well be dependent upon the *Epistula*, demonstrates that the

---

[54] Some Mss have the optional spelling, *ḥamame*, but there is no difference in meaning.
[55] Cf. also Justin, *1Apol.* 38.1.
[56] The manuscript is fragmentary and the crucial verb uncertain. Schmidt, *Gespräche Jesu*, 51–2, considered the reading printed above, ⲁⲥⲣ̄ⲡⲗⲁⲥⲥⲉ ⲛ̄ⲙⲁⲓ̈ ('she formed me'), but rejected it on doctrinal grounds for ⲁⲓ̈ⲣ̄ⲡⲗⲁⲥⲥⲉ ⲛ̄ⲙⲁⲓ̈ ('I formed myself'). I prefer the former as the more difficult (theological) reading and better Coptic, but it would not materially change the argument made here if the latter reading is preferred.
[57] Wajnberg, in Schmidt, *Gespräche Jesu*, 50–2.
[58] 'In the last times he changed the earth and, coming late / as a new light, he rose from the womb of the Virgin Mary. / Coming from heaven, he put a mortal form. / First, then Gabriel was revealed in his strong and holy person. / Second, the archangel also addressed the maiden in speech: / "Receive God, Virgin, in your immaculate bosom." / Thus speaking, he breathed in the grace of God, even to one who was always a maiden. / Fear and, at the same time, wonder seized her as she listened. / She

reading 'she laughed' is unquestionably ancient. Second, the sequence of the Coptic makes little sense: Mary's heart accepts the message and she believes, she forms Christ (presumably in her womb) and then, finally, he enters her womb, where he has already been formed. This cannot be correct. The Ethiopic is much more straightforward: Mary's heart accepts the message and she believes, she laughs, and Christ enters her womb. It seems inescapable, the Greek original read ἐγέλασεν (ΕΓΕΛΑϹΕ[Ν]), but was misread by the Coptic translator as ἔπλασεν (ΕΠΛΑϹΕ[Ν]), who then emended the text to speak of Mary 'forming' Christ in her womb.[59]

These three possible mistranslations have an accumulative force. It is easy to dismiss one as not a mistranslation at all, but merely a different reading. But three together strengthen the impression that we are dealing with a Greek exemplar – and only a Greek exemplar – behind both the Coptic and the Ethiopic. This is especially so as all three can be explained merely on the supposition of Greek to Ethiopic; there is no reason in any of the three instances to posit an Arabic stage of transmission.

Literary relations and early circulation

One final consideration seems to add further support to the emerging case for a Greek *Vorlage*. The probability that the *Epistula* shares a literary relationship with the *Testamentum Domini*, on the one hand, and with the apocalyptic material which prefaces the *Epistula* in the Ethiopic *Nagar ba-Galilā*, on the other, is best explained by a Greek context, rather than an Ethiopic one.[60] The *Testamentum Domini*, a work of the second half of the fourth century or later,[61] opens with an apocalyptic section in which the disciples question the risen Christ about 'signs of the end'. The opening scene of the *Testamentum Domini*, an appearance of the risen Christ to his disciples, is in a number of details reminiscent of *Ep.Apost*. 11–12. In an allusion to Luke 24.39 and 1 John 1.1, both *Test.Dom*. Prol. and *Ep.Apost*. 12 affirm that the disciples touched or handled the risen Christ. Both portray the disciples falling 'on their faces' before him (*Test.Dom*. Prol.; *Ep.Apost*. 12), both attribute this reaction to the disciples' fear (although this is only implicit in *Ep.Apost*. 12), and in both Jesus is styled

---

stood trembling. Her mind fluttered / while her heart was shaken by the unfamiliar things she heard. / But again she rejoiced, and her heart was healed by the voice. / The maiden *laughed* (κουρίδιον δ' ἐγέλασσεν [some mss: ἐγέλασεν]) and reddened her cheek, / rejoicing with joy and enchanted in heart with awe. / Courage also came over her. A word flew to her womb. / In time it was made flesh and came to life in the womb, / and was fashioned in mortal form and became a boy / by virgin birth.' (Collins' translation from *OTP* I.428.)

[59] I owe a debt of thanks to Francis Watson for conversations over this interesting passage.

[60] This argument was also first suggested to me by Francis Watson. I am indebted to him for his original suggestion and for the email conversation which followed.

[61] The *Testamentum Domini* has been dated 'about 350 A.D.' or, alternatively, '361–363 A.D.' (Cooper and Maclean, *Testament*, 25 and 41, respectively); 'sometime in the second half of the fourth century, probably before 381' (G. Sperry-White, *The Testamentum Domini: A Text for Students, with Introduction, Translation, and Notes* (Nottingham: Grove Books, 1991), 6); 'probably from the fifth century' (J. Quasten, *Patrology*, 3 Vols. (Utrecht: Spectrum, 1962), II.185; and 'the fifth century' (C. Moreschini and E. Norelli, *Early Christian Greek and Latin Literature: A Literary History*, 2 Vols., M. J. O'Connell (trans.) (Peabody, MA: Hendrickson, 2005), II.195).

'Teacher' or 'Master' (*Ep.Apost.* 11: *mamhərkəmu*; [ⲡⲉⲧⲛⲥⲁϩ];[62] *Test.Dom.* Prol.: *liq ena* [Ethiopic], *mallpānan* [Syriac]).[63] The difference in meaning between *liq* and *mamhər* is not great; both could be a translation of either διδάσκαλος or καθηγητής, although the former is more likely. All four of these elements have parallels in early accounts of resurrection appearances: touching/handling Jesus (Lk 24.39; Ignatius, *Smyrn.* 3.2); the face to the ground posture (Mt 28.9); the fearful reaction (Mk 16.8; Mt 28.8, 10) and Jesus addressed as 'Teacher' (Jn 20.16), and none of them in isolation from the others would elicit comment. It is, however, the collocation of all four in so brief a compass which suggests the author of the *Testamentum*[64] was here drawing on the *Epistula*. That this is indeed the case seems to be confirmed by a passage latter in the apocalyptic section of the *Testamentum*. In *Test.Dom.* 6–7 Christ tells his disciples of 'signs in heaven' which will precede the end. They will include 'a bow ... and a horn and lights'. This parallels *Ep.Apost.* 34 where we read that 'those who do not believe will see a horn from heaven, the appearance of great stars, visible (even) during the daytime'. The sighting of a horn in heaven, rather than hearing the blast of a horn, is striking and in itself suggests the possibility of dependency. However, in the *Testamentum*, this list of heavenly signs is immediately followed by earthly ones, including 'the birth of dragons from mankind', which strikes me as a grotesque domestication of the heavenly sign which immediately follows in *Ep.Apost.* 34: 'a dragon which reaches from heaven to the earth'. It is important to note, however, that this last parallel, between *Test.Dom.* 6 and *Ep.Apost.* 34, is absent from the Ethiopic version of the *Testamentum*: the Ethiopic omits 'the horn', and reads 'moon and stars' for 'lights'. With the dropping of the difficult sighting of a horn in the heavens and with the natural specification of lights as 'moon and stars', the Ethiopic version appears to be the later, smoother reading.[65]

If all this is accepted, then the author of the *Testamentum Domini*, or his apocalyptic source, had the text of the *Epistula* before him, or in his memory, when he constructed his account of resurrection appearance and his list of eschatological signs. Moreover, as noted above, the material which precedes the *Epistula* in the Ethiopic version (or the *Nagar ba-Galilā*, to use its Geʿez name) includes a passage which clearly parallels *Test.Dom.* i.9–11, as well as another which parallels *Ep.Apost.* 34. The very fact that these eleven chapters, which precede the *Epistula*, are present in all Ethiopic manuscripts suggests that they became attached to the *Epistula* early on, either before the *Epistula* was translated into Ethiopic, at the time of the translation, or very shortly thereafter.

How do we account for this complex of relationships: first, the *Testamentum Domini*'s dependence on the *Epistula*; second, the literary relationship between *Test. Dom.* i.9–11 and the *Nagar ba-Galilā*; and third, the fact that in Ethiopia the *Epistula* most often, but not always, was copied alongside the *Testamentum Domini*? It is

---

[62] The Coptic manuscript is fragmentary and ⲡⲉⲧⲛⲥⲁϩ ('your teacher/master') is supplied on the basis of the Ethiopic.
[63] 'Our teacher/master.'
[64] Or, perhaps, the author of the apocalyptic source which was taken up by the compiler of the *Testamentum*.
[65] The author of the apocalyptic introduction added to the *Epistula*, which also includes this passage, goes a step further and omits all reference to the dragon.

certainly possible that the *Epistula* was a source for the *Testamentum Domini*, and the latter was then a source for the author of the 'little apocalypse' which makes up the introduction of the *Nagar ba-Galilā*, and that, by sheer coincidence, in Ethiopian tradition this apocalyptic introduction is combined with a work which served as a source for its own source. The dependence of the 'little apocalypse' on the *Testamentum Domini* could then be limited to the Ethiopic translation of the latter, for after all, our only evidence for the 'little apocalypse' are the Ethiopic manuscripts of the *Nagar ba-Galilā*. Such a scenario could be set out as follows:

Ep.Apost. → *Test.Dom.* → 'little apoc.' → *Nagar ba-Galilā* ('little apoc.' + *Ep.Apost.*) [in most Mss copied alongside *Test.Dom.*]

However, it is simpler and more straightforward to suppose that the *Epistula* already acquired its apocalyptic introduction before it was translated into Ethiopic and before the author of the *Testamentum* drew on both. We would then have the following scenario:

Ep.Apost. → 'little apoc.' + *Ep.Apost.* → *Test.Dom.* ⤳ Eth. translation of *Nagar ba-Galilā*
⤳ Eth. translation of *Test.Dom.*

This would fit with the above observation that, as all the Ethiopic manuscripts of the *Epistula* also contain the 'little apocalypse', it must have been added early on.

If the scenario set out immediately above is correct, then it follows that the author/compiler of the *Testamentum Domini* had a Greek copy of the *Epistula* (with its added apocalyptic introduction) before him, for the original language of the *Testamentum* was almost certainly Greek. The *Testamentum*'s author/compiler borrowed from the Greek *Epistula* for his opening scene and his signs of the end, *and* from the Greek apocalyptic introduction for i.9–11.

Now, it is not impossible that the combined text of the *Epistula*, with its added introduction, circulated widely, was at one point translated into Arabic and it was this version that served as the *Vorlage* of the Ethiopic version. That could be schematized as follows:

Ep.Apost. → 'little apoc.' + *Ep.Apost.* → *Test.Dom.* → Ar. translation ⤳ Eth. translation of *Nagar ba-Galilā*
⤳ Eth. translation of *Test.Dom.*

While there are many possible variables, and an Arabic stage of the *Nagar ba-Galilā* is not impossible (there is, after all, an Arabic version of the *Testamentum*), we have no positive evidence for such a stage. What we do have is clear evidence for literary borrowing by the author/compiler of the *Testamentum* from the *Epistula and* from the 'little apocalypse' at the Greek stage. The *Epistula*, with or without its added introduction, must have circulated rather widely at that early stage. It was known in Egypt (Coptic manuscript), in the West (Latin version), in Syria (*Testamentum*) and, perhaps, in Asia (if it was indeed composed there). Later, our only evidence for it is in Ethiopia. An Arabic version and stage of transmission are not impossible, but the likelihood, given its early wide circulation, is that the *Epistula* entered Ethiopia early on, and that means a Greek *Vorlage*.

Conclusions

All of the above – the distance of many of the NT allusions from the Ethiopic NT; the evidence of Greek loan words, especially *Qarānyo*; the three possible examples of mistaken translation, especially when considered together; and the evidence for the early widespread circulation of the *Epistula* over against its more restricted circulation later – altogether make a strong case for a Greek *Vorlage*, and consequently an early date for the translation into Ethiopic. I can find no correspondingly strong arguments for an Arabic (or Coptic) *Vorlage*. Moreover, new evidence has now shown that Wajnberg's sole argument was based on an error. The *Epistula Apostolorum* did not always circulate with the *Testamentum Domini* in Ethiopia; our earliest manuscript of the *Epistula* does not contain the *Testamentum*. I conclude that Wajnberg's conjecture of an Arabic version must now be seriously questioned – if not rejected outright.

Nonetheless, it is clear that in the Ethiopic we do not possess a witness equal in value to the Coptic. The many differences between the two, the looseness of the Ethiopic, especially in difficult passages, the not infrequent occasions when none of the Ethiopic variant readings seem to be correct and the few occasions when the Ethiopic has smoothed over and corrected the less than orthodox theology of the Coptic (e.g. chapter 18), all bear witness to three interrelated facts: the Ethiopic translator worked later than and was less gifted than his Coptic counterpart, and the product of his labours has suffered through centuries of less than careful scribes. Nevertheless, the evidence offered here points to the conclusion that the Ethiopic version of the *Epistula* is most likely not a late medieval work, but rather belongs to the period of the evangelization of Ethiopia. It follows that it should be regarded as a more reliable textual witness to the text of the *Epistula Apostolorum* than it has been since Wajnberg.

Appendix 1 Ethiopic manuscripts of the *Epistula Apostolorum*

Place	Date	Symbol	Contents[66]
Paris: Abbadianus 51	15th–16th cent.[67]	A	*Kidān*; *Nagar*
Paris: Abbadianus 90	16th cent.[68]	B	*Kidān*; *Nagar*
Paris: Abbadianus 199	17th–18th cent.[69]	C	*Kidān*; *Nagar*
Dāgā Esṭifānos 66[70]	14th–15th cent.[71]	E	*Nagar*
London: B.L. Or. 795	mid.-18th cent.[72]	K	*Kidān*; *Nagar*
London: B.L. Or. 793	mid.-18th cent.[73]	L	*Kidān*; *Nagar*
EMML 370	19/20th cent.[74]	M	*Kidān*; *Nagar*
EMML 1945	18th cent.[75]	N	*Kidān*; *Nagar*
EMML 2358	1575–1590[76]	O	*Kidān*; *Nagar*
EMML 6925	17th–18th cent.[77]	P	uncertain; *Nagar*
EMML 7021	19th cent.[78]	Q	*Kidān*; *Nagar*
EMML 7204	18th cent.[79]	R	*Kidān*; *Nagar*
Stuttgart: Or. fol. 49	17th or 18th cent.[80]	S	*Kidān*; *Nagar*
Lake Ṭānā 35	18th cent.?[81]	T	*Kidān*; *Nagar*
Vatican: Cerulli Eth. 151	20th cent.[82]	V	*Kidān*; *Nagar*

[66] Here I list not all the contents of each Ms., but only note whether or not they contain the *Kidān*, as well as the *Nagar*.
[67] M. Chaîne, *Catalogue des manuscripts éthiopiens de la Collection Antoine d'Abbadie* (Paris, 1912), 34–7, avers that it was copied in the sixteenth century. Wajnberg in Schmidt, *Gespräche Jesu*, 9, prefers fifteenth/sixteenth century. Cf. also S. Uhlig, *Äthiopische Paläographie* (Stuttgart: Franz Steiner Verlag, 1988), 333.
[68] So Chaîne, *Catalogue Antoine d'Abbadie*, 58. Cf. also Wajnberg in Schmidt, *Gespräche Jesu*, 9.
[69] So Uhlig, *Äthiopische Paläographie*, 729–30. Interestingly, Chaîne, *Catalogue Antoine d'Abbadie*, 119, dated this Ms. to the nineteenth century.
[70] Or Lake Ṭānā 177.
[71] Six, *Äthiopische Handschriften vom Ṭānāsee 3*, 233–7.
[72] So Wajnberg in Schmidt, *Gespräche Jesu*, 8.
[73] So Wajnberg in Schmidt, *Gespräche Jesu*, 8. Cf. also Uhlig, *Äthiopische Paläographie*, 562–3, who discusses this Ms. in connection with his fifth period, i.e. mid-seventeenth to second half of the eighteenth century, but does not date it precisely.
[74] W. F. Macomber and Getatchew Haile, *A Catalogue of Ethiopian Manuscripts microfilmed for the Ethiopian Manuscript Microfilm Library, Addis Ababa, and for the Hill Monastic Manuscript Library, Collegeville*, Vol. 2 (Collegeville, MN: St John's Abbey and University, 1976), 83.
[75] My estimate, on the basis of comparison of the microfilm with K, L, and S. So also Pérès, *L'Épritre des Apôtres*, 58.
[76] So S. Uhlig, *Introduction to Ethiopian Palaeography* (Stuttgart: Franz Steiner Verlag, 1990), 77–9. Cf. also idem, *Äthiopische Paläographie*, 466–7.
[77] So Pérès, *L'Épritre des Apôtres*, 58.
[78] So the cover page of the microfilm supplied by EMML.
[79] So the cover page of the microfilm supplied by EMML.
[80] Wajnberg (Schmidt, *Gespräche Jesu*, 13) dates this manuscript to the eighteenth century, but Veronika Six (*Äthiopische Handschriften III: Handschriften deutscher Bibliotheken, Museen und aus Privatbesitz*, (Stuttgart: Steiner Verlag, 1994), 461–6) suggests that it might belong rather to the seventeenth century.
[81] So E. Hammerschmidt, *Äthiopische Handschriften vom Ṭānāsee 1: Reisebericht und Beschreibung der Handschriften in dem Kloster des Heiligen Gabriel auf der Insel Kebrān* (Wiesbaden: Steiner Verlag, 1973), 163–7.
[82] So Pérès, *L'Épître des Apôtres*, 58.

Appendix 2 A simplified stemma of the Ethiopic manuscripts of the *Epistula Apostolorum*

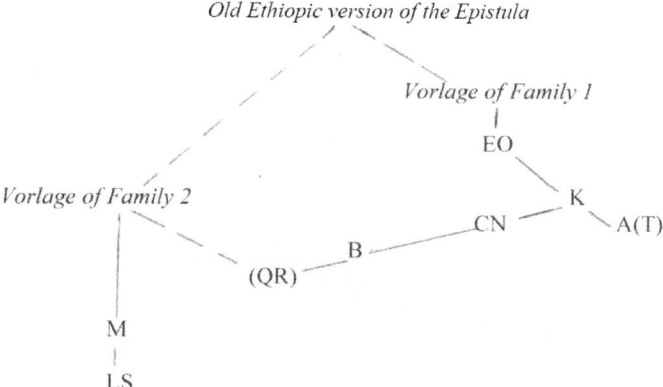

8

The Apocalypse of Peter: The Relationship of the Versions

Eric J. Beck

At least three texts go by the name of the Apocalypse of Peter. There is the Apocalypse of Peter discovered at Nag Hammadi, variably called the Coptic Apocalypse of Peter or the Gnostic Apocalypse of Peter. There is also an Arabic text designated as either the Arabic Apocalypse of Peter or the Book of the Rolls, the latter of which is the title given by the work itself.[1] The final text, to which this study is devoted, might be called the Early Christian Apocalypse of Peter or the Second-Century Apocalypse of Peter, but it is predominantly referred to simply as the Apocalypse of Peter without any adjectival descriptor.[2] Texts such as the Muratorian Fragment and Clement of Alexandria's *Extracts from the Prophets* invariably refer to this third document when discussing Peter's apocalypse, and it is right for current scholarship to retain the simple title for the work, even if it necessitates an initial discussion clarifying terminology.[3]

The Apocalypse of Peter (Apoc Pet) is extant today in five manuscripts. The first is part of a Greek codex discovered in the winter of 1886/87 in Akhmīm Egypt and published in 1892.[4] In 1910, Sylvain Grébaut published the text of manuscript d'Abbadie 51 from the *Bibliothèque nationale* in Paris, which includes a version of the Apoc Pet in Ethiopic.[5] That same year, M. R. James published the text of a Greek fragment of the Apoc Pet, MS Gr. theol. f. 4 (P), known as the Bodleian fragment.[6] Just over a decade later, in 1924, Charles Wessely published the text of a fragmentary Greek text from the

---

[1] A Mingana, *Woodbrooke Studies* (Cambridge: W. Heffer & Sons, 1931), 393–450.
[2] A brief discussion on these three texts and their relationship to each other can be found in Dennis D. Buchholz, *Your Eyes Will Be Opened: A Study in the Greek (Ethiopic) Apocalypse of Peter* (SBLDS 97; Atlanta: Scholars Press, 1988), 1–19.
[3] The *SBL Handbook of Style* (2nd ed.) does little to alleviate this confusion by suggesting the same abbreviation (Apoc. Pet.) for both the Coptic/Gnostic Apocalypse of Peter (referred to as VII 3 Revelation of Peter in the Handbook) as well as the Early Christian/Second-Century Apocalypse of Peter.
[4] Urbain Bouriant, 'Fragments du texte grec du livre d'Enoch et de quelques écrits attribués à Saint-Pierre', in *Mémoires publiés par les membres de la Mission archéologique française au Caire*, t. 9, fasc. 1 (Paris: Ernest Leroux, 1892), 91–147.
[5] Sylvain Grébaut, 'Littérature éthiopienne pseudo-clémentine', *Revue de l'Orient chrétien* 15 (1910): 198–214, 307–23, 425–39.
[6] M. R. James, 'Additional Notes on the Apocalypse of Peter', *JTS* 12 (1910): 157.

Rainer collection in Vienna, P. Vindob.G 39756, which also contains a portion of our text and is referred to as the Rainer fragment.[7] It is important to note that the Bodleian and Rainer fragments likely come from the same manuscript.[8] Finally, in 1968 Ernst Hammerschmidt photographed and catalogued a number of Ethiopic manuscripts from the monastery of Saint Gabriel on the island of Kebrān in Lake Tānā in Ethiopia. Number 35 in his catalogue contains some of the same texts found in d'Abbadie 51, including an Ethiopic version of the Apoc Pet.[9]

Of these five extant documents, only the two Ethiopic manuscripts contain the complete text of the Apoc Pet. The Bodleian and Rainer fragments consist of only a few verses each, and the Akhmīm text lacks roughly eleven of the seventeen chapters preserved in the Ethiopic manuscripts. That the extra chapters in the Ethiopic are not later additions is confirmed by the abrupt beginning and ending of the Akhmīm text as well as the close correlation between the length of the Ethiopic text of the Apoc Pet and the length recorded in Codex Claromontanus and the Stichometry of Nicephorus.[10] The apparent completeness of the Ethiopic manuscripts, however, does not necessarily equate to their reliability as witnesses to the earliest version of the text. Instead, it is clear upon analysing the text and placing it within the context of other early Christian documents that the Ethiopic manuscripts constitute a later, edited version of the Apoc Pet distinct from the other extant recensions.

Following a discussion of what constitutes the Ethiopic Apocalypse of Peter (Eth Apoc Pet), this chapter will offer a comparative analysis of the various recensions of the Apoc Pet in order to ascertain the reliability of the Ethiopic text as a witness to the earliest version of the Apoc Pet. The first point of comparison is the different understandings of *apokatastasis* between the Eth Apoc Pet and the Rainer fragment. This comparison will show that the Eth Apoc Pet did not entirely remove the doctrine of *apokatastasis*, but rather it made changes to the portrayal of the doctrine that reveal particular editorial motives. The second point of comparison is between the transfiguration accounts of the Eth Apoc Pet and the Akhmīm Apocalypse of Peter (Akh Apoc Pet). This comparison suggests that the high Christology and inclusion of narrative elements from the Synoptic Gospels in the Eth Apoc Pet were later additions to the text. The conclusion drawn from these comparisons is that the Eth Apoc Pet constitutes an edited version of the Apoc Pet, not unlike the Akh Apoc Pet, that is not a consistently reliable witness to the oldest version of the text.

---

[7] Charles Wessely, 'Les plus anciens monuments du christianisme écrits sur papyrus II', *PO* 18 (1924): 482–3.

[8] M. R. James, 'The Rainer Fragment of the Apocalypse of Peter', *JTS* 32 (1931): 278; Thomas J. Kraus and Tobias Nicklas, *Das Petrusevangelium und die Petrusapokalypse: Die griechischen Fragmente mit deutscher und englischer Übersetzung* (Berlin: de Gruyter, 2004), 121–2.

[9] Ernst Hammerschmidt, Äthiopische Handschriften vom Ṭānāsee 1: Reisebericht und Beschreibung der Handschriften in dem Kloster des Heiligen Gabriel auf der Insel Kebrān, Verzeichnis der Orientalischen Handschriften in Deutschland 20.1 (Wiesbaden: Franz Steiner, 1973), 163–7.

[10] Hugo Duensing and Christian Maurer, 'Apocalypse of Peter', in *New Testament Apocrypha*, eds Wilhelm Schneemelcher and Robert McL. Wilson (London: Lutterworth, 1965), 2.665.

The Ethiopic recension of the Apocalypse of Peter

In order to discuss the content of the Ethiopic manuscripts of the Apocalypse of Peter, it is first necessary to establish how much of the manuscript evidence is under consideration. In this regard, it is important to note that while the Akh Apoc Pet is a truncated version of the document, the Eth Apoc Pet is lengthened. Neither of the Ethiopic manuscripts present the Apoc Pet as its own text. Rather, both manuscripts incorporate the Apoc Pet as the beginning of a larger, Pseudo-Clementine text titled in accordance with its opening words: 'The Second Coming of Christ and the Resurrection of the Dead'. The shift from the Apoc Pet to the Pseudo-Clementine additions occurs, in manuscript d'Abbadie 51, at the end of F137rb when the narrative perspective changes from Peter to Clement: 'And he [Peter] opened his mouth and said to me, "Listen, my son Clement, everything that he created is for his glory".'[11] It is clear that at this point the text of the Apoc Pet ends and the Pseudo-Clementine additions begin due to the sudden introduction of Clement as the new narrator and the change in writing style that commences from this point forward.[12] This does not mean, however, that one can simply remove the Pseudo-Clementine additions from the text and obtain an accurate understanding of the Apoc Pet as it existed prior to its incorporation into this larger work. As suggested by Dennis Buchholz, the extent to which the Apoc Pet was incorporated into the Pseudo-Clementine text goes beyond merely adding material to the end, but instead includes editorial changes to the Apoc Pet itself.[13] The result is that, contrary to Buchholz's interpretation, the additional material at the end of the Apoc Pet is not merely a commentary on the text but the second part of a newer, longer version of the Apoc Pet.

While scholars agree that the Apoc Pet was incorporated into a longer Pseudo-Clementine text, the precise boundaries for what constitutes the Eth Apoc Pet have yet to be clearly defined. Even while recognizing the Pseudo-Clementine additions to the text, the vast majority of scholarship works exclusively with only the part of the text which resembles the original Apoc Pet. However, Roger Cowley claims that to speak of an Eth Apoc Pet, one must refer to the entire text of 'The Second Coming of Christ and the Resurrection of the Dead' as well as the text which follows it in both Ethiopic manuscripts called 'The Mystery of the Judgment of Sinners'.[14] Alessandro Bausi likewise groups these texts together as individual treatises that are part of a larger dossier, which in turn is part of a four-work collection containing two additional texts called 'The Testament of Our Lord' and 'The Testament of Our Lord Jesus Christ in Galilee'.[15] The arguments of Bausi and Cowley are plausible, but are unfortunately largely unverifiable for most scholars at the present time. The only editions of the

---

[11] All translations of the Apoc Pet, regardless of the recension, and The Second Coming of Christ and the Resurrection of the Dead are my own.
[12] Buchholz, *Your Eyes Will Be Opened*, 378–80.
[13] Buchholz, *Your Eyes Will Be Opened*, 382–6.
[14] Roger W. Cowley, 'The Ethiopic Work Which Is Believed to Contain the Material of the Ancient Greek Apocalypse of Peter', *JTS* 36 (1985): 151–3.
[15] Alessandro Bausi, 'Towards a Re-Edition of the Ethiopic Dossier of the Apocalypse of Peter: A Few Remarks on the Ethiopic Manuscript Witnesses', *Apocrypha* 27 (2016): 179–96.

Ethiopic text of the Apoc Pet which consider both extant manuscripts, d'Abbadie 51 and Kebrān 35, are that of Buchholz[16] and Paolo Marrassini.[17] However, neither edition contains any of the additional Pseudo-Clementine material. In addition, there is currently no translation of the Pseudo-Clementine dossier available in any language that utilizes both available manuscripts. All that is available is Grébaut's original publication of manuscript d'Abbadie 51 and its accompanying French translation from 1910. This would be adequate for the task of verifying Bausi's and Cowley's claims, except that some of their arguments include the unreliability of Grébaut's text as well as the use of Kebrān 35 instead of d'Abbadie 51.[18] Therefore, until a critical edition of the entire Pseudo-Clementine dossier based upon both extant manuscripts or facsimiles of both manuscripts themselves become available, their claim that the Eth Apoc Pet should be understood as a combination of both 'The Second Coming of Christ and the Resurrection of the Dead' and 'The Mystery of the Judgment of Sinners' lacks a great deal of applicability. Thankfully, this should be remedied in the near future, as (at time of writing) such a critical edition is apparently planned for the Corpus Christianorum: Series Apocryphorum.[19]

Even though it is currently not possible to verify all the claims of Bausi and Cowley, it is undeniable that the Apoc Pet, as it is preserved in Ethiopic, is part of 'The Second Coming of Christ and the Resurrection of the Dead'. No scholar disputes this point, but few make the logical secondary claim that to speak of an Eth Apoc Pet, one should at the very least maintain an awareness of the treatise within which the Apoc Pet is now contained in the Ethiopic tradition. In the process of incorporating the Apoc Pet into this Pseudo-Clementine text, the former underwent editorial changes. This chapter will show that while some of these changes are apparent upon comparing the different recensions of the Apoc Pet, the rationale behind some of them at times relies on an analysis of the subsequent Pseudo-Clementine text. Therefore, when one's goal is to analyse the Apoc Pet within its Ethiopic context, as it is here, the Eth Apoc Pet should be studied together with 'The Second Coming of Christ and the Resurrection of the Dead'. With this understanding of the Eth Apoc Pet in mind, it is now possible to discuss some of its distinct features compared to the other recensions of the text.

Apokatastasis in the Eth Apoc Pet

The first feature with a unique portrayal in the Eth Apoc Pet compared to the other recensions is its approach to the doctrine of *apokatastasis*. None of the recensions

---

[16] Buchholz, *Your Eyes Will Be Opened*, 162–243.
[17] Paolo Marrassini, 'L'Apocalisse di Pietro', in *Etiopica e oltre. Studi in onore di Langranco Ricci* (Studi Africanistici, Serie Etiopica 1, eds Yaqob Beyene et al.; Napoli: Instituto universitario orientale, 1994), 221–32.
[18] Bausi, 'Towards a Re-Edition of the Ethiopic Dossier of the Apocalypse of Peter', 190–1; Cowley, 'The Ethiopic Work Which Is Believed to Contain the Material of the Ancient Greek Apocalypse of Peter', 152.
[19] Bausi, 'Towards a Re-Edition of the Ethiopic Dossier of the Apocalypse of Peter', 181–3.

mention this doctrine by name, but two of them make use of the concept. The word ἀποκατάστασις itself refers to restoration, 'but as a Christian and a late-antique philosophical doctrine, it came to indicate the theory of universal restoration, that is, of the return of all beings, or at least all rational beings or all humans, to the Good, i.e. God, in the end'.[20] The Rainer fragment clearly utilizes this doctrine in its offer of post-mortem salvation for the wicked when it says:

> I will give to my called and my elect whomever they ask of me out of punishment, and I will give them a good baptism in the salvation of the so-called Acherusian Lake in the Elysian Field, a part of righteousness with my holy ones. And I will depart, I and my elect, rejoicing with the patriarchs to my eternal kingdom. And I will accomplish with them my promises, which I promised to them, I and my father who is in heaven.

Two details in this portrayal of *apokatastasis* deserve mention: 1) it is only through the request of the righteous that the wicked are able to obtain salvation, and 2) the wicked only receive a part of the salvation reserved for the righteous. This same understanding of how *apokatastasis* functions eschatologically also appears in book 2 of the Sibylline Oracles.

> To these pious ones imperishable God, the universal ruler, will also give
> another thing. Whenever they ask the imperishable God
> to save men from the raging fire and deathless gnashing
> he will grant it, and he will do this.
> For he will pick them out again from the undying fire
> and set them elsewhere and send them on account of his own people
> to another eternal life with the immortals
> in the Elysian plain where he has the long waves
> of the deep perennial Acherusian lake.
>
> Sib. Or. 2.330–338[21]

The Sibylline Oracles 2.194–338 are heavily reliant upon the Apoc Pet, so it is unsurprising to see such a parallel here.[22] This does, however, confirm that the Rainer fragment reliably preserves an older version of the Apoc Pet at this point. This is important, because the Eth Apoc Pet is markedly different in these verses.

> And then I will give to my elect and to my righteous ones the baptism and salvation which they have asked of me in the field of Acherusia, which is called Elysium. A portion of the righteous ones has bloomed and I will depart when I will rejoice

---

[20] Ilaria L. E. Ramelli, *The Christian Doctrine of Apokatastasis: A Critical Assessment from the New Testament to Eriugena* (VCSup 120; Leiden: Brill, 2013), 1.
[21] John J. Collins, 'Sibylline Oracles', in *The Old Testament Pseudepigrapha*, (ed. James H. Charlesworth; New York: Doubleday, 1983), 1.353.
[22] M. R. James, *The Apocryphal New Testament* (Oxford: Clarendon, 1953), 521.

with them. I will lead the nations into my eternal kingdom. And I will do for them what I promised them eternally, I and my heavenly father.

Eth Apoc Pet 14.1–3a

Clearly in the Eth Apoc Pet, the post-mortem salvation for the wicked was removed from this section. According to Buchholz, its removal was likely a result of theological objections to the doctrine.[23] While this would be unsurprising due to the somewhat marginal position of the doctrine of *apokatastasis* throughout church history, particularly among those with an interest in hell, it is not an entirely accurate assessment of the Eth Apoc Pet within the context of its Pseudo-Clementine additions.

The doctrine of *apokatastasis* was indeed removed from Eth Apoc Pet 14, but it was not removed from 'The Second Coming of Christ and the Resurrection of the Dead'. In the Pseudo-Clementine additions of the Eth Apoc Pet, Peter is in great distress, having seen the horrible fate of the wicked. By way of comforting him and answering his questions, Jesus reveals to Peter that there will be mercy for the wicked, but that he must not tell them, for they would simply sin all the more as a result of obtaining this knowledge. Jesus' explanation is long and abstruse, but it can be summarized with a few key sentences from folio 142 of d'Abbadie 51:

> As for mercy, my father is merciful and I also show mercy, because that which is my father's is mine, and everything which is mine is my father's. And when the sinners who believed in me begged, [and] I also will beg my father with them while I seek mercy for them from my father ... And therefore, the father will give to everyone life, honour, and a kingdom which will not end, and his judgment which will not be divided, and a crown of honour which is beautiful and shining, and glory ... And now again, you will not reveal (this) to those who are not able to bear it, so that they might not sin against their neighbour.

This section of the Pseudo-Clementine text adheres to the doctrine of *apokatastasis* just as clearly as does the Rainer fragment. However, the expression of the doctrine is not consistent between the two recensions. Whereas the Rainer fragment has salvation for the wicked come through the request of the righteous, the Eth Apoc Pet, with its Pseudo-Clementine additions, teaches that salvation for the wicked is a direct result of the mercy of Jesus. Likewise, 'The Second Coming of Christ and the Resurrection of the Dead' makes no mention of the wicked receiving only partial salvation, but instead offers the same afterlife bliss to everyone. Finally, the text adds the important caveat that this doctrine is not to be shared with those who will simply continue sinning as a result. These differences show that while both recensions of the Apoc Pet adhere to the doctrine of *apokatastasis*, their understandings of how the doctrine is best conveyed diverge significantly.

It is clear from the parallels between the Rainer fragment and book 2 of the Sibylline Oracles that the Eth Apoc Pet bears witness to a later, edited version of the Apoc Pet. It is also clear from Jesus' repeated warning to Peter not to tell the foolish

---

[23] Buchholz, *Your Eyes Will Be Opened*, 348.

about post-mortem salvation lest they sin even more, as well as Peter's reaffirmation of this warning to Clement at the end of the text, that the description of post-mortem salvation in Eth Apoc Pet 14 was changed, at least in part, to relegate the doctrine to a hidden teaching rather than a blatant part of the tour of hell. What is not readily apparent, however, is how these changes found their way into the text during the transmission process. It is impossible to offer anything more than speculation to this query, but it is perhaps feasible that the Eth Apoc Pet was influenced by Origenian thought. The idea that the Eth Apoc Pet contains Origenian influences is not new.[24] Some have even hypothesized that Origen himself knew the Apoc Pet and viewed it as inspired, but such a claim is unfounded.[25]

As one of the most well-known proponents of the doctrine of *apokatastasis*, the writings and thought of Origen may have circulated in some of the same circles as the Apoc Pet. Unlike the Apoc Pet, Origen occasionally showed some hesitancy to discuss his thoughts on the afterlife. In one of his homilies on Luke, prior to discussing the topic, Origen says:

> I do not know whether we should bring out such mystical things before this kind of an audience, especially among those who do not examine the marrow of the Scriptures but are fascinated by the superficial sense alone. It is risky; but I have to touch on it cursorily and briefly.
>
> *Hom. Luc.* 23.5[26]

Perhaps those reading the Apoc Pet shared in Origen's hesitation to preach the doctrine of *apokatastasis* to those who would not be able to handle it appropriately. Likewise, the Apoc Pet and Origen differ when describing the source of salvation for the wicked. Origen founded his understanding of *apokatastasis* on the incarnation, sacrifice and resurrection of Jesus.[27] However, while the Apoc Pet views the post-mortem salvation of the wicked as a mystery of the Son of God according to the prologue, it is enacted through the mercy of the righteous. In this way, post-mortem salvation for the wicked in the Apoc Pet relies equally on divine and human mercy. In both these instances, the Christological foundation of *apokatastasis* and the hesitancy to openly share the doctrine, the Eth Apoc Pet shows a move toward Origenian thought.

The Eth Apoc Pet is not properly Origenian in its portrayal of *apokatastasis*, however. One of the changes made from the Rainer fragment to the Eth Apoc Pet is a shift from granting only a part of salvation to the wicked to an equal share for both the righteous and the wicked. This change actually goes against what was already something Origen shared with the Apoc Pet. As Origen explains in his *First Principles*, although all human

---

[24] Giangrancesco Lusini, 'Tradizione Origeniana in Etiopia', in *Origeniana Octava: Origene e la Tradizione Alessandrina* (ed. L. Perrone, BETL 164; Leuven: University Press, 2003), 1177–84.
[25] Ramelli, *The Christian Doctrine of Apokatastasis*, 68, 273.
[26] Origen, *Homilies on Luke* (trans. Joseph T. Lienhard; Washington, DC: Catholic University of America Press, 1995).
[27] Ilaria L. E. Ramelli, 'Origen's Doctrine of Apokatastasis: A Reassessment', in *Origeniana Decima: Origen as Writer* (ed. Sylwia Kaczmarek and Henryk Pietras, BETL 244; Leuven: Peeters, 2011), 660–9.

beings will eventually be fully reconciled with God, one's eschatological abode is contingent upon whether such reconciliation came before or after death:

> In this heaven and earth the end and perfection of all things may find a safe and most sure abode. There, for instance, those who have for their offences endured the sharp reproof of punishments by way of purgation and have fulfilled and discharged every obligation may be found worthy of a dwelling-place in the earth; while those who have been obedient to the word of God and have already here by their submission shown themselves receptive of his wisdom may be said to gain the kingdom of that heaven or heavens.
>
> Princ. 2.3.7[28]

The idea that the wicked who receive salvation after death remain on the new earth while the righteous are taken to heavenly paradise closely aligns with the Rainer fragment. In the older recension of the Apoc Pet, the wicked, after receiving baptism in the Acherusian Lake, remain in the Elysian Field, while the righteous depart with Jesus to the eternal kingdom. Therefore, while it appears as though the Eth Apoc Pet may have acquired some more Origenian conceptions of *apokatastasis* than what was originally in the Apoc Pet, it also lost others. This suggests that during its transmission, the Eth Apoc Pet was not purposefully made to adhere to the doctrine of *apokatastasis* as it was taught by Origen, but through the years it was edited to better align with various thoughts on the doctrine that were deemed important at the time, some of which adhere better with Origen's theology than that of the original Apoc Pet.

The transfiguration in the Eth Apoc Pet

Upon the publication of the Eth Apoc Pet in 1910, the two primary topics of discussion were the relationship between the Eth Apoc Pet and the Akh Apoc Pet, and the relationship between the transfiguration accounts in Eth Apoc Pet 15–17 and the Synoptic Gospels.[29] Concerning the first topic, M. R. James supported the superiority of the Eth Apoc Pet over the Akh Apoc Pet almost immediately upon its publication.[30] This notion has since become the majority view among scholarship, with the following three arguments forming the basis for the position:

1. The Ethiopic is longer and more closely adheres to the length recorded in Codex Claromontanus and the Stichometry of Nicephorus.
2. The Ethiopic text contains nearly all of the early quotations of the Apoc Pet, while the Akhmīm text only contains one.

---

[28] Origen, *On First Principles* (trans. G. W. Butterworth; Notre Dame, IN: Ave Maria, 2013).
[29] Buchholz, *Your Eyes Will Be Opened*, 106–7.
[30] M. R. James, 'A New Text of the Apocalypse of Peter', *JTS* 12 (1911): 573–83; M. R. James, 'The Recovery of the Apocalypse of Peter', *CQR* 80 (1915): 1–36.

3. The Bodleian and Rainer fragments as well as the second Sibylline Oracle confirm the general reliability of the Ethiopic text in content, as well as its more original use of the future tense within the tour of hell over the past tense used in the Akhmīm text.[31]

It must be noted, however, that while these arguments confirm the reliability of the Eth Apoc Pet in general terms – that is regarding length, verb tense and overall content – they in no way address the finer details of the text. Such a comparative analysis is an important aspect of the second topic mentioned above: the relationship between the transfiguration accounts in Eth Apoc Pet 15–17 and the Synoptic Gospels. Therefore, before analysing the thematic connections between Eth Apoc Pet 15–17 and the Synoptic transfiguration accounts, a detailed comparison of the parallel passages of Akh Apoc Pet 4–20 and Eth Apoc Pet 15.1–16.4 will first be given.[32]

The first difference between the two recensions is how they refer to Jesus.[33] The proper name of Jesus is only used four times in the Ethiopic text, all in chapters 15 and 16. In addition to the sudden use of Jesus' name, Eth Apoc Pet 15–16 also introduces new titles for Jesus, king (nəguś) and God ('əgzi'abəḥer) which occur nowhere else in the material that aligns with the ancient Apoc Pet.[34] The use of such titles in these chapters reveals a high Christology that, along with the name of Jesus and the his titles God and king, do not exist elsewhere in the Eth Apoc Pet or any of the Greek fragments.[35] Robert Helmer believes the different forms of address for Jesus between chapters 15–16 and the rest of the Eth Apoc Pet reveals a threefold structure in the narrative.[36] He does not seem to consider that such inconsistency may indicate corruption in the text. Buchholz, however, recognizes this possibility when he says: 'By their very form these titles must be under suspicion, but the Akhmīm is also different and may preserve the more original titles. In that case "Jesus Christ our King" is an addition.'[37] The Akh Apoc Pet refers to Jesus as the Lord, ὁ κύριος, in the parallel material, which is the same title used throughout the Eth Apoc Pet, save for chapters 15–16.[38] The use of ὁ κύριος in Akh Apoc Pet 4–20 maintains both verbal and

---

[31] Richard Bauckham, 'The Apocalypse of Peter: A Jewish Christian Apocalypse from the Time of Bar Kokhba', in *The Fate of the Dead: Studies on the Jewish and Christian Apocalypses* (NovTSup 93; Leiden: Brill, 1998), 162–4; Buchholz, *Your Eyes Will Be Opened*, 419; Duensing and Maurer, 'Apocalypse of Peter', 665–7.

[32] This analysis is drawn from Eric J. Beck, *Justice and Mercy in the Apocalypse of Peter: A New Translation and Analysis of the Purpose of the Text*, WUNT 427 (Tübingen: Mohr Siebeck, 2019), 88–92.

[33] The text of Akh Apoc Pet 4–20 and Eth Apoc Pet 15.1–16.4 are given in parallel columns in the Appendix.

[34] While 'əgzi'abəḥer occurs elsewhere in the Eth Apoc Pet, only in chapter16 does it apply to Jesus.

[35] Buchholz, *Your Eyes Will Be Opened*, 363.

[36] Robert C. Helmer, '"That We May Know and Understand": Gospel Tradition in the Apocalypse of Peter' (PhD diss., Marquette University, 1998), 44–5. He gives no explanation for the lack of such titles for Jesus in chapter 17, which he includes as part of the third narrative section along with chapters 15–16.

[37] Buchholz, *Your Eyes Will Be Opened*, 363.

[38] The Ethiopic word used for 'Lord' is 'əgzi'.

theological consistency with the remainder of the narrative, where Eth Apoc Pet 15–16 does not.

The second significant difference between the texts is the description of the two men who appear on the mountain. Buchholz claims the difference between the Akh Apoc Pet and the Eth Apoc Pet is that the Akhmīm text describes both men together and the Ethiopic text describes each separately. While he admits on his reading that the issue of which is more original cannot be resolved, he prefers the reading of the Eth Apoc Pet.[39] Contrary to Buchholz's claims, however, the Eth Apoc Pet does not consistently describe both men separately. The description begins in 15.2 with 'from one of them was coming a light which was shining more than the sun'. The description continues in 15.3–4, but is now applied to both men:

> And even their clothes were bright, and it is not possible to say. And there is nothing which can be compared with them here in the world. And a mouth is not able to say (in) simplicity the beauty of their splendour, because their appearance was stupefying and a wonder.

Then in vv. 5–7, the text describes 'the other' man, with two exceptions:

> And the other, great I say, was shining more than snow in his appearance. Like a rose was the beauty of his appearance and his flesh and the hair on his head. And down from his shoulders and upon their foreheads were garlands of spikenard woven with beautiful flowers. Like a rainbow in water was his hair. Thus was the charm of his face. And (he was) adorned with every adornment. And when we saw them suddenly, we marvelled.

As such, the text does not describe one and then the other, as Buchholz claims, but switches back and forth rather indiscriminately. This confusion in the text could be a result of the inconsistency in differentiating between the singular and the plural that is common throughout the Eth Apoc Pet, but also could reveal that the Ethiopic text is corrupt in this section. If the Eth Apoc Pet truly described first one man then the other, Buchholz would be correct that the matter of which is a more original reading could not be decided. As it stands, however, the Eth Apoc Pet awkwardly switches between the singular and plural, and Akh Apoc Pet reads far smoother by applying the whole description to both men. This suggests the Apoc Pet originally described both men together. Furthermore, as Philipp Vielhauer explains, it is unlikely that these two men were originally designated as Moses and Elijah.[40] It is doubtful that the editor of the Akh Apoc Pet would have stripped such notable characters of their names.

Thirdly, the Eth Apoc Pet and the Akh Apoc Pet also differ greatly in their descriptions of paradise. On the one hand, the Ethiopic text is poorly written and often

---

[39] Buchholz, *Your Eyes Will Be Opened*, 364–5.
[40] Philipp Vielhauer, *'Geschichte der urchristlichen Literatur: Einleitung' in das Neue Testament, die Apokryphen und die Apostolishcen Väter* (Berlin: de Gruyter, 1975), 510–11; Philipp Vielhauer, *Historia de la literatura cristiana primitiva: Introducción al nuevo testamento, los apócrifos y los padres apostólicos* (Salamanca: Ediciones Sígueme, 1991), 526.

requires some degree of emendation in order to make it comprehensible. The most common change is emending 'its aroma was coming to it (ḥabehu)' to 'its aroma was coming to us (ḥabena)' in 16.3.[41] The Akh Apoc Pet, on the other hand, is significantly longer than the Ethiopic text. This is the only place where the Akhmīm text contains notably more material than the Ethiopic. Theophilus' *Ad Autolycum* may witness to the originality of some of the additional material found in the Akh Apoc Pet. Theophilus writes: 'After forming man, God chose a place for him in the eastern regions, excellent for its light, brilliant with brighter air, most beautiful with its plants' (2.19).[42] Gilles Quispel and Robert Grant believe Theophilus used the Apoc Pet as his source for this passage, because it exhibits close parallels with Akh Apoc Pet 15:

And the Lord showed me a large place outside of this world exceedingly bright with light, and the sky there was illuminated by the rays of the sun and the ground itself blooming with unfading flowers and full of fragrant things and plants beautifully blooming and imperishable and bearing blessed fruit.[43]

Buchholz, however, does not believe the evidence is compelling enough to prove a relationship between the texts.[44] He nevertheless uses the parallels between these texts to suggest that the Akh Apoc Pet was expanded with traditional material. Buchholz instead suggests the Eth Apoc Pet contains parallels with descriptions of paradise such as those in 1 Enoch 24.4 and 32.3–6. While he admits these similarities may have found their way into the Eth Apoc Pet during its transmission, he believes they were original to the Apoc Pet.[45] As both recensions reflect traditional understandings of paradise, neither the parallels with 1 Enoch nor Theophilus' *Ad Autolycum* are compelling enough to determine which recension may be more original.

The fourth difference between the two recensions is in how they portray Jesus responding to Peter. The descriptions of paradise in each text are introduced with a question from Peter requesting to know the fate of the righteous dead. While both utilize the description of paradise as the answer to this question, only the Akh Apoc Pet actually describes the righteous who live in the garden. The Eth Apoc Pet makes no mention of the inhabitants of paradise. It does, however, conclude its depiction of paradise with Jesus saying: 'You have seen the nation of the fathers, and thus is their rest' (16.4). This is a perplexing claim, for the text gives no indication that the disciples saw anyone in paradise. If Buchholz is correct that 'aḥzāba 'abaw, nation of the fathers, is a unique way of referring to the patriarchs in the Eth Apoc Pet, then Jesus could be referring back to Moses and Elijah.[46] Jesus' statement then encompasses all of chapters 15–16 by telling Peter he has seen the glorified form of Moses and Elijah (15.2–7) and

---

[41] Hugo Duensing, 'Ein Stücke der urchristlichen Petrusapokalypse enthaltender Traktat der äthiopischen Pseudoklementinischen Literatur', *ZNW* 14 (1913): 73n11.
[42] Theophilus of Antioch, *Ad Autolycum* (trans. Robert M Grant; OECT; Oxford: Clarendon, 1970), 59.
[43] G. Quispel and Robert M. Grant, 'Note on the Petrine Apocrypha', *VC* 6 (1952): 31–2.
[44] Buchholz, *Your Eyes Will Be Opened*, 49.
[45] Buchholz, *Your Eyes Will Be Opened*, 367–8.
[46] Buchholz, *Your Eyes Will Be Opened*, 369–70.

their paradisiacal abode (16.2-3). This still fails to answer Peter's question, however, even not taking into account the likelihood that the references to Moses and Elijah are later additions. In Eth Apoc Pet 16.1, Peter does not ask for details regarding the abode of the righteous, but about the righteous themselves, naming Abraham, Isaac and Jacob in particular. In the Akhmīm text, the disciples first ask to see the righteous who have died (Akh Apoc Pet 5), and then Peter follows this with a question regarding where the glorified righteous reside (Akh Apoc Pet 14). Jesus' response in Akh Apoc Pet 15-19 is then a robust answer to Peter's question, which not only describes paradise but even the inhabitants who live there. The inadequate response to Peter's question in the Ethiopic compared to the detailed description in the Akhmīm text suggests the earliest form of the Apoc Pet likely included a reference to the inhabitants of paradise.

Of the four major differences between Eth Apoc Pet 15.1-16.4 and Akh Apoc Pet 4-20, three indicate that the Akh Apoc Pet may be a better witness to the older version of the Apoc Pet, and one is inconclusive. The conclusion this suggests is that in the case of the transfiguration account of the Apoc Pet, the Akh Apoc Pet contains the more original version. Such a conclusion has important implications for understanding the Apoc Pet in the Ethiopic context. Before delving into those implications, however, it must first be clarified that although this discussion and many that came before have consistently referred to the transfiguration account of the Apoc Pet, strictly speaking the Apoc Pet does not contain a transfiguration account. Neither recension actually describes Jesus being transfigured. Nevertheless, they do both share similar themes with the transfiguration accounts in the Synoptic Gospels.[47] The Akh Apoc Pet, as the likely more original version, shares the mountainous setting and references to shining faces and clothing also found in the Gospel accounts (Akh Apoc Pet 4, 7, Mt 17.1-2, Mk 9.2, Lk 9.28-29), but these shared themes do not necessarily indicate that the Apoc Pet was dependent upon the Synoptic Gospels in creating its account.[48] The evidence for dependence increases drastically in the Eth Apoc Pet, however.

In addition to sharing the mountainous setting and the references to shining faces and clothing (15.1-6), the Eth Apoc Pet shares multiple additional other themes with the Synoptic Gospels as well. First, the two men, who were likely nameless in the original Apoc Pet, have been identified in the Eth Apoc Pet as Moses and Elijah (16.1, 7; 17.2-3). This parallels the Gospel accounts (Mt 17.3, Mk 9.4, Lk 9.30), but, unlike in the Synoptics, Peter only knows the identity of these men in the Eth Apoc Pet after Jesus names them. Second, the Eth Apoc Pet includes Peter's question from the Synoptics regarding whether he should build dwellings for Jesus, Moses and Elijah (Eth Apoc Pet 16.7, Mt 17.5, Mk 9.5, Lk 9.33). Third, Jesus' rebuke of Peter in Eth Apoc Pet 16.8, 'And he said to me in anger, "Satan is attacking you" and has veiled your understanding, and the affairs of this world are overcoming you"', perhaps draws from the similar rebuke in Matthew 16.23 and Mark 8.33.[49] Fourth, Eth Apoc Pet 17.1

---

[47] Bauckham, 'The Apocalypse of Peter', 240; idem, 'The Apocalypse of Peter: An Account of Research', *ANRW* 2.25.6 (1988): 4735.
[48] Bauckham, 'The Apocalypse of Peter: An Account of Research', 4735.
[49] Buchholz, *Your Eyes Will Be Opened*, 371; Enrico Norelli, 'Pierre, le visionnaire: la réception de l'épisode de la transfiguration en 2 Pierre et dans l'Apocalypse de Pierre', *Foi Vie* 106.4 (2007): 36.

includes the voice from heaven referring to Jesus as the beloved Son similar to the Synoptic Gospels (Mt 17.5, Mk 9.7, Lk 9.35). Fifth, a cloud appears on the mountain in each text (Eth Apoc Pet 17.2, Mt 17.5, Mk 9.7, Lk 9.34). Sixth, and finally, Eth Apoc Pet 17.2 describes Peter as trembling with fear, which parallels the description of the disciples in Matthew 17.6, Mark 9.6 and Luke 9.34. The existence of six additional parallels between the Eth Apoc Pet and the Synoptic Gospels that are not present in the Akh Apoc Pet indicates that the text of the Eth Apoc Pet was likely edited in order to incorporate Gospel material.

Conclusions

The Eth Apoc Pet is known to be a corrupt text for those who wish to recreate the oldest possible version of the second-century Apoc Pet.[50] At the same time, it is widely, and paradoxically, viewed as though it is a reliable witness to the earliest form of the text.[51] While this may be true regarding its length and verb tense, it is not necessarily so for the finer details of its content. By comparing the different recensions and drawing upon thematic connections between the Eth Apoc Pet and other early Christian texts, it is possible to see that in the Ethiopic context, or in whatever context the Ethiopic recension was first edited to its current form, the text of the Apoc Pet was influenced by other texts and ideas. Some of these influences arose from direct dependence and are easy to identify, such as the use of one or more of the Synoptic Gospels to expand the material in Eth Apoc Pet 15–17. Other changes likely did not derive from direct dependence on a source, but they still show some similarities with other documents and ideas circulating among early Christians. This is exhibited by the Eth Apoc Pet's similarities with a more Origenian understanding of *apokatastasis* than that found in the older Rainer fragment.

The intrusion of other texts and ideas into the Eth Apoc Pet during its transmission not only highlights the fluidity of such documents, but brings further caution to those attempting to recreate an original version from only a few extant manuscripts. The Eth Apoc Pet may reflect an ancient version of the Apoc Pet in certain ways, but it also exists as its own, unique text distinct from the original second-century document and the other extant recensions. These unique features of the Eth Apoc Pet, particularly its role as part of the Pseudo-Clementine 'The Second Coming of Christ and the Resurrection of the Dead', call into question the scholarly consensus regarding the superiority of the Ethiopic text over the Akh Apoc Pet. Apart from length and verb tense, the Akh Apoc Pet may at times be a better witness to the oldest version of the text.

---

[50] Buchholz, *Your Eyes Will Be Opened*, 119.
[51] Bauckham, 'The Apocalypse of Peter: An Account of Research', 4718.

Appendix

Eth Apoc Pet 15.1–16.4	Akh Apoc Pet 4–20
And my lord, Jesus Christ our king, said to me, 'Let us proceed to the holy mountain.' And his disciples came with him while they were praying.	And continuing the Lord said, 'Let us go to the mountain and pray.' And going with him we, the twelve disciples, requested that he might show us one of our righteous brothers who has departed from the world, so that we might see what manner of form they are, and having taken courage, me might also encourage those people who hear us.
And behold, (there were) two people. And we were powerless to look at their face, because from one of them was coming a light which was shining more than the sun. And even their clothes were bright, and it is not possible to say. And there is nothing which can be compared with them here in the world. And a mouth is not able to say (in) simplicity the beauty of their splendour, because their appearance was stupefying and a wonder. And the other, great I say, was shining more than snow in his appearance. Like a rose was the beauty of his appearance and his flesh and the hair on his head. And down from his shoulders and upon their foreheads were garlands of spikenard woven with beautiful flowers. Like a rainbow in water was his hair. Thus was the charm of his face. And (he was) adorned with every adornment. And when we saw them suddenly, we marvelled.	And while we were praying, suddenly two men appeared standing in front of the Lord, at whom we were not able to look. For a ray like the sun was coming from their face and their clothing was radiant, of what sort a person's eye has never seen. Neither is a mouth able to describe nor heart express the glory that they were wearing and the beauty of their appearance. When we beheld them, we were amazed. For their bodies were whiter than any snow and redder than any rose. But their red was blended with white, and I am simply not able to describe their beauty. For not only was their hair curly and splendid but it also suited their face and shoulders as though it were a crown woven of spikenard and many coloured flowers, or as a rainbow in the sky. Such was their fine appearance. Therefore, when we beheld their beauty, we became utterly astonished by them, because they appeared suddenly.
And I approached near to God, Jesus Christ, and I said to him, 'Lord, who is this?' And he said to me, 'This is Moses and Elijah.' And I said to him, '(What about) Abraham, and Isaac, and Jacob, and the other righteous fathers?'	And approaching the Lord, I said, 'Who are these?' He said to me, 'These are your brothers, the righteous whose forms you wanted to see.' And I said to him, 'And where are all the righteous or of what sort is the age in which they have this glory.'
And he showed us an open, large garden full of fruitful trees and blessed fruit, full of the aroma of perfume. Its aroma was delightful. And its aroma was coming to it and from within it I saw a wonder: abundant fruit.	And the Lord showed me a large place outside of this world exceedingly bright with light, and the sky there was illuminated by the rays of the sun and the ground itself blooming with unfading flowers and full of fragrant things and plants beautifully blooming and imperishable and bearing blessed fruit. And so great was the fragrance that it carried from there even to us. And the inhabitants of that place were clothed in the clothes of radiant angels, and their clothing was like their place. And angels moved about them there. And the glory of the inhabitants there was equal and with one voice they loudly praised the Lord God, rejoicing in that place. The Lord said to us, 'This is the place of your high priests, the righteous people.
And my Lord and my God, Jesus Christ, said to me, '[And] You have seen the nation of the fathers, and thus is their rest.'	

9

Gospel Writing in Transition: A Look at the Ethiopic *Ta-'ammərä 'Iyasus*

Meron T. Gebreananaye

The Ethiopic book of *Ta-'ammərä 'Iyasus* (Miracles of Jesus)[1] is made up of a collection of 'miracles' generally beginning with the formulaic opening; *Tā-ammər za-gabra 'Egzi'əna wa-Madḫāni-na 'Iyasus Krəstos*... ('A miracle performed by our Lord and our Saviour Jesus Christ...') likely from which the title given to the work is derived. Each miracle also ends with a closing benediction; *barakat, ṣagga-hu... la-'ālam 'ālam 'amen* ('blessing and grace... unto the end of the ages, amen'). At first glance, the formulaic opening and closing, in conjunction with the use of individual or selected miracles from this corpus in the devotional and liturgical literature of the Ethiopian Orthodox Tawāḥədo Church (EOTC)[2], gives the impression that each episode constitutes a standalone account. This, however, disguises the fact that the *Ta-'ammərä 'Iyasus* (TI) is itself a coherent narrative, covering the entirety of the life and ministry of Jesus organized in the form of the canonical gospels. Based on these features, Stephen Gero rightly suggests that the *Ta-'ammərä 'Iyasus* is best understood as a 'Gospel' account.[3] He goes on to note that this makes the TI a rare example of a complete apocryphal gospel, which generally tend to focus on one aspect of the Jesus tradition (Infancy, Ministry, Passion, Resurrection).

In spite of this, however, the limited amount of research that has been conducted on the TI to date has mainly dealt with questions of textual development and source criticism. While it would be wrong to underestimate the significant contributions made by such research, the primary focus on identifying and/or reconstructing sources has meant that the TI is yet to receive adequate attention as a literary whole.

In this chapter, I hope to make a preliminary attempt to redress this neglect by looking at the reception and appropriation of gospel traditions in the TI toward

---

[1] Clavis *Christian Apocrypha* 45 (hereafter referenced as CANT.) M. Geerard, Clavis Apocryphorum Novi Testamenti, Turnhout, 1992/ *e-Clavis: Christian Apocrypha*.
[2] For example, components of the TI can be discovered as part of the Gəbra Həmamat, the lectionary for passion week, as well as in a separate compilation known as the *Ta-'ammərä 'Iyasus wa-Marəyam*.
[3] Stephen Gerö, 'THE TA'ĀMRA 'ĪYASŪS: A Study of Textual and Source-Critical Problems' in *Proceedings of the Eight International Conference of Ethiopian Studies* (ed. Taddese Beyene; Addis Ababa: Institute of Ethiopian Studies, 1988), 165.

offering some insight into the literary characteristics and interpretative processes that are employed by this text. In doing so, I hope to highlight continuities with interpretative traditions that are already present in the source texts – including the canonical gospels – as well as looking at some of the more innovative elements that are introduced in the development of the TI.

Texts and sources

I will begin here by offering a very brief introduction to the textual history and sources of the TI. Outside of the biblical corpus, the TI is one of the most well-attested texts in the Ethiopic tradition.[4] This is borne out by even the most cursory review of the catalogues of the *Bibliothèque nationale de France*, the Hill Monastic Manuscript Library (HMML) and the British Library.[5] The oldest attestation of the TI is discovered in a fifteenth-century manuscript *Vaticano Cerulli Etiopico* 238.[6] As noted by Andre Caquot, the TI (*le livre des miracles de son fils, appelé el aqfar*) is also referenced in the inventory of the books bequeathed by the Emperor *Zara Yaqob* (1434–68) to *Dabəra Kerbe*, suggesting that this work was translated and in circulation before this date.[7] Despite this evidence for a relatively early attestation, however, there is no indication that the text of the TI was ever standardized. As a result, what is largely the same body of material is arranged diversely in different manuscripts. The most recent version of the TI published by the EOTC, for example, lists 150 miracles,[8] although most Mss witnesses range from forty to eighty. As noted by Witold Witakowski, however, 'the growing number of episodes is not a result of text expansion but only of changes in the division of the same text', likely for liturgical or devotional convenience.[9] This peculiarity makes the TI a difficult text to study as a literary whole. I will here for ease of reference utilize text from the incomplete critical edition, with French translation, published in increments by Sylvain Grébaut in the early twentieth century.[10] All references to the TI will follow the structure of d'Abbadie 168 – the primary manuscript used by Grébaut's in the development of his incomplete edition – outlined by Witakowski (see Appendix for complete outline).

---

[4] With more and more witnesses being identified and catalogued by several projects currently underway, it is as yet not possible to precisely state the number of known Mss, other than to note that there are now many more that the eighty manuscripts identified by Witakowski, three decades ago. Witold Witakowski, 'The Miracles of Jesus: An Ethiopian Apocryphal Gospel', *Apocrypha* 6 (1995): 280.
[5] In addition to complete witnesses to the TI, partial witnesses are also discovered in Mss of liturgical texts such as in the lectionary of the Passion Week.
[6] Andre Caquot, 'Aperçu préliminaire sur le Maṣḥafa Ṭēfut de Gechen Amba', *Annales d' Éthiopie* 1 (1955): 107. Witakowski notes that 'el aqfar' here is likely a corruption of the Arabic word for apocrypha – 'al-abuqrifa'. Witakowski, 'The Miracles of Jesus', 286.
[7] Caquot, 'Aperçu préliminaire', 107.
[8] ተአምረ ኢየሱስ፤ ግእዝና አማርኛ (አዲስ አበባ፤ ኢትዮጵያ ኦርቶዶክስ ቤተ ክርስትያን በትንሣኤ ዘጉባኤ ማተሚያ ቤት) 2007 ዓ.ም። It is not clear what Mss were used as a basis for this edition.
[9] Witakowski, 'The Miracles of Jesus', 288.
[10] Grébaut based his edition on five Mss (d'Abbadie 168; 226; British Museum Or. 623; 624; 712) dated from the seventeenth to the nineteenth centuries.

Efforts to identify the main sources included in the TI have established that the core section of the narrative is made up of the Arabic Apocryphal Gospel of John (CANT 44).[11] The Apocryphal Gospel of John (AGJ) is itself a compilation of the canonical gospels and earlier apocryphal[12] traditions discovered in texts such as Jubilees, the Testament of Adam, the Proto-Evangelium of James [CANT 50], the Acts of Pilate, the Cave of Treasures and the Apocalypse of Pseudo-Methodius. The earliest extant witness of this Arabic text is dated to the late twelfth century.[13] With the identification of the AGJ as the primary source of the TI, earlier theories as to a possible Syriac *Vorlage* for the entirety of the TI were laid to rest.[14] An Arabic *Vorlage*, in turn, suggests that this material was likely translated in Ethiopia during the period of literary revival in the fourteenth century, when major translations from Arabic are known to have taken place.

In addition to the AGJ, the Ethiopic TI also includes other earlier apocryphal writings including the Infancy Gospel of Thomas[15] (CANT 57) and the correspondence of Abgar and Jesus (CANT 88).[16] The Infancy materials that are incorporated in the TI include eleven that are discovered in other traditions, including the Syriac, and one which is only attested in the Ethiopic (8.xii).[17] In some witnesses, including d'Abbadie 168, the Correspondence of Abgar and Jesus is attached at the end, seemingly as a standalone text (56).

Having briefly looked at the textual history and sources of the TI, I will now look more closely at the literary characteristics and hermeneutical processes it employs.

---

[11] So, Witakowski, 'The Miracles of Jesus', 279–98; Stephen Gerö, 'THE TA'ĀMRA 'ĪYASŪS', 166. Similar content is also discovered in the Arabic Miracles of Jesus. W. Scott Watson, 'A Syriac-Arabic Narrative of the Miracles of Jesus', *American Journal of Semitic Languages*, 16 (1899/1900): 37–46.

[12] I use the term apocryphal here in line with the definition of Christian Apocrypha offered by Tony Burke: 'non-biblical Christian literature that features tales of Jesus, his family and his immediate followers. They are similar in content and genre to texts included in the New Testament; ... [but] not selected for inclusion in the Bible' (Tony Burke, *Secret Scriptures Revealed: A New Introduction to the Christian Apocrypha* (Grand Rapids: Eerdmans, 2013), 6).

[13] Ms. Sinai Arabic 441, dated 1196.

[14] Arthur Vööbus, 'Ta'ämera 'Iyasus: Zeuge eines älteren äthiopischen Evangelientypus', *Orientalia Christiana Periodica* 17 (1951): 462–7. Vööbus, notably, concluded that the divergence of gospel quotations in the TI from the standard Ethiopic New Testament text serves as evidence that an ancient Syriac Gospel Manuscript was behind the Miracles.

[15] Stephen Gerö argues that the Ethiopic IGT 'closely corresponds to the old Syriac version ... which was current in the 5th–6th centuries'; this claim, however, is yet to be conclusively proven (Gerö, 'THE TA'ĀMRA 'ĪYASŪS', 165).

[16] The Abgar tradition enjoys a unique status among Christian apocryphal writings in that it contains material purporting to be written by Jesus himself. Eusebius (*Hist. eccl.* 1.13.5–22) claimed to have discovered original Syriac documents that preserved this correspondence in the public archives of Edessa, although this is likely a later legendary account. Getatchew Haile notes that versions of the text preserved in the Ethiopic are quite close, in content, to the earliest witnesses to the tradition discovered in Eusebius and in the Doctrine of Addai (CANT 89). Getachew also notes that there are four versions of the Legend of Abgar in Ethiopic literature: 'These are the 1) the longer versions, 2) the Synaxary version, 3) the shorter version, and 4) the older version' (Getachew Haile, 'The Legend of Abgar in Ethiopic Tradition', *Orientalia Christiana Periodica* 55 (1989): 376).

[17] Gerö, 'THE TA'ĀMRA 'ĪYASŪS', 165.

Narrative techniques and interpretative processes

The internal literary characteristics and narrative techniques employed by the TI serve to highlight some of the interpretative processes by which the TI brings together diverse traditions to create a complete apocryphal gospel account. While it is impossible to offer a full analysis of the complex narrative of the TI within the confines of this short study, I will in this section look at some extracts from different sections as a preliminary exploration, before offering my reflections on the hermeneutical processes that are revealed.

Introductory materials

The very first miracle of the TI repurposes material from its core source the AGJ to establish its authorship and literary character.

> And John prepared the mysteries (*məṣṭirāt*) which his Lord gave him to understand in many books. And he placed all the books in the land of Rome ... And of the books of mysteries that John the beloved disciple wrote, this is the book which is called the Book of *Ala Tqarfa*.

The ascription of authorship that is established here – at the very outset of the narrative – clearly seeks to derive legitimacy and authority by appropriating the figure of the Apostle John. The utility of appropriating the figure of this apostle in developing a gospel account is apparent when we note that he is not only believed to be the author of the fourth canonical gospel, but that he is also the direct recipient of post-ascension 'divine mysteries' as discovered in the canonical book of the Apocalypse.

The reference to 'many books' in this context could also be an echo of John 21.25: 'But there are also many other things that Jesus did; if every one of them were written down, I suppose that the world itself could not contain the books that would be written' (NRSV). The writer of the TI thus positions his narrative as one which describes the 'many other things' that had not been included in the Gospel of John.

The reference to 'many books' in relation to the 'books of mysteries' could also serve to recall the wider literary corpus – non-canonical and canonical – associated with the Apostle John. If, as noted by Witakowski, *Ala Tqarfa* is here an Arabic corruption of the Greek word apocrypha (literally things that are hidden or secret), the writer of the TI may also be seeking to align this text with other self-identified apocryphal gospels (e.g. Gospel of Thomas, Gospel of Judas). It bears noting, however, that such an identification is not borne out by the narrative proper inasmuch as claims of secret or specialized knowledge are not made or maintained.[18]

---

[18] Markus Bockmuehl notes that the use of the term apocryphal as a self-designation generally correlates with claims of hidden knowledge or an alternative Jesus tradition. Markus Bockmuehl, *Ancient Apocryphal Gospels* (Interpretation: Resources for the Use of Scripture in the Church; Louisville: Westminster John Knox Press, 2017), 39.

Through its authorship claims, therefore, the TI both appropriates the authority of the canonical literature, as well as retaining the fluidity or openness of the wider body of literature that presents itself as Johannine.

In addition to establishing important matters such as authorship, the prologue of the TI also serves to establish the narrative setting which foreshadows the primary conflict of the narrative:

> By his word (*lit. mouth*) he made armies of holy angels, that they declare his name holy and glorify his power ... One angel, called Satan, was made prince over these Archangels and he caused the adoration of all the angels to ascend to the Lord ... When this creature knew with certainty that he was created of spirit and eternal light, he began to think in his mind and in his soul, 'Why should I give my glory to another?' ... Many angels fell with him from their degrees ... they became impure spirits ...
>
> Prologue, 3-4

As we can see from this short extract, the writer of the TI establishes that its narrative plays out on the metaphysical as well as on the physical plane. The metaphysical setting is characterized by the rebellion of the 'holy angels' against their creator. The physical world, and humanity in particular, came into being and continues to exist within the context of this grand conflict.

The larger context of the cosmic struggle introduced in the prologue foreshadows the central plot of the gospel narrative and reveals the rebellious Archangel Lucifer (Satan) as the primary antagonist. In this role, Satan features rather significantly in the TI as the source of all resistance to the life and ministry of the protagonist Jesus, as well as periodically featuring as a 'hostile witness' to the divine identity of Christ, which is one of the central motifs of the narrative, as we will see below. Of particular interest, if for nothing more than literary merit and rarity, the TI delivers first-hand accounts of events from Satan's perspective. A good example in this regard is the episode describing Satan's reaction to the events surrounding the nativity (Miracle 4). Through this reflection, the TI manages to indicate the manifestation of the cosmic struggle in the physical realm by revealing Satan's role as the main antagonist of the ministry of the Old Testament prophets. In this account, his fear and trepidation at the birth of the holy infant also serves to highlight that this new character was a 'game-changer' in the ongoing conflict that ensued as a result of Satan's rebellion.

Interpretative reframing

An important element of the literary development of the TI is how it reframes different traditions to create a narrative whole. The processes by which different episodes – variously placed in the source materials – are brought together into miracles, as well the sequential arrangement of miracles, serves to reflect the interpretative decisions made by the writer. I will next look at some examples of the TI's interpretative reframing of gospel episodes.

The nativity in the TI

The nativity narrative in the TI offers a very interesting example of the reception and interpretation of both canonical and non-canonical gospel traditions. This narrative unfolds in the following sequence:

Miracle 1: Mary the Mother of Jesus
Miracle 2: The Birth of Jesus
Miracle 3: The Hymn of the Midwife Salome
Miracle 4: The Fear of Satan and the Demons
Miracle 5: The Presentation of Jesus in the Temple
Miracle 6: The Coming of the Magi and the Flight to Egypt

The first miracle draws heavily upon the Proto-Evangelium of James (P^EJ)[19] to offer a preamble to the birth of Christ by establishing the unique pedigree (e.g. the status, wealth and piety of her parents) and sanctity of Mary the mother of Christ, before going on to recount the Annunciation and conception of Jesus. The nativity story proper, which begins in Miracle 2, also follows the P^EJ's retelling of the Lukan narrative. Accordingly, Mary and Joseph are on their way to Bethlehem for the census registration when she goes into labour and they are forced to find shelter in the nearest cave. Following this, however, the TI introduces its own innovation by omitting the first midwife who attends to the birth of Jesus in the Proto-Evangelium while focusing and developing the second and named midwife, Salome.

The hymn of Salome (Miracle 3) serves as a substitute for the Lukan hymn of Mary, which is not discovered in either the P^EJ or the TI, and is particularly interesting in that it encapsulates the TI's commitment to highlight and assert the divine nature of the Christ child. This interpretative priority also seems to be reflected in that the TI, like the P^EJ, omits the genealogical accounts. The decision behind this omission seems to be more significant than the writer choosing to follow one source more closely when we take into consideration the TI's practice of including details from all sources, even when some elements may be contradictory or repetitive. Evidence for this preference on the part of the writer and/or editor(s) of the TI can be discovered even within the nativity pericope, when we look at how it inserts the account of the Magi discovered in another apocryphal source (the Revelation of the Magi) in between the sections of the P^EJ dealing with the birth of Jesus and the arrival of the Magi in Jerusalem. This account elaborates the identity of the Magi as Eastern mystics who were custodians of a Christological prophecy transmitted from Seth the son of Adam. The prophetic and universal nature of the acclamation of the Christ child here clearly serves to support the interpretative interests of the writer more than the canonical genealogical accounts.

A second important motif of the TI that is revealed in this pericope can be discovered in the miracle dealing with the reaction of Satan and the Demons to the incarnation. According to the TI, it was not just the angels of the traditional scene that

---

[19] In the Ethiopic tradition preserved mainly as the Mäshafä Lədäta lä Maryam.

attended the birth of Jesus, but also Satan and his demonic horde. Here, Satan himself is made aware of the momentous event by eavesdropping on the good news delivered to the shepherds by the angelic cohort (Lk 2.8–21). This episode serves to place the gospel narrative in relation to the larger story of creation and the cosmic struggle of Satan against the sovereignty of God. As briefly noted above in my discussion of the introductory materials, the TI establishes the significance of this motif by taking up accounts from Jubilees and other texts of the OT pseudepigrapha in its prologue to establish this as the primary conflict informing its interpretation of the gospel narrative.

Last Suppers?

In some instances, the editor(s) of the TI allow diverse accounts of the same event to coexist with no effort to harmonize or explain the ensuing inconsistencies. A good example of this can be seen in the three separate accounts of the Last Supper preserved in the TI.[20]

The first account brings together traditions from the Gospel of Luke, the Gospel of John and the Book of the Cock. The narrative starts with Jesus sending out the disciples to prepare for the Passover (Lk 22.7–13), during which he proceeds to wash his disciples' feet (Jn 13.5ff). These two episodes from the canonical accounts are woven together with redactional supplements reminding the reader of the dramatic context – which is the opposition of the Jewish leaders – and the impending plot climax: the crucifixion. To supplement the editor(s)' characterization of Judas during this episode, the TI utilizes a tradition, from the (Ethiopic) Book of the Cock, that describes how Judah is denounced as the traitor by a moving and speaking pillar.[21]

The second account of the Last Supper found in the TI utilizes a different set of elements from the Book of the Cock, including the setting of the Passover meal at the house of a certain Alexander and his wife Akrosənna and Alexander's initial reluctance to let Judas in. The account in the TI, however, does not include the motif of the rooster[22] which is central to the source material and is instead supplemented by an indictment of Judah delivered by the doorkeeper who delays Judas: 'I see a big and black snake around your neck stretching his tongue to kiss your mouth and to harden your heart.'

The third account picks up from the washing of the feet of the disciples and recounts the throwing of lots among the disciples to identify the traitor and the confirmation by Jesus that it is indeed Judas by giving him a piece of bread dipped in sauce. This account

---

[20] These miracles are unnumbered in d'Abbadie 168 and 226.
[21] '... Jesus was speaking to his disciples on the Mount of Olives, concerning his passion and betrayal. He told a stone pillar to point out his betrayer, and it indicated Judas, son of Simon Iscariot. Judas reproved Jesus as a sorcerer ...' (Cowley, 'Ethiopic Book of the Cock, 17).
[22] According to the Book of the Cock, a rooster that was slain and cooked by Akrosənna for the Passover meal was resurrected by Jesus to spy on Judah as he made and acted on plans to betray Jesus in Jerusalem. The rooster reports his activities to Jesus and the other disciples, and he is sent to heaven as reward for his services.

seems to be a basic conflation of accounts discovered in the canonical gospels, in this instance from John 13.5ff and Matthew 26.23–25.

The Last Supper narratives reveal several interesting interpretative choices made by the editor(s) of the TI. The first is the contrast between the creative redaction that brings together different traditions within one account (miracle) and the minimal editorial interference in the preservation of inconsistent accounts about the same event with little to no attempt to resolve tensions. In addition to helping us understand the editorial processes of the TI, these accounts also reveal tantalizing insight into what are potentially different interpretations, or innovative adaptions of the same set of traditions. Second, we can note that for the editor(s) of the TI, all the sources included enjoyed equal authenticity and authority. Third, the editor(s)' (re)use of all traditions with impunity and little concern for historical or narrative consistency suggests that the TI has little to no polemical concern other than that which it receives and retains from its sources. These factors suggest that this text is primarily intended as a vehicle to present as thorough as possible a compilation of the gospel traditions available to its editor(s).

The writings of Jesus

Another example of the process of the reframing of separate traditions into the TI can be discovered in the compilation of the independent Abgar correspondence into the narrative frame of the Ethiopic TI.[23] Witakowski notes that in d'Abbadie 168 and 226 'this episode is compiled alongside the TI but as a separate composition, not as part of the MJ [Miracles of Jesus]'.[24] At first glance, this seems a fair assessment, particularly when we note that this episode is discovered after the primary gospel narrative has come to its conclusion and that in these two witnesses the formulaic introduction is also absent.

Based on manuscript evidence and internal witness, however, I would like to argue for an alternative conclusion. First, manuscript witnesses from the same period as d'Abbadie 168 and 226 reveal that the Abgar correspondence is preserved with the introduction *Tāmәra za-gabәra 'Egzi'әna wa-Madḫāni-na 'Iyasus Krәstos* ('A miracle performed by our Lord and our saviour Jesus Christ'). Examples of such witnesses include those used by Getachew Haile – EMML 2050 (nineteenth century) and EMML 2180 (eighteenth century), both copies of the Gәbra Hәmamat – in his critical edition and translation of the Abgar correspondence. These manuscripts are particularly significant because they serve to demonstrate that the formulaic introduction, which identifies episodes (miracles) of the TI, is also used as a preface to the Abgar material when it is preserved independently. This suggests that this material was recognized to be a part of the 'Miracles' even where it is not placed alongside the TI. Second, as we have seen briefly above, the internal literary practice of the TI indicates that traditions are brought together with little editorial input. Therefore, the absence of a redactional

---

[23] I will briefly look at the inclusion of the IGT below in relation to the use of this material to develop the theological thesis of the TI.
[24] Witakowski, 'The Miracles of Jesus', 290n.

bridge between the last miracle and the Abgar correspondence does not necessarily suggest that the latter is not a part of the narrative of the TI.

Finally, if more circumstantially, the literary and theological utility of this writing within the broad narrative framework of the TI suggests a reason why it would have been appropriated as a part of this tradition. The repeated reiteration of the different 'miracles' performed by Jesus as part of Abgar's epistle, for example, resonates rather well with the title of the entire work, serving as a summary of the events of Jesus' life that are the key literary focus of the TI. The unique status of the God-man Jesus, which Abgar infers from the miracle accounts that had reached him and Jesus' response to him affirming his understanding, coheres with and further develops the characterization of the divine Jesus, which is a central motif of the TI, as noted above.

On these bases, it is possible to argue that the Abgar Legend is not included within or alongside the TI by happenstance, but through a process of judicious reframing and editing toward developing the gospel narrative further. Assuming that this conclusion is correct, the inclusion of the Abgar correspondence offers an example of the creative adoption of a less well-known 'act' of Jesus within the traditional framework for the gospel narrative.

Interpretative supplementing

Berfsinya (the Samaritan woman)

Another literary process that is employed in the narrative development of the TI is that of supplementing. Much like other canonical and non-canonical gospel writings, the TI finds creative inspiration in narrative gaps. The following short extract from the rather long section that covers the TI's retelling of Jesus' encounter with the Samaritan woman (Jn 41–42) serves as a good example for this:

> And the Lord Jesus said; Truly I know all that you have done; [of] the four men who were with you before and this person who is with you now. The first was called *Səlti*, the second *Yokan*, the third Lewi, the fourth *Helot* and the fifth is called *Rafsay* ... And this woman, called *Berfsinya* ... And many from amongst them followed Jesus. And from amongst them, the learned men of Samaria came out and went to the land of Palestine to preach in his name, without the command of the Lord Jesus, and to return many people to the true faith.
>
> Miracles 16.2–7

The account of the Samaritan woman, already dripping with human interest in its canonical form, leaves unanswered questions that allow the writer to unleash creative/ interpretative imagination. It is, of course, impossible to assert if the details provided in the short example above come from other sources or oral traditions. Their usefulness in answering obvious literary questions, however, would suggest that this at least serves as a record of the efforts made by readers or listeners of the original traditions to fill in the gaps – for example, what were the names of the Samaritan woman and her husbands? The section also concludes by offering a revised ending to the episode by offering what the narrator believes to be the proper response to the revelation of the Messiah: to go out to preach and convert many. This creative supplementing of narrative gaps opens a window into one or more instances of the reception of the New Testament, revealing both the questions being asked by interpreters and the homiletic implications they sought to draw in their engagement.

The Ethiopic episode of the Infancy Gospel of Thomas

As noted by Andries G. Van Aarde, the depiction of Jesus in the Infancy Gospel of Thomas (IGT) by no means seeks to portray an ideal or conventional child, but rather seeks to demonstrate the extent to which Jesus, the God-child, contravened social expectations of human children.[25] This depiction aligns very much with the overall focus of the characterization of Jesus in the TI and is carried through in the one episode which is likely 'an Ethiopic elaboration of the legend'.[26]

> Again, the Lord Jesus did a miracle. When the sun entered through the window, the Lord Jesus rode on the sunbeam and went to the east and west, as far as the sunbeam came.
>
> Miracles 8.12

This episode, which has no parallels in the witnesses of the IGT that exist in other traditions, serves as an example of creative supplementing and development of both the motif as well as the style of the source material likely to enhance the characterization aims of the TI. This episode seems to allude to a wider tradition which made use of the sun as an illustration for the Trinity; according to this analogy, the essence of the Sun is God the Father, the light beam is Jesus and the heat can represent the Holy Spirit. In utilizing this imagery, the TI thus seems to seek to place the miraculous God-child firmly within the context of Christian Trinitarian conceptions.

In doing so, the Ethiopic editor follows the example of the even more spectacular creativity of the AGJ, which includes similarly oriented episodes that are believed to be original to it. According to Witakowski, original compositions in the AGJ are 'marked by a certain naivety, [that seems to characterize] the original inventions of the author of the apocryphon'.[27] While these original episodes are indeed characterized by talking plants, beasts and resurrected saints, all suggesting a certain literary simplicity, it bears noting that these narratives build upon material that is already present in older canonical gospel traditions. I will look at one such example here to further elaborate this point:

> And the Lord Jesus moved away from them for a while and with a great voice uttered: 'Sarah, Rebecca, and Rachel I order you to arise from the dead and come

---

[25] Van Aarde Andries, 'The infancy Gospel of Thomas: Allegory or myth? Gnostic or Ebionite?' *Verbum et Ecclesia* 26 (2005): 826–50.
[26] Gerö, 'THE TA'ĀMRA 'ĪYASŪS', 167.
[27] Witakowski, 'The Miracles of Jesus', 295.

out from inside of the grave and come to where I am'. At this time there was a great earthquake, much noise was heard, and the rocks split apart. These pure [women] came out from there. Sarah, Rebecca, and Rachel prostrated themselves before Jesus; their faces shone bright like the sun.

Miracle 22

This episode builds upon the Lazarus episode but supplements it with a more prestigious and recognizable cast of characters. Jesus' resurrection of the matriarchs of the Israelites and their prostration before him further develop his characterization as a divine being owed worship by all. It is also interesting to note that the earthquake, the shining faces and the prostration in this account all come together not only to evoke the depiction of theophanies in the Old Testament, but also to echo the imagery of the Matthean resurrection account:

At that moment the curtain of the temple was torn in two ... the earth shook, and the rocks were split. The tombs also were opened, and many bodies of the saints who had fallen asleep were raised.

Mt 27.51–52 NRSV

This echo serves to strengthen the TI's central focus on the manifestations of divinity and miraculous power in the life and ministry of Jesus Christ. To this interpretative end, the TI brings forward post-crucifixion events, generally believed to portend the eschatological resurrection, and populates them with well-known characters. Thus, what at first reading may come across as literary naivety may in actuality reveal more sophisticated techniques that elaborate upon strategies and content already present in earlier materials.

It is, therefore, possible to at least tentatively suggest that the use of interpretative supplementing in the TI that I have attempted to look at here serves to reveal: 1) the creative liberty to augment and explicate existing traditions that is a characteristic of not only apocryphal but also canonical gospel traditions; and 2) the significance of theological priorities, as seen in this case with the focus on the identity of Jesus as the God-man who has absolute sovereignty over the entire cosmos.

Concluding thoughts

In conclusion, I would like to highlight a few of the interesting characteristics of the TI that are revealed through this brief look at its narrative techniques and interpretative processes. First, we can note the extent to which the TI brings together a diverse, and at times divergent, set of witnesses into one account. This effort suggests that rather than seeking to rewrite or supplant other earlier gospel narratives, this text seeks to transmit its sources within a new framework. Second, in addition to bringing together sources, the TI also exhibits a creative reimagining that utilizes original supplements. Third, the narrative forwards specific theological motifs that serve to reinterpret and organize its content.

In this light, we can argue that the writer(s) of the TI reflect continuity and development of literary and interpretative practices present in earlier gospel traditions including the canonical gospels. In doing so, the TI does not only assume the authority and authenticity of these traditions, but also establishes itself as a participant in the broader sacred tradition.[28] The question of authority in this context is an interesting one, which may, with further study, serve to illuminate further the definition of 'canon' in the EOTC and possibly other earlier Christian traditions. This understanding of canon defers from the traditional assumption of a set of books being more concerned about the rule of faith. In the case of the TI, for example, coherence with its overarching theological or Christological motif seems to take precedence over any potential questions of 'authenticity'.

Appendix: An outline of the *Ta-'ammərä 'Iyasus* (Miracles of Jesus)[29]

Introduction: The creation of the angels and of Adam; the rebellion of the angels; the fall of Adam; Abel and Cain.

1. The choosing of Mary; the Annunciation and Conception of Jesus; the trial of Mary and Joseph by the 'bitter' water.
2. The birth of Jesus; the midwife Salome doubting Mary's virginity.
3. Salome's hymn to Jesus.
4. The fear of Satan and the demons at Jesus' birth.
5. The presentation of Jesus in the Temple.
6. The coming of the Magi; the Flight to Egypt.
7. The return of the Holy Family from Egypt and the meeting with three brigands.
8. The miracles of Infancy (Infancy Gospel of Thomas):

    i. Jesus makes 12 bird figures on the Sabbath day and causes them to fly.
    ii. The son of the scribe Hanna is punished with withering of his body for letting the water of Jesus' pools run away.
    iii. The death of a child who struck Jesus' breast.
    iv. Jesus at school with the teacher Zacchaeus.
    v. Jesus resuscitates a boy who was killed by falling from a roof.
    vi. Jesus brings water in his cloak when the jar is broken.
    vii. Jesus works as a carpenter to help Joseph.
    viii. The death of a teacher who struck Jesus at school.
    ix. Jesus astonishes another teacher with his knowledge.
    x. The healing of Jacob, Joseph's son, bitten by a snake.

---

[28] Hindy Najman develops this idea of later and/or pseudonymous writings as participants in earlier sacred traditions. Hindy Najman, *Seconding Sinai: The Development of Mosaic Discourse in Second Temple Judaism* (JSJSup 77; Leiden: Brill, 2003).

[29] This outline was developed by Witakowski on the basis of d'Abbadie 168 (see Witold Witakowski, 'The Miracles of Jesus: An Ethiopian Apocryphal Gospel', *Apocrypha* 6 (1995): 288–90).

    xi. Jesus teaches in the temple in Jerusalem.
    xii. Jesus rides a sunbeam.
    xiii. The miraculous harvest from five grains of barley sown by Jesus.
9. The theft of the cattle of the righteous Tetmena.
10. The theft of fish from a fisherman of Tiberias.
11. The theft of a heifer.
12. Joseph and a lion, which confesses Jesus' divinity.
13. Jesus makes a flooded field dry.
14. The four beasts of Ezekiel's vision, and the patriarchs (Abraham, Jacob and Moses) testify to Jesus' divinity.
15. The adulteress.
16. Berfsinya, the Samaritan woman.
17. The calling and baptism of Simon (Peter) and Andrew; Peter is given priestly authority.
18. The healing of the deaf, dumb and blind man.
19. The resurrection of the son of the widow of Nain.
20. The resurrection of a dead man and the glorification of Jesus by sheep and an ox.
21. Zacchaeus's olive branch blessed by Jesus yields abundantly.
22. Sara, Rebecca and Rachel testify to Jesus' divinity.
23. The miraculous harvest of melons.
24. The healing of the woman suffering from a haemorrhage; a talking gazelle testifies to Jesus' divinity.
25. The healing of the deaf-mute suffering from elephantiasis.
26. The expulsion of locusts from Galilee and Judaea, and the question of the Sabbath.
27. The lions of Ascalon leave the region at the behest of Nathaniel.
28. Eschatological discourse of Jesus in Jericho.
29. Jesus' sermon to the apostles on the Mount of Olives.
30. The Baptism and Temptation of Jesus.
31. The wedding feast at Cana.
32. The resurrection of Lazarus.
33. Jesus' sermon to the apostles on Mount Sinai.
34. Jesus' speech concerning Jerusalem.
35. Jesus' entry into Jerusalem.
36. Mary (Magdalene) anoints Jesus.
37. The Last Supper.
38. Judas leaves the cenacle.
39. Gethsemane: Jesus is arrested.
40. Jesus before Pilate.
41. Pilate delivers Jesus to the Jews; Peter's denial.
42. The Crucifixion.
43. Titus the good thief; the Death of Jesus.
44. The Burial of Jesus.
45. Judas hangs himself; the priests of the Jews consult Nicodemus about Jesus.

46. The Resurrection.
47. The women and the disciples at Jesus' tomb; Pilate interrogates the guards of the tomb who have been bribed by the Jews.
48. Jesus and the disciples at Emmaus.
49. The imprisonment of Joseph of Arimathea and of many of the seventy disciples; their miraculous deliverance.
50. The appearance of Jesus to the apostles on the Sea of Tiberias; the miraculous draught of fishes; the appearance to Peter and John.
51. Jesus' appearance to the apostles in the cenacle; doubting Thomas.
52. The Ascension.
53. The Pentecost.
54. The missionary regions of the apostles.
55. The apostles and the disciples spread the Gospel in the world; the Assumption of Mary.
56. The correspondence between King Abgar and Jesus.

10

'The House of the Gospel': Text, Image and Sacred Space

Francis Watson

The architecture of a gospel book

A few miles west of Aksum, ancient capital of Ethiopia, and near the town of Adwa, lies the Abunä Gärima Monastery. The monastery is named after its founder, one of the 'nine saints' traditionally supposed to have renewed the church of Ethiopia in around the sixth century CE.[1] Visitors are taken to see the rocky platform on which the saint is believed to have resided, high above the present monastery itself. Tradition also names the saint as the scribe responsible for writing the monastery's oldest and most revered gospel book, a task completed within a single day – although sunset had to be supernaturally delayed to allow him to do so.[2]

In reality the monastery houses not one but three ancient Ethiopic gospel books, at least two of which appear to be older than any known to have survived elsewhere. These manuscripts are foundational for modern critical editions of the gospels in Geʻez, representing an early text-form (A) which, in the case of Matthew, predates a revision aimed at a more accurate rendering of the Greek original (B). In the dominant later textual tradition, variant A and B readings are systematically conflated (C).[3] The C text-form can be traced back to the late thirteenth century, and the B- and A-forms which it conflates must be older than this.[4] Two of the three ancient Abunä Gärima

---

[1] On the tradition of the 'nine saints', believed to have arrived in Ethiopia from various eastern provinces of the Byzantine empire, see *Encyclopaedia Aethiopica* (*EAe*), 5 vols, ed. S. Uhlig and A. Baussi (Wiesbaden: Harrassowitz Verlag, 2003–14), 3.1188–91. The life of Gärima (also known as Yəṣḥaq) is recounted in a homily by John bishop of Axum, dating from the fifteenth century – around 900 years after the saint's supposed lifetime.

[2] Antonella Brita, *I racconti tradizionali sulla seconda cristianizzazione dell'Etiopia : il ciclo agiografico dei nove santi* (Napoli : Istituto universitario orientale, 2010). There is a brief illustrated description of an illustrated life of Gärima in A. Brita, 'With the Saints came the Manuscripts', https://www.manuscript-cultures.uni-hamburg.de/mom/2012_11_mom_e.html (accessed 28 May 2018).

[3] Rochus Zuurmond, *Novum Testamentum Aethiopice, Part III: The Gospel of Matthew* (Aethiopistische Forschungen 55; Wiesbaden: Harrassowitz Verlag, 2001), 1–19.

[4] See my discussion of the textual evidence for early dating of the older Ethiopic manuscripts, in Judith McKenzie and Francis Watson, *Early Illuminated Gospel Books from Ethiopia* (Oxford: Manar

gospel manuscripts have been carbon dated to around the sixth century,[5] preserving a gospel translation that may itself date back to the fourth or fifth century.[6] These manuscripts (Gärima I and III) contain artwork of extraordinary quality, greatly superior to that of the somewhat later Gärima II.[7] Like other ancient Christian gospel books, they all contain an elaborately decorated set of 'canon tables', the remarkable cross referencing system and analysis of gospel parallels devised by Eusebius of Caesarea.

Analysing gospel parallels with the help of an older gospel synopsis,[8] Eusebius discovered four primary categories of gospel relationships, two of which could be further subdivided to give a total of ten such categories. Some passages occur in all four gospels, others in three, others in two, others in a single gospel. Passages occurring in all four gospels are listed numerically in Eusebius's canon I. Within the second category, passages occurring in three gospels, Eusebius uncovered three different combinations: Matthew–Mark–Luke (canon II), Matthew–Luke–John (canon III) and Matthew–Mark–John (canon IV). Passages occurring in two gospels are found in the combinations Matthew–Luke (canon V), Matthew–Mark (canon VI), Matthew–John (canon VII), Luke–Mark (canon VIII) and Luke–John (canon IX). Passages distinctive to each of the gospels are all gathered into the four sections of canon X. The tables were designed to be accommodated within an eight-page sequence, with a full page for the longer lists of parallels (canons I, II and V), two tables to a page for the shorter ones (canons III and IV, VI and VII, VIII and IX) and two pages for the lists of distinctive passages in canon X. Above the grid that houses the enumerated parallels, the names of the relevant evangelists were enclosed within an arcade, above which the title of the canon in question was set within a further arch. The eight-page canon table sequence was prefaced by an explanatory 'letter' addressed by Eusebius to an otherwise unknown individual named Carpianus, which explains why these tables of gospel parallels were compiled and how they are to be used. The formatting as well as the content of the tables must go back to Eusebius himself.[9] A simple, clear format along these lines would

---

al-Athar, 2016), 205–9. Early datings are proposed on paleographical grounds by Donald M. Davies (eighth–tenth century) and on art-historical grounds by Marilyn Heldman (sixth century?). See Donald M. Davies, 'The Dating of Ethiopic Manuscripts', *Journal of Near Eastern Studies* 46 (1987): 287–307, at 287; Marilyn Heldman et al., *African Zion: The Sacred Art of Ethiopia* (New Haven & London: Yale University Press, 1993), 129.

[5] McKenzie and Watson, *Early Illuminated Gospel Books*, 40–1.
[6] 'Not later than the 6th century A.D.', according to R. Zuurmond, 'The Textual Background of the Gospel of Matthew in Ge'ez', *Aethiopica* 4 (2001): 32–41, at 32. However, Zuurmond dates the Gärima manuscripts that attest the A text of Matthew to 'the 12th century or earlier' (33), failing to explain why a long-superseded text-form was still being copied at so late a date.
[7] The enumeration of the three Gärima volumes stems from William F. Macomber, *Catalogue of Ethiopian Manuscripts from Abbā Garimā . . . from Microfilms in the Collection of Dr Donald Davies, De Land, Florida and Godfrey, Ontario, and of the Hill Monastic Manuscript Library, St John's University, Collegeville, Minnesota* (Collegeville, Minnesota: Privately reproduced). Until recent restoration work, the three books were bound into two volumes with many leaves displaced.
[8] See Matthew R. Crawford, 'Ammonius of Alexandria, Eusebius of Caesarea, and the Beginnings of Gospels Scholarship', *NTS* 61 (2015): 1–29.
[9] Evidence for the earliest canon table format is analysed by Carl Nordenfalk, *Die spätantiken Kanontafeln: Kunstgeschichtliche Studien über die eusebianische Evangelien-Konkordanz in den vier ersten Jahrhunderten ihrer Geschichte* (with accompanying *Tafelband*) (Göteborg: Oscar Isacsons

be essential if scribes were to adopt the system and reproduce it accurately. What is less clear is whether Eusebius was in any way responsible for the remarkable transformation of a cross-referencing system into artwork, attested in gospel books from all over the Christian world of the second half of the first millennium.

The Gärima I gospel book allocates three pages to the prefatory letter, rendered in an eccentric and inaccurate Ge'ez translation that makes it impossible to use the canon tables as Eusebius intended.[10] As if in compensation for this deficiency, both the letter and the tables are accompanied by artwork of such quality that they cease to function as scholarly tools and become instead objects of contemplation in their own right, symbolizing the harmonious order underlying the surface complexity of gospel interrelations. This symbolic function becomes explicit in an image that follows the canon table sequence (Figure 1). Like the canon table frames, it combines architectural features with upper zones inhabited by flowers and birds, an allusion perhaps to the Garden of Eden. Unlike the canon table frames, there are here four pillars rather than two, of which the two inner pillars are linked together by their brown shading just as the outer ones are by their blue shading. The outer pillars presumably symbolize the apostolic first and fourth gospels, Matthew and John, while the inner ones symbolize the post-apostolic Mark and Luke.[11] Use of a four-pillared structure to close the canon

Figure 1

Boktryckeri, 1938), 65–72. Nordenfalk believes that the Eusebian archetype distributed the prefatory letter over 3 pages and the canon tables over 7 (as in Garima I). In my view, the 2 + 8 page format of Garima III is more likely to represent Eusebius's original design.

[10] See my presentation of Greek and Ge'ez texts and translations in McKenzie and Watson, *Early Illuminated Gospel Books*, Appendix III (221–7).

[11] This distinction between apostolic and post-apostolic gospels is present in Tertullian, *adv. Marc.* iv.2.1–5, where the authority of the *apostolici* (Luke and Mark) is subordinated to that of the *apostoli* (Matthew and John). See also my discussion of the iconography of the fifth-century Galla Placidia Mausoleum, Ravenna (Francis Watson, *Gospel Writing* (Grand Rapids: Eerdmans, 2013), 577–83).

table sequence is attested in later gospel books,[12] and may already have been traditional at the time of Gärima I. The image of the four pillars derives ultimately from Irenaeus, who argues that

> since the world in which we live has four regions and four main winds [Gk τέσσαρα καθολικὰ πνεύματα], and the church is spread out across all the world, and the pillar and foundation of the church is the gospel together with the Spirit of life [Gk πνεῦμα ζωῆς] – it is proper that it should have four pillars [Gk στύλους; Lat *columnas*], everywhere breathing out immortality and rekindling people to life.[13]

The four pillars in the Gärima I image also seem to breathe out life, sustaining the roof-garden they support, with its flowers and birds.

In the Gärima III gospel book, the canon table sequence is preceded by a portrait of Eusebius (Figure 2). Here Eusebius's probable original formatting – two pages for the prefatory letter, eight for the canon tables – is preserved, in contrast to the three-plus-seven format of Gärima I. The artistry of these Gärima III pages is, if anything, on a still higher level than that of Gärima I (Figure 3). The colouring is less vivid, but the

Figure 2

---

[12] For example, the Armenian 'Etchmiadzin Gospels' (989 CE; Yerevan, Matenadaran ms. 2374, fol. 5v). In some other gospel books the number of pillars varies, so that the association with the four gospels is lost: examples in Paul A. Underwood, 'The Fountain of Life in Manuscripts of the Gospels', *Dumbarton Oak Papers* 5 (1950), 41–138, figs. 34–8, 26, 30, 53–5.

[13] Irenaeus, *Adv. haer.* iii.11.8.

'The House of the Gospel': Text, Image and Sacred Space 149

Figure 3

design is more intricate. The basic form of the two sets of images is similar, however. In both cases, a simple grid is set between two outer pillars with elaborate bases and capitals in contrasting colours. The grid is unbroken by the intervening pillars inserted by canon table artists elsewhere. In both cases, a set of three concentric arcs is supported by a long lintel which extends beyond the edges of the capitals. It is striking, then, that the image that follows the canon table sequence in Gärima III is so different from its four-pillared equivalent in Gärima I (Figure 4).

The Gärima III image depicts a building with a high pitched roof decorated with rows of projecting curved tiles extending up to a set of five spherical ornaments on the ridge of the roof. There are three rows of these tiles to left and to right of the steep central pediment, and the inner rows converge at the ridge, echoing and enclosing the triangle of the pediment below. The lowest part of the pediment seems to be open to the building's interior; from it a lamp is suspended. The main part of the building is set on a platform, approached by a flight of steps. The entrance is marked by two tall pillars, behind the lower parts of which open doors are located. Between the upper parts of the pillars a curtain suspended from five curtain rings is tied in the middle so that the interior of the building is visible. If the curtain were to be untied and the doors closed, the whole entrance would be covered. As depicted here, they indicate that access to the building is open. To left and right of the pillars, arcades separate the hewn stone wall from its roof. Their arches serve as windows, and from each a lamp is suspended like the one in the pediment, giving a total of seven lamps in all. Below, small square windows are set into the wall. The platform on which the building is set features a central flight of ten steps with what seems to be water flowing down in well-defined channels on either side. The movement of the water is depicted by rows of wave-like curves which echo the rows of curved tiles on the roof. To left and right of the steps, the grey hewn stones of the upper building continue down into the platform, but its walls are broken on both sides by openings occupied by

Figure 4

long-necked animals of indeterminate species. To the left, one animal appears to be exiting the opening while another enters it, leaving only its hindquarters and tail visible. The animal on the right displays its elaborate antlers as it steps forth from the opening. Like its companion on the other side of the steps, it stretches its elongated head up towards the entrance of the building on the platform above. Although the building and its stonework are directly facing the viewer, the steps, water channels and emerging animals are depicted at oblique angles that create some ambiguity in the perspective.

Some features of the Gärima III building may reflect Aksumite architectural practice. The square windows in the main building recall the ones carved into Aksumite stelai. Churches and other edifices were built on stone platforms with flights of steps. A curtain tied in the middle can still be seen in Ethiopian churches. Yet the Gärima image depicts a fantasy building, not a credible structure: the animals, the water flowing from the entrance, and the perspectival oddities make that clear. In the case of the Gärima I image of the four-pillared structure, a possible literary source was found in Irenaeus. Even without Irenaeus, a structure with two pairs of columns is, in this context, an obvious symbol of the fourfold gospel. Decoding the more complex Gärima III image is, however, much less straightforward. Given its positioning at the end of a canon table sequence, it must still somehow represent the fourfold gospel; yet it is not clear how it can do so. There are two water channels here, three large white mammals, seven lamps and ten steps, but the number four is represented only in the insignificant form of the square windows. To answer the question how this image represents the fourfold gospel, it is necessary to trace it back to its scriptural roots – in 1 Kings (3 Kgdms LXX), in Ezekiel, and above all in the Book of Enoch.

The Enochic temple

The building is the Jerusalem temple, originally constructed by King Solomon, destroyed by the Babylonians, and then rebuilt both in prophetic imagination and in reality. The Gärima III image combines selected features from the scriptural description of Solomon's temple with prophetic depictions of its eschatological restoration: one from the perspective of Ezekiel, who anticipates a restored temple in the near future; the other from the more distant perspective of Enoch, who foresees the whole future history of Israel with the restored temple at its eschatological climax.

1. The description of Solomon's temple in 3 Kingdoms 6 LXX (Hebrew, 1 Kgs) has influenced the Gärima III image at three main points:

    (i) In 3 Kingdoms 6.2, it is said that 'the house that King Solomon built for the Lord was 40 cubits in length, 20 cubits in breadth, and 25 cubits in height'. In the Masoretic text, in contrast, the figures are 60 cubits for the length, 20 for the breadth, and 30 cubits for the height. In the LXX figures, the ratio of breadth to height is therefore *4:5* (*20:25*), in the Hebrew and Syriac ones *2:3* (*20:30*). Even without measuring its dimensions, it is obvious that the Gärima image depicts a structure whose height (from the platfom) is slightly greater than its breadth. In fact, the Ethiopic artist scrupulously observes the Septuagintal ratio of *4:5*.[14]
    (ii) The pillars on either side of the porch are based on the bronze pillars cast for Solomon by Hiram of Tyre (3 Kgdms 7.1–9).[15] Here the Hebrew and Greek texts agree that the height of the pillars and their capitals was 18 + 5 cubits, only a little less than the height of the building (Gk *23:25*). This ratio the artist does not attempt to reproduce, choosing instead to set the pillars between the high roof and the platform on which the main building is set.
    (iii) The temple was provided with windows 'with recessed frames' according to the Hebrew (1 Kgs 6.4), or for peering in at the mysteries according to the Septuagintal Greek, where these are θυρίδας παρακυπτομένας κρυπτάς, which may mean 'windows [small doors] for secret observation'.[16] Here too

---

[14] Both MT and LXX differ here from the Ge'ez text printed in A. Dillmann, *Veteris Testamenti Aethiopici Tomus I: Octateuchus Aethiopicus* (Leipzig: Vogelius, 1853), where the equivalent dimensions are 8 x 8 x 8 cubits (3 Kgs 6.6 Eth). These figures imitate the cube-shaped Holy of holies (3 Kgdms 6.20 LXX) and indicate an assimilation of the Temple, the Holy of holies, and the Ark of the Covenant.
[15] 1 Kgdms 7.1–9 LXX = 1 Kgs 7.13–22.
[16] Hebrew חַלּוֹנֵי שְׁקֻפִים אֲטֻמִים (probably 'recessed windows').

the Gärima artist responds to the cues of the scriptural text, as well as to local architectural practice. Why he thinks that the temple is an appropriate image for the fourfold gospel remains unclear, however.

2. In the final chapters of the Book of Ezekiel, the prophet is taken on an angelically guided tour of a future restored temple (Ezek 40–48). The oldest extant Ethiopic manuscripts of this Old Testament book omit about three-quarters of the contents of Ezekiel 42–46, much of which is concerned with priestly duties, and attention is focused instead on the temple's architecture (Ezek 40–41) and on the river that flowed forth from its threshold (47).[17] In his vision the prophet sees that water was flowing down from below the threshold of the temple toward the east (47.1). At the same time, water was also flowing 'from below the south end of the threshold of the Temple' (47.2). The temple has become a spring or source, and the double source produces a river at first ankle deep, then waist deep, and finally deep enough to swim in (47.3, 5). The river will be a rich resource for fishermen; evergreen fruit trees will grow on its banks, and their leaves will have healing properties (47.7–10, 12).[18] In the Gärima image, too, water flows forth from the threshold of the temple, a feature that can only derive from Ezekiel. It is possible that the oblique perspective of the two channels represents the double source flowing from beneath the temple threshold to the south (on the left) and to the east (on the right). In early Christian symbolism and iconography, the fourfold gospel is often associated with the four rivers that flow out into the world from the Garden of Eden. If there is a connection with the two channels or rivers in the Gärima image, however, it remains unclear. Four rivers can effectively symbolize a fourfold gospel, but two cannot.

3. If the two Gärima rivers are inspired by Ezekiel, the unusual animals seem to derive from Enoch – specifically, from the 'Animal Apocalypse' that constitutes the second and longer of Enoch's two 'Dream-Visions' (1 Enoch 83–84, 85–90) and from the conclusion of the 'Apocalypse of Weeks' that follows (1 Enoch 91.12–13).

In the Animal Apocalypse, Enoch recounts a dream to his son Methuselah that he had experienced long ago, before his marriage, in which the entire preordained course of scriptural history was revealed. From Enoch's standpoint, some events of that history have already taken place – notably the creation of Adam and Eve, Cain's murder of Abel, the birth of Seth, the angel marriages, and the birth of the giants (1 Enoch 85.3–86.6). Adam is depicted as a white bull, Eve as a female calf, Cain and Abel as black and red calves respectively.[19] Enoch saw how

---

[17] M. A. Knibb, 'Hebrew and Syriac Elements in the Ethiopic Version of Enoch?' *JSS* 33 (1988): 11–35; 23.

[18] Ethiopic omissions from Ezekiel 47.1–12 are confined to vv. 1b–2a, 4, 11 (Knibb, 'Hebrew and Syriac Elements', 23). The result is a more succinct and coherent text.

[19] Translations here and elsewhere are my own. Ge'ez text in R. H. Charles, *The Ethiopic Version of the Book of Enoch* (Oxford: Clarendon Press, 1906); M. A. Knibb, *The Ethiopic Book of Enoch, Vol. I*:

a bull came forth from the ground, and that bull was white, and after it there came forth a single female calf and with her there came forth two [male] calves, and one was black and one was red. And the black calf struck the red one and pursued him from the ground.

85.3-4[20]

The surprising assimilation of the creation of Eve to the birth of Cain and Abel introduces the theme of conflict between animals that will dominate the whole apocalypse. Cain and his wife produce a posterity of black bulls; Eve gives birth to a white bull, Seth, whose posterity are white (85.5, 8-10), but white and black bulls alike are attacked and devoured by the elephants, camels and asses that result from the angel marriages (86.4-6). The other white bull figures are Noah (a white bull who becomes human, 89.1),[21] Shem (89.9), Abraham (89.11) and Isaac (89.11). As Eve's offspring consisted of a black, a red and a white bull, so it is with Noah (89.9): the red and the black bulls are Ham and Japheth, who produce every kind of species, both animals (lions, dogs, hyenas, and so on) and birds (vultures, eagles, crows, and so on; 89.10). The reference is to the 'table of nations' of Genesis 10, with Shem (the white bull) responsible solely for the line that leads to Abraham (another white bull).[22] It is not only the black and red bulls who produce offspring of other species. In the midst of the post-diluvian menagerie, the white bull that is Abraham begets a wild ass (Ishmael)[23] and a white bull (Isaac), who in turn begets a black wild boar (Esau) and – rather than a white bull – a white sheep (Jacob, 89.12). The boar begets many boars, the sheep twelve sheep, Jacob's twelve sons who are also the ancestors of Israel's twelve tribes (89.12). From this point on, the Animal Apocalypse is dominated by the relationship between the sheep (the people of Israel) and animals or birds hostile to them (the Gentiles). Shortly after the emergence of the twelve sheep, a further character is introduced: the Lord of the sheep, the God of Israel (89.14-16).

Text and Apparatus (Oxford: Clarendon Press, 1978). Charles's English translation is available in *Apocrypha and Pseudepigrapha of the Old Testament* (ed. R. H. Charles; 2 vols.; Oxford: Clarendon Press, 1913), 2.188–281; Knibb's, most accessibly in *The Apocryphal Old Testament* (ed. H. F. D. Sparks; Oxford: Clarendon Press, 1984), 184–319. Other English translations include E. Isaac, in *The Old Testament Pseudepigrapha, Volume 1: Apocalyptic Literature and Testaments* (ed. J. H. Charlesworth; 1983), 13–89; George W. E. Nickelsburg and James C. VanderKam, *1 Enoch: A New Translation Based on the Hermeneia Commentary* (Minneapolis: Fortress, 2004). For a German translation, see S. Uhlig, *Der äthiopische Henochbuch* (JSHRZ V.6; Gütersloh: Gütersloher Verlagshaus, 1984).

[20] References to the 'ground' (*mədr*) in connection with Adam's origin and Abel's blood echo Genesis 2.7 (*mareta mədr*) and 4.10 ('*emenna mədr*). Like Cain and Abel, Eve is introduced as a 'calf' (*ta'wa*), a connection that is lost in Knibb's translation, where the 'heifer' is differentiated from the 'two bullocks' (*Enoch*, 2.195). In 1 Enoch 85.4, *wusət mədr* probably means 'into the ground', although some manuscripts read *diba mədr*, 'on the earth'. Accepting the latter reading, Nickelsburg suggests that it was Abel who pursued Cain 'across the earth, like a Greek fury, seeking vengeance' (George W. E. Nickelsburg, 1 Enoch 1 (Hermeneia, Minneapolis: Fortress, 2001, 371). But that would require an unlikely switch of subject and object.

[21] Noah and Moses become human in connection with their building activity (89.1, 36); so Nickelsburg, 1 Enoch 1, 375.

[22] Here the primary scriptural sources are Genesis 10.1-20 + 11.10-26, with the second ('P') genealogy of Shem preferred to the first ('J', Gen 10.21-31).

[23] Ishmael is already depicted as a 'wild ass of a man' (פֶּרֶא אָדָם) in Genesis 16.12 MT.

Underlying the apparent complexities is a simple schema. 'Bulls' represent the generically human, prior to the differentiation between Israel and the Gentiles. Righteous individuals in the first half of Genesis are white bulls: Adam, Seth and his posterity, Noah, Shem, Abraham and Isaac. Black bulls represent Cain and his posterity and Noah's son Ham, the red bulls Abel and Japheth. Since 'Israel' is Jacob, it is Jacob rather than Abraham or Isaac who is the first of the sheep. In this taxonomy of the animal world, there are bulls, sheep, and all other creatures (including birds). The bulls disappear from the picture throughout the theriomorphized history of Israel that follows, although (as we shall see) they become highly relevant again at the very end.

Where does the idea of replacing the human agents of scripture with animal ones originate? The association of the people of Israel with a flock of sheep, with YHWH as their shepherd is, of course, a scriptural commonplace. The identification of the nations of Genesis 10 with animals and birds may be influenced by the story of Noah's Ark, specifically the exit from the ark of Noah and his family but also of all the animals, reptiles and birds (Gen 8.19, cf. 9.18). The Enochic author does not mention the animals in the ark, although Noah's three sons are represented as bulls; Noah himself was born a white bull and became a man. As animals and birds come forth from the ark in Genesis, so animals and birds come forth from the ark's red and black bulls (Ham and Japheth) in the Enochic text. The non-human cargo of the ark is thus associated with the Gentile nations of Genesis 10, and this association may have been the origin of the Animal Apocalypse.[24]

In Enoch's dream, animal agents pre-enact the scriptural history of Israel, with sheep playing the role of the people of Israel and the other animals and birds that of their successive enemies. The Egyptian oppressors are 'wolves' (89.13–27), the Philistines are 'dogs' (89.42–49), the Babylonians are 'lions' (89.56). The Lord of the sheep overthrows the wolves in the Red Sea, raises up a pair of rams (Saul and David) to counter the dogs, but subjects his flock to near-destruction at the hands of the Babylonian lions and their allies, in punishment for their blindness (89.54–58). At this point, the Lord of the sheep abandons his role as shepherd of his people and hands them over to seventy shepherds – angelic rulers of Gentile nations – who will successively oppress the sheep, surrendering them to their animal enemies and going far beyond the limited punitive role assigned to them (89.59–90.8). An epic battle ensues between the wild animals and birds on the one hand and a ram, perhaps representing Judas Maccabeus (90.6–19). At this point in the story, the Lord of the sheep intervenes directly. The hostile animals and birds are swallowed up into the earth (90.15, 18) or slaughtered by sword-wielding sheep (90.19); a throne is set up for the divine judge (90.20), who inflicts judgement on the imprisoned Watchers (90.21, 24), on the seventy shepherds (90.22, 25) and on the blinded among the sheep themselves (90.26–27).

It is in its final scenes that the Animal Apocalypse becomes relevant to the temple-and-animal image of the gospel book known as Gärima III – and thus, somehow, relevant to the fourfold gospel which is represented in that image. The Enochic author notes that the temple has its prototype in Moses' tabernacle (89.36) and proceeds to tell

---

[24] 1 Enoch 89.10 might be translated 'And there arose from them every community of Gentiles [*zaʾəmkʷəllu ḥəbr ʿaḥzāb*] rather than 'every kind of species' (Knibb). For the animal kingdom as representing Gentiles, compare Acts 10.12, 11.6.

how Solomon built a great house for the Lord of the sheep (89.50), how the Lord abandoned his house to punish his sheep for their blindness (89.56), how it was destroyed by the Babylonians (89.66–67), and how it was unsatisfactorily rebuilt after the exile (89.72–73). With the conclusive divine victory over all hostile powers, the way is open for both the temple and the surviving animals to attain their eschatological perfection.[25]

After the judgement scenes, it is time for reconstruction. The new era requires a new temple, and Enoch describes how it replaced the old one:

> And I stood up to look until he folded up the old house, and they removed all the pillars; and all the beams and ornaments of that house were folded up with it, and they removed it and laid it in a place in the south of the land. And I looked until the Lord of the sheep brought a new house, larger and higher than the first one, and he set it up on the site of the first one which had been wrapped up. And all its pillars were new and its ornaments were new and larger than those of the first one, the old one which he had removed. And all the sheep were within it.
>
> 90.28–29[26]

The sheep within the house are the righteous elect of the new age, but there are still surviving sheep and others animals and birds outside the house to do homage to them and to their Lord:

> And I saw all the sheep that were left, and all the animals on the earth and all the birds of heaven as they fell and prostrated themselves before those sheep, and entreated them and obeyed them in every matter.
>
> 90.30

Here the distinction between sheep (Israel) and wild animals and birds (Gentiles) has been modified. The fundamental distinction is now between the sheep within the temple and the sheep, wild animals and birds outside who are no longer hostile and who acknowledge the temple's occupants and its Lord. Yet these outsiders do not continue as such, for:

> all the beasts of the field and all the birds of heaven gathered together in that house, and the Lord of the sheep rejoiced with great joy because they were all good and had returned to his house.
>
> 90.33

---

[25] According to Nickelsburg, the 'house' refers not to the temple but to the New Jerusalem (1 Enoch 1, 404–405). 'House' (*bet*) initially refers to the tabernacle erected by Moses (89.36), but the house is later differentiated from a 'high tower' although the two are closely associated (89.50, 66–67, 72–73). The house/tower distinction serves only to indicate the destruction and rebuilding of both city and temple in the Babylonian era. In 90.29, the new 'house' is 'larger and higher' than its predecessor, and both are envisaged as pillared buildings; it is probably the temple that is in view.

[26] Charles (187) emend *ṭawamo* ('he folded [it] up') to *ṭāməwo* ('they folded [it] up'). Charles (187) and Uhlig (703) accept the reading *wakʷəllomu ʾabāgəʿ māʾəkalā* ('All the sheep were within it'); Knibb (1.336) *waʾəgziʾ ʾabāgəʿ māʾəkalā* ('The Lord of the sheep was within it').

Remarkably, these symbols of the Gentile world are given precedence over those Israelite sheep who had been blind but now see; these too are invited in, but it is doubtful if the house has the capacity to hold them all (90.34–35). The distinction between Israel and the Gentiles is wearing thin. The Lord is no longer Lord only of the sheep, and the seventy shepherds who once lorded it over the Gentiles have been despatched to their eternal fiery punishment.

In the Gärima image as in the Enochic apocalypse, the temple is unexpectedly occupied by animals, as though it were a second Noah's Ark. In the image, however, there are no sheep. The mysterious Gärima animals with their elongated necks, heads, legs, tails and antlers are white but otherwise entirely unsheeplike. The reason for this is clear: there are no sheep in the image because they disappear from the text itself, transformed into white bulls. Thus the distinction between Israel and the Gentiles is abolished, and we are returned to the generic humanity that existed in the beginning:

> And I saw how a white bull was born, and its horns were great, and all the beasts of the field and all the birds of heaven were afraid of it and entreated it continually. And I looked until all their species were transformed, and they all became white bulls, and the first among them was a *nagar*, and that *nagar* was a large animal and had great black horns on its head. And the Lord of the sheep rejoiced over them and over all the bulls.
>
> 90.37–38[27]

What kind of creature is a *nagar*? The Ge'ez term means 'word' or 'speech', although it is not the equivalent of *logos* and has no clear christological connotations. According to an old and attractive theory, this Enochic animal came to be known as a 'speech', *nagar*, as a result of a double translation failure. On this theory, the Greek text underlying the Ge'ez transliterated the Hebrew word *rēm*, a wild ox, as *rēm*, which the Ethiopic translator misread as *rēma*, word.[28] Whatever the explanation, the Enochic bestiary now includes the great-horned *nagar*, which is said to be the first among the white bulls. This, no doubt, is the impressive white creature on the right of the Gärima image.

At this point the Animal Apocalypse comes to a close. Shortly afterwards, in the next chapter, Enoch resumes his testament-like address to his son Methuselah in which is embedded a displaced fragment of the brief 'Apocalypse of Weeks'. When reassembled in its original form, this Apocalypse can be read as a schematic summary of the Animal Apocalypse. There are no animals here, but in the account of the eighth week there is a close parallel to the temple scene at the close of the longer work:

---

[27] On this remarkable passage Nickelsburg writes (1 Enoch *1*, 407): 'With the universal transformation, the perennial enemies of Israel are eliminated, and the world returns to its created unity ... An unprecedented situation exists. All the bulls are white. There is no red bull to be slain or any black bull to slay him. The creation cannot go awry as it did with the first two beginnings.' The birth of the white bull 'triggers the transformation of the whole human race, Israelites and Gentiles, into primordial righteousness and perfection ... The closest analogy is in the two-Adams theology of the apostle Paul.'

[28] For other possible explanations see Nickelsburg, 1 Enoch *1*, 403.

And after this there shall be another week, the eighth, that of righteousness, and a sword shall be given to it so that righteous judgment may be executed on the oppressors, and the sinners will be delivered into the hands of the righteous. At its end they will acquire houses through their righteousness, and the house of the great king shall be built in glory for ever.

91.12–13

In contrast to the Animal Apocalypse, it is said here that the glorious house of the great king will be built *before* the final judgement, which will take place only in the following week, the ninth.[29] Christian readers of the Book of Enoch could then associate the building of the house not with the eschaton but with the incarnate life of Christ. Similarly, the Gärima image draws from the final scene of the Animal Apocalypse to create a symbolic representation not of the eschaton but of the gospel history. The house broad enough to accommodate the whole of redeemed humanity is the fourfold gospel.

The House of the Gospel

The eschatological temple of the Animal Apocalypse is not described in any detail. The text speaks only of pillars and ornaments (90.29); as we have seen, the Gärima artist has also drawn inspiration from the scriptural accounts of Solomon's temple for certain architectural features, and on the Book of Ezekiel for the streams of water flowing down from the threshold. Nevertheless, the unexpected presence of animals in a temple setting confirms that the Enochic scene is primary here. Given its context in a gospel book, at the close of the canon table sequence, the image must presuppose a strongly christological interpretation of the Enochic text. If the Gärima book dates from around the sixth century CE, as carbon dating and textual history suggest, we are unlikely to find contemporary evidence for such an interpretation from within Ethiopia itself. Aksumite culture was to some degree literate and literary, but there is no equivalent here to the mass of surviving patristic literature from the Greek, Latin and Syriac language areas. Yet broad exegetical traditions can survive for centuries. It is possible that echoes of the early Ethiopic reception of Enoch may still be perceptible in a collection of homilies commissioned and authorized by Zär'a Ya'əqob, a king belonging to the so-called 'Solomonic' dynasty who ruled from 1434 to 1468.[30] In these homilies, passages from different parts of Enoch are extensively cited and the book's canonical status is defended.

The collection is entitled the *Mäṣḥäfä Milad*, the 'Book of the Nativity', and the homilies are meant to be preached on the penultimate day of every month, when Christ's birth was celebrated.[31] The tone is generally polemical, and favoured targets

---

[29] 'And after this in the ninth week the righteous judgment will be revealed to the whole world, and all the deeds of the wicked will depart from the whole earth. And the world will be written down for destruction, and all people will look to the straight paths' (91.14).

[30] On Zär'a Ya'əqob, see *EAe* 5.146–50 and literature cited there.

[31] K. Wendt, *Das Mäṣḥāfa Milād (Liber Nativitatis) und Mäṣḥāfa Sellāsē (Liber Trinitatis) des Kaisers Zar'a Yā'qob* (henceforth *MM*) (CSCO, Scriptores Aethiopici 41, 43 (Ge'ez text), 42, 44 (German translation); Louvain: Peeters, 1962–3).

include Christians who hold a tritheistic version of the doctrine of the Trinity and Jews who deny the divinity and messiahship of Jesus. These rhetorical opponents are frequently addressed directly. A long citation from 1 Enoch 71.12–17 is introduced with the apostrophe,

> Hear, O Jew, from the prophet Enoch what he prophesied about Jesus Christ, son of Mary and Son of God![32]

At the conclusion of the citation, the scope of the address is broadened:

> Hear, O man, whether you are a Christian or whether you are a Jew: you cannot contradict Enoch! For he prophesied before all other prophets in the world, before all those who prophesied Christ's birth from Mary doubly Virgin and also his baptism and his epiphany, his death and his resurrection and his ascension and his session at the right hand of the Father...[33]

Enoch, then, is valued as the proto-prophet, and indeed 'the first of the prophets' is a standard epithet.[34] The homilist acknowledges that there are some who dispute Enoch's status, but he refutes them vigorously.[35] Enoch is affirmed by the Law, where it is said that he 'pleased God and was no longer seen, because the Lord took him' (Gen 5.24).[36] Moses' succinct statement summarizes Enoch's own testimony as to how he had been 'carried off by a whirlwind' (1 Enoch 52.1; cf. 14.8) and how no one knew what had happened to him (1 Enoch 12.1). Enoch's canonical status is also confirmed by the apostles, who speak of him as 'the seventh from Adam' (Jude 14, citing 1 Enoch 60.8 [cf. 93.3]) and who appeal to his visionary account of the Lord's coming in judgement (Jude 14–15, citing 1 Enoch 1.9).[37] Further impressive endorsements of Enoch and his prophetic book are found in the Book of Jubilees.[38] Enoch's messianic prophecies are closely associated with his comprehensive account of time – time in its entirety, from creation to eschaton, but also the years, months and days that make up time's individual units. For the homilist, there would be no liturgical year without Enoch, and in that sense one cannot be a Christian or a Jew without him.[39] The book is like rain falling upon thirsty ground; the world could not exist without it.[40] The book is as essential as the sun itself, without which the world would be plunged into darkness.[41]

---

[32] *MM* I, 62.14–15. References are to the first or second volume of Wendt's Ge'ez text with page and line numbers. The pagination of these volumes is noted in the margins of the German ones.
[33] *MM* I, 63.4–9.
[34] *henok qadāmihomu lanabiyāt, MM* I, 14.14; 123.15. Repeated reference is also made to 'the prophet Enoch who ascended in a whirlwind' (*nabəy zaʿārga banako[r]kʷāra*), I, 53.12–13; 122.24; cf. 1 Enoch14.8; 52.1). The two epithets are combined at *MM* II, 81.23.
[35] Extended defences of the Book of Enoch are found at *MM* I, 66.5–67.25; II, 101.4–103.14.
[36] *MM* I, 66.6–8.
[37] *MM* I, 66.8–17, where reference is also made to the apostolic *Didaskalia*.
[38] *MM* I, 66.17–67.15.
[39] *MM* I, 67.15–22.
[40] *MM* II, 101.4–11.
[41] *MM* II, 103.8–10.

Two main sections of Enoch's book are interpreted christologically in these homilies: (i) the second and third of the Parables (1 Enoch 45–59, 60–64); (ii) the Animal Apocalypse (1 Enoch 85–90) together with the displaced conclusion of the Apocalypse of Weeks (1 Enoch 91.12–17).

(i) In the course of the fourth homily of this series, an extensive passage from Enoch's second Parable is quoted in full (46.1–51.5), along with a substantial part of the third (62.1–17).[42] At various points the text evokes a christological interpretation from the homilist. The second Parable begins with a vision of the Danielic Ancient of Days, accompanied by another, a human figure identified by the interpreting angel as 'the Son of man who has righteousness and with whom righteousness dwells' (1 Enoch 46.1, 3). On the Day of Judgement there will be no help for the unrighteous, 'for they denied the Lord of spirits and his Messiah' (1 Enoch 48.10): that is, according to the homilist's gloss, Jesus Christ.[43] When, similarly, the ancient prophet tells how 'the Chosen One will sit on his throne, and all the secrets of wisdom will flow out from the counsel of his mouth' (1 Enoch 51.3), the homilist explains that 'the Chosen One, as the prophet Enoch calls him, is Christ'.[44]

The application to Jesus of passages speaking of a Son of man, Messiah, or Chosen One alongside God is virtually inevitable if the reader is a Christian who accepts Enoch's scriptural authority. Such passages as these are no doubt in Tertullian's mind when – like the later Ethiopic homilist – he defends Enoch's canonical status against Jewish rejection of this book. It is, Tertullian claims, precisely because Enoch speaks of Christ that it is rejected by Jews. For the same reason, Christians should accept his authority: 'Enoch in this same writing speaks of the Lord, and nothing at all should be rejected by us that pertains to us.'[45] For the same reason, Christians should accept it. Like the homilies, Tertullian provides further support for this claim by appealing to the testimony of the apostle Jude.[46] In its christological and polemical orientation, the fifteenth-century Ethiopic reading of Enoch has a prior history extending back for more than a millenium.

(ii) Developing an otherwise traditional exegetical argument about the presence of the Trinity in the Old Testament, the Ethiopic homilies call for support upon the Books of Jubilees and of Enoch. Jubilees features the august figure of the 'Angel of the Presence', and there is a comparable figure in the Enochic Animal Apocalypse, where the exalted 'Lord of the sheep' appears in glory to defeat his enemies at the Red Sea and to instruct his flock at Mount Sinai (1 Enoch 89.17–30, cited in full).[47] According to the homilist, the Angel of the Presence and the Lord of the sheep are one and the same: no created

---

[42] *MM* I, 54.26–58.11; 59.17–60.27.
[43] *MM* I, 57.8–9.
[44] *MM* I, 58.6–7.
[45] *de cul. fem.* iii.2: Sed cum Enoch eadem scriptura etiam de domino praedicarit, a nobis quidem nihil omnino reiciendum est quod pertineat ad nos. (*Tertullien, la toilette des femmes*, Sources Chrétiennes 173, ed. Marie Turcan, Paris: Cerf, 1971).
[46] *de cul. fem.* iii.2: Eo accedit quod Enoch apud Iudam apostolum testimonium possidet.
[47] *MM* II, 81.22–82.25.

being, but 'the Son' who is 'God from God'.[48] Here, too, Enoch (the first of the prophets) speaks of the one who was to become flesh of a pure virgin.[49] It follows that the eschatological temple with which the Animal Apocalypse ends will be the dwelling-place of Christ, the Lord of the sheep. For Christian readers, this will not be a literal temple, built on the site of Solomon's temple and its inferior post-exilic successor. The 'new house' established by the Lord of the sheep will refer instead to one aspect or another of the spiritual reality created by Christ.

In the *Epistle of Barnabas*, the author quotes with approval from the Enochic account of the destruction of the temple, when the Lord of the sheep abandoned his flock and his 'tower' to the onslaught of the wild animals (1 Enoch 89.55–56):

> For the scripture says, 'And it shall come to pass in the last days that the Lord will hand over the sheep of his pasture and the sheepfold and their tower to destruction'.
>
> *Barn.* 16.5

For this author, the Enochic text speaks of the events of 70 CE, far more important for Christian readers than the destruction of Solomon's temple centuries earlier. The question now arises of a new temple, and at this point the author turns to the Apocalypse of Weeks:

> Let us inquire whether there is a temple of God. There is indeed, one that he himself says he will make and perfect. For it is written, 'And it shall come to pass when the week is ended that a temple of God will be built gloriously, in the name of the Lord'.
>
> *Barn.* 16.6

The author here cites freely from the Enochic account of the eighth week, at the end of which 'a house will be built for the great king in glory for ever' (1 Enoch 91.13). For Barnabas, Enoch's prophecy of a new temple is fulfilled in the Christian prophet whose heart is the dwelling-place of God.[50]

The Ethiopic homilist understands the new temple of the eighth week differently, in a manner that approximates to the intention of the Gärima image. In contrast to Barnabas's selective and inaccurate citations, he quotes the Enochic passage about the eighth week in full before adding his interpretation of it:

> 'And after this there shall be an eighth week, that of righteousness, and a sword shall be given to it so that judgment and justice may be executed on the oppressors, and the sinners will be delivered into the hands of the righteous. At its end they will acquire houses through their righteousness, and the house of the great king shall be built in glory for ever.' This is the time of Christ, when according to Enoch a new sword shall be given to us Christians and the House of glory is built, the

---

[48] *MM* II, 81.20–21.
[49] *MM* II, 81.18–23.
[50] *Barn.* 16.7–10.

House of the Gospel [*bet wangəl*]. The Jewish temple he does not enter, nor does he see it, but he turns away from it.[51]

If the animals in the Gärima image represent the redeemed humanity of the Animal Apocalypse, the temple itself represents 'the House of the Gospel'. The homilist probably used this expression to refer to the place where the gospel is read and heard – that is, the church. For the Gärima artist, the House of the Gospel is the fourfold text itself, in which all may find a home and from which living water flows for them to drink.

---

[51] *MM* I, 53.18–25, citing 1 Enoch 91.12–13.

Afterword

Michael A. Knibb

This interesting and important collection of essays is focused on a number of apocryphal and pseudepigraphical writings[1] from the late Second Temple and Early Christian periods for which the version in Classical Ethiopic (Ge'ez) happens to provide the only, or a major source of, the textual evidence, and which raise a number of questions about relationships and interconnections – between theological ideas, between documents (including different versions of the same document), between canonical and non-canonical writings, and between Jewish and Christian texts.

The first five chapters are, to a greater or lesser extent, concerned with 1 Enoch and Jubilees. There is much of interest in these essays, and much with which one would agree; but they also illustrate some of the unresolved problems in making use of this material, particularly the disparity between the fact that 1 Enoch and Jubilees are in origin Jewish documents, but the great bulk of the textual evidence is Christian. Western scholarship has primarily been concerned to interpret 1 Enoch and Jubilees as Jewish documents that may be compared with the more or less contemporary New Testament writings, and the discovery at Qumran of the Aramaic fragments of Enoch and the Hebrew fragments of Jubilees seemingly confirmed the correctness of this view. One consequence of this has been that scholars have found it difficult to resist the temptation to fill out the substantial gaps in the Qumran fragments of Enoch and Jubilees on the basis of the Greek evidence for Enoch and the Ethiopic evidence for Enoch and Jubilees, and to treat the resultant reconstructions as if they represented the original Jewish text.[2] But there are differences between the fragments from Qumran and the later Greek and Ethiopic texts,[3] and in any case each version needs to be treated separately in the first instance and to be read and interpreted in its own theological context – in the case of the Ethiopic 1 Enoch and Jubilees, as part of the biblical canon

---

[1] The terms 'apocryphal' and 'pseudepigraphical' need unpacking and explaining, but I use them here as a matter of convenience.
[2] I note in contrast James Hamrick's decision to 'engage with the Ethiopic text, making use of VanderKam's critical Ethiopic text, rather than relying on the heavily reconstructed Hebrew fragments from Qumran'.
[3] Cf. Michael A. Knibb, '*The Book of Enoch* or *Books of Enoch*? The Textual Evidence for 1 Enoch', in *Essays on the Book of Enoch and other Early Jewish Texts and Traditions* (Studia in Veteris Testamenti Pseudepigrapha 22; Leiden: Brill, 2009), 36–55, particularly 43–4, 54–5.

of the Ethiopian Orthodox Täwaḥədo Church.[4] There clearly is a problem here, in that it makes no sense to ignore the evidence of the later Greek and Ethiopic versions in the restoration and interpretation of the Aramaic and Hebrew fragments or for the purposes of comparison with New Testament material. But in comparing, say, a passage in the New Testament with one in Enoch or Jubilees, it needs always to be borne in mind that the New Testament evidence and the evidence of Enoch and Jubilees are not on the same footing.

These issues are addressed directly by Loren Stuckenbruck, the editor of the new edition of the Ethiopic Enoch in preparation in Munich. He discusses the textual evidence for four passages from across the length of 1 Enoch in an attempt to establish some principles for distinguishing between Jewish and Christian elements in the text. His conclusions are very helpful for clarifying the distinctions that need to be made in the textual and exegetical study of the text, particularly the second conclusion that he believes is highlighted by his analysis: 'the need to distinguish between text-criticism within the Ge'ez itself, and text-criticism that more broadly (and eclectically) attempts to recover a non-Christian Jewish text-tradition from the Second Temple period.'[5] It is a distinction that has not always been made in editions of, and commentaries on, 1 Enoch.

The question of a proper method for employing texts such as 1 Enoch or Jubilees in relation to the New Testament forms the focus of the chapter by Logan Williams and is also raised in the chapters by Sofanit Abebe and James Hamrick. Logan Williams provides a very important critique of much recent, and indeed older, work on the Son of Man, which has been dominated by the view that the Son of Man figure in the Synoptic Gospels is dependent on that in the Parables (Similitudes) of Enoch. Inspired by Samuel Sandmel's classic paper 'Parallelomania', Williams maintains that the arguments used to support the idea of dependence are methodologically flawed and involve a misinterpretation of the evidence, and he suggests that the presentation of the Son of Man in the Gospels and the presentation in the Parables represent alternative reinterpretations of the Son of Man figure in Daniel 7 that can be brought into dialogue with one another. The dialogical method he proposes is surely correct. It offers the possibility of exploring differences as well as similarities between the Synoptic Gospels and the Parables, and also of bringing other texts into consideration, notably in this instance 4 Ezra 11–12, 13. The method is helpful whatever date is finally assigned to the Parables or to the Synoptic Gospels.

Sofanit Abebe does not talk about a dialogical method, but speaks of the need for 'conversations' between the two texts with which she is concerned, 1 Enoch 91–108, particularly 1 Enoch 108, and 1 Peter. After noting that eschatological material from 1 Enoch has often been seen as a background to material in 1 Peter, and that in both texts suffering is seen as an adjunct to the pious life, she argues that there is a need for a thoroughgoing comparative analysis that would treat the material in 1 Enoch on a par

---

[4] Cf. the comments of James Hamrick in Section 3 of his paper 'Ethiopian Reception and its Implications'.
[5] Cf. Michael A. Knibb, 'Interpreting the *Book of Enoch*: Reflections on a Recently Published Commentary', in *Essays on the Book of Enoch*, 82–3.

with the New Testament text. She provides just such a comparative analysis of the eschatological perspectives of 1 Enoch 91–108 and 1 Peter and rightly sees this approach as making possible a more nuanced discussion of the Enochic material.

James Hamrick's chapter on the treatment of non-human animals in Ethiopic Jubilees is interesting because of his stated aim of experimenting with different ways of engaging with this book and of avoiding treating the text just as background for the New Testament or other texts. He first provides an analysis of the material in Jubilees relevant to his theme 'in its own right' and only then attempts to bring the material into 'creative conversation' with early Christian texts. He suggests, for example, that the Jerusalem decree (Acts 15.20, 29) is 'an especially interesting conversation partner for Jubilees'; it provides the impetus for productive discussion of the interpretation both of the passage in Acts and of the relevant passages in Jubilees.

Philip Esler is also concerned, but in a more conventional way, with the comparison of 1 Enoch with the New Testament in his discussion of the status of Israel and the nations at the end time in 1 Enoch, in Paul, and in Matthew. In relation to the much-discussed passage Matthew 25.31, he argues that similarities with 1 Enoch indicate use of that text or of other traditions very similar to it.

The complexity of the relationship between Jewish and Christian traditions is highlighted by Jan Dochhorn's interesting chapter on the trial of Isaiah in the Ascension of Isaiah. In common with most of those who have written on the Ascension in recent years, he rejects the view that the narrative of the Ascension incorporates a written Jewish source.[6] But he also rejects the view that the motive of the trial and martyrdom derives from Jewish traditions, and his argument here seems less certain. However, he does also accept that Judaism may still form the background to the Ascension of Isaiah and suggests that 'the specific profile of Manasseh in the Ascension of Isaiah indicates that the dominating – and mostly threatening – cultural power in the world of its author still may have been a kind of Judaism that was in conflict with Christians'.

The *Epistula Apostolorum* and the Apocalypse of Peter, discussed respectively by Darrell Hannah and Eric Beck, have a number of similarities with one another and are linked also by the Ethiopic textual evidence. Thus in the two Ethiopic manuscripts (out of the five textual witnesses) that contain the Apocalypse of Peter, Abbadianus 51 and Lake Ṭānā 35, both writings occur in a dossier of four documents, the *Epistula Apostolorum* in the second place in the dossier as the major part of a document entitled 'The Testament of our Lord and Saviour Jesus Christ ... in Galilee', the Apocalypse of Peter within a document in the third place in the dossier entitled 'The Second Coming of Christ and the Resurrection of the Dead'. The dossier also includes the *Testamentum Domini* and an Ethiopic writing entitled 'Description of the Mystery concerning the Judgment of the Sinners'. When the dossier is properly published it will be interesting to have more information about its origin and purpose in the Ethiopian context. In the present work, Darrell Hannah provides a nuanced discussion of the evidence in favour of the view that the *Vorlage* of the Ethiopic version of the *Epistula Apostolorum* was

---

[6] Cf. Michael A. Knibb, 'Isaianic Traditions in the Apocrypha and Pseudepigrapha', in *Essays on the Book of Enoch*, 292–303 (here 293).

Greek, and Eric Beck evaluates the relationship of the Ethiopic and Greek versions of the Apocalypse of Peter.

Both the *Epistula Apostolorum* and the Apocalypse of Peter are in the form of dialogues between Jesus and the disciples and date in origin from the second century, and both have passages that recall the Synoptic Gospels. But the work known as the *Ta'amməra Iyäsus* ('the Miracles of Jesus') is a complete gospel account, a retelling of the life of Jesus by means of a series of miracle stories. It is based primarily on the Arabic Apocryphal Gospel of John, but incorporates material from other sources, and Meron Gebreananaye provides a good account of the editorial principles at work in the formation of the work. It is much later in origin than the *Epistula Apostolorum* and the Apocalypse of Peter, and it was only translated into Ethiopic in the fourteenth century. It is extremely popular in Ethiopia, and its form – and relatively late date – raise the question of what a gospel was understood to be in the Ethiopian Church.

Francis Watson draws on Ethiopian Christological interpretations of the Book of Enoch (the Parables, the Vision of the Animals, the Apocalypse of Weeks) in his analysis of the image of the eschatological temple in Abba Garima III. He shows convincingly how, given its position at the end of a canon table sequence, the image of the temple must represent the fourfold gospel, the House of the Gospel to which all may come. His chapter provides a very fitting conclusion to this collection. But it is perhaps worth adding that these interesting contributions also show how much there is still worth doing in the study of this literature.

Bibliography

Acerbi, Antonio. *Serra Lignea. Studi sulla fortuna della Ascensione di Isaia*. Rome: Editrice A.V.E., 1984.
Achtemeier, Paul J. *1 Peter*. Minneapolis: Augsburg Fortress, 1996.
Allison, Dale C. *Testament of Abraham*. Commentaries on Early Jewish Literature. Berlin: Walter de Gruyter, 2003.
Andries, Aarde. 'The Infancy Gospel of Thomas: Allegory or Myth? Gnostic or Ebionite?' *Verbum et Ecclesia* 26 (2005): 826–850.
Barclay, John M. G. 'Constructing a Dialogue: 4 Ezra and Paul on the Mercy of God'. Pages 3–22 in *Anthropologie und Ethik im Frühjudentum und im Neuen Testament*. Edited by M. Konradt and E. Schläpfer. Wissenschaftliche Untersuchungen zum Neuen Testament 322. Tübingen: Mohr Siebeck, 2014.
Barrett, C.K. *A Critical and Exegetical Commentary on the Acts of the Apostles*. International Critical Commentary. 2 vols. London: Clark, 2010.
Barth, Fredrik. 'Introduction'. Pages 9–38 in *Ethnic Groups and Boundaries: The Social Organization of Culture Difference*. Edited by Fredrik Barth. London: George Allen and Unwin, 1969.
Barton, Carlin A. and Daniel Boyarin. *Imagine No Religion: How Modern Abstractions Hide Ancient Realities*. New York: Fordham University Press, 2016.
Bauckham, Richard. 'The Apocalypse of Peter: A Jewish Christian Apocalypse from the Time of Bar Kokhba'. Pages 160–258 in *The Fate of the Dead: Studies on the Jewish and Christian Apocalypses*. Supplements to Novum Testamentum 93. Leiden: Brill, 1998.
—. 'The Apocalypse of Peter: An Account of Research'. *ANRW* 25.6: 4712–50, Part 2, Principat 25.6. Edited by H. Temporini and W. Haase. New York: de Gruyter, 1988.
—. 'The Ascension of Isaiah: Genre, Unity and Date'. Pages 363–390 in *The Fate of the Dead: Studies on the Jewish and Christian Apocalypses*. Supplements to Novum Testamentum 93. Leiden: Brill, 1998.
Bausi, Alessandro. 'Towards a Re-Edition of the Ethiopic Dossier of the Apocalypse of Peter: A Few Remarks on the Ethiopic Manuscript Witnesses'. *Apocrypha* 27 (2016): 179–196.
Beck, Eric J. 'Perceiving the Mystery of the Merciful Son of God: An Analysis of the Purpose of the Apocalypse of Peter'. PhD diss., University of Edinburgh, 2018.
Beers, H. *The Followers of Jesus as the 'Servant': Luke's Model from Isaiah for the Disciples in Luke-Acts*. Library of New Testament Studies. London: T&T Clark, 2015.
Black, Matthew. *Apocalypsis Henochi Graece: Fragmenta Pseudepigraphorum quae Supersunt Graeca*. Leiden: Brill, 1970.
—. *The Book of Enoch or 1 Enoch: A New English Edition with Commentary and Textual Notes*. Studia in Veteris Testamenti Pseudepigraphica 7. Leiden: Brill, 1985.
Boccaccini, Gabriele. 'The Enoch Seminar at Camaldoli: Re-entering the Parables of Enoch in the Study of Second Temple Judaism and Christian Origins'. Pages 3–16 in *Enoch and the Messiah Son of Man: Revisiting the Book of Parables*. Edited by Gabriele Boccaccini. Grand Rapids: Eerdmans, 2007.

—. 'Finding a Place for the Parables of Enoch within Second Temple Jewish Literature'. Pages 263–289 in *Enoch and the Messiah Son of Man: Revisiting the Book of Parables*. Edited by Gabriele Boccaccini. Grand Rapids. Eerdmans, 2007.

—. 'Jesus the Messiah: Man, Angel, or God? The Jewish Roots of Early Christology'. *Annali di Scienze Religiose* 4 (2011): 193–220.

—. 'Forgiveness of Sins: An Enochic Problem, a Synoptic Answer'. Pages 153–167 in *Enoch and the Synoptic Gospels: Reminiscences, Allusion, Intertextuality*. Early Jewish Literature 44. Edited by Loren T. Stuckenbruck and Gabriele Boccaccini. Atlanta: Society of Biblical Literature, 2016.

Bock, Darrell. 'The Use of Daniel 7 in Jesus' Trial with Implications for his Self-Understanding'. Pages 78–100 in *Who is this Son of Man? The Latest Scholarship on a Puzzling Expression of the Historical Jesus*. Edited by Larry Hurtado and Paul Owen. London: T&T Clark, 2011.

Bockmuehl, Markus. *Ancient Apocryphal Gospels*. Interpretation. Louisville: Westminster John Knox Press, 2017.

Bouriant, Urbain. 'Fragments du texte grec du livre d'Enoch et de quelques écrits attribués à Saint-Pierre'. Pages 91–147 in *Mémoires publiés par les membres de la Mission archéologique française au Caire*. Paris: Ernest Leroux, 1892.

Boyarin, Daniel. 'How Enoch can Teach us About Jesus'. *Early Christianity* 2 (2011): 51–76.

Brita, Antonella. *I racconti tradizionali sulla seconda cristianizzazione dell'Etiopia: il ciclo agiografico dei nove santi*. Napoli: Istituto universitario orientale, 2010.

—. 'With the Saints Came the Manuscripts . . .'. *Manuscript of the Month* (2012). Cited 28 May 2018. Online: https://www.manuscript-cultures.uni-hamburg.de/mom/2012_11_mom_e.html.

Brock, Sebastian P. 'A Fragment of Enoch in Syriac'. *Journal of Theological Studies* 19 (1968): 626–631.

Buchholz, D. D. *Your Eyes Will Be Opened: A Study of the Greek (Ethiopic) Apocalypse of Peter*. Society of Biblical Literature Dissertation Series 97. Atlanta: Scholars Press, 1988.

Burch, Vacher. 'The Literary Unity of the Ascensio Isaiae'. *Journal of Theological Studies* 20 (1919): 17–23.

Burke, Tony. *Secret Scriptures Revealed: A New Introduction to the Christian Apocrypha*. Grand Rapids: Eerdmans, 2013.

Cameron, R. *The Other Gospels: Non-Canonical Gospel Texts*. Louisville: Westminster John Knox Press, 1982.

Caquot, Andre. 'Aperçu préliminaire sur le Maṣḥafa Ṭēfut de Gechen Amba'. *Annales d' Éthiopie* 1 (1955): 89–108.

Chaîne, M. *Catalogue des manuscripts éthiopiens de la Collection Antoine d'Abbadie*. Paris, 1912.

Charles, R. H. *The Ethiopic Version of the Book of Enoch*. Oxford: Clarendon, 1906.

—. '1 Enoch'. Pages 188–281 in *Apocrypha and Pseudepigrapha of the Old Testament in English, Volume 2: Pseudepigrapha*. Edited by R. H. Charles. Oxford: Clarendon Press, 1913.

Charlesworth, James H. 'Foreword'. Pages ix-xi in *The Parables of Enoch: A Paradigm Shift*. Jewish and Christian Texts 11. Edited by Darrell Bock and James H. Charlesworth. London: T&T Clark, 2013.

—. 'Preface: The Books of Enoch: *Status Quaestionis*'. Pages xiii–xvii in *The Parables of Enoch: A Paradigm Shift*. Jewish and Christian Texts 11. Edited by Darrell Bock and James H. Charlesworth. London: T&T Clark, 2013.

—. 'Did Jesus Know the Traditions in the *Parables of Enoch*? ΤΙΣ ΕΣΤΙΝ ΟΥΤΟΣ Ο ΥΙΟΣ ΤΟΥ ΑΝΘΡΩΠΟΥ; (Jn 12:34)'. Pages 173–217 in *The Parables of Enoch: A Paradigm Shift*. Jewish and Christian Texts 11. Edited by Darrell Bock and James H. Charlesworth. London: T&T Clark, 2013.
—. 'The Date and Provenience of the Parables of Enoch'. Pages 37–57 in *The Parables of Enoch: A Paradigm Shift*. Jewish and Christian Texts 11. Edited by Darrell Bock and James H. Charlesworth. London: T&T Clark, 2013.
Charlesworth, James H. and Darrell Bock. 'Conclusion'. Pages 364–72 in *The Parables of Enoch: A Paradigm Shift*. Jewish and Christian Texts 11. Edited by Darrell Bock and James H. Charlesworth. London: T&T Clark, 2013.
Chialà, Sabino. 'The Son of Man: The Evolution of an Expression'. Pages 153–178 in *Enoch and the Messiah Son of Man: Revisiting the Book of Parables*. Edited by Gabriele Boccaccini. Grand Rapids: Eerdmans, 2007.
Collins, A. Y. 'The Early Christian Apocalypses'. *Semeia 14: Apocalypse: The Morphology of a Genre*. Edited by John J. Collins. Atlanta: Society of Biblical Literature, 1979.
—. *Mark: A Commentary*. Hermeneia. Minneapolis: Fortress, 2007.
Collins, John J. 'Sibylline Oracles'. Pages 317–472 in *The Old Testament Pseudepigrapha, Volume 1: Apocalyptic Literature and Testaments*. Edited by James H. Charlesworth. New York: Doubleday, 1983.
—. 'Wisdom, Apocalypticism and Generic Compatibility'. Pages 165–185 in *In Search of Wisdom: Essays in Memory of John G. Gammie*. Edited by L. G Perdue, B. B. Scott, and W. J. Wiseman. Louisville: Westminster John Knox Press, 1993.
—. *Apocalypse, Prophecy, and Pseudepigraphy: On Jewish Apocalyptic Literature*. Grand Rapids: Eerdmans, 2015.
Cooper, J. and A. J. Maclean, *The Testament of our Lord: Translated into English from the Syriac with Introduction and Notes*. Edinburgh: T & T Clark, 1902.
Cowley, Roger W. 'The Ethiopic Work Which Is Believed to Contain the Material of the Ancient Greek Apocalypse of Peter'. *Journal of Theological Studies* 36 (1985): 151–153.
Crawford, Matthew R. 'Ammonius of Alexandria, Eusebius of Caesarea, and the Beginnings of Gospels Scholarship'. *New Testament Studies* 61 (2015): 1–29.
Daiber, T. '"Wisset!" Zu einem angeblichen Anakoluth in Mk 2,10 bzw. zum ὅτι recitativum'. *Zeitschrift für die neutestamentliche Wissenschaft und die Kunde der älteren Kirche* 104 (2013): 277–285.
Dalton, William J. *Christ's Proclamation to the Spirits: A Study of 1 Peter 3:18–4:6*. 2d edition. Analecta biblica 23. Rome: Pontifical Biblical Institute, 1989.
Davenport, Gene L. *The Eschatology of the Book of Jubilees*. Leiden: Brill, 1971.
Davies, Donald M. 'The Dating of Ethiopic Manuscripts'. *Journal of Near Eastern Studies* 46 (1987): 287–307.
Davila, James R. '(How) Can We Tell if a Greek Apocryphon or Pseudepigraphon Has Been Translated from Hebrew or Aramaic?'. *Journal for the Study of the Pseudepigrapha* 15 (2005): 3–61.
—. *The Provenance of the Pseudepigrapha: Jewish, Christian, or Other?* Supplements to the Journal for the Study of Judaism 105. Leiden: Brill, 2005.
DeSilva, David A. 'The *Testaments of the Twelve Patriarchs* as Witnesses to Pre-Christian Judaism: A Reassessment'. *Journal for the Study of te Pseudepigrapha* 23 (2013): 21–68.
Dibelius, Martin. *Die Geisterwelt im Glauben des Paulus*. Göttingen: Vandenhoeck & Ruprecht, 1909.
Dillmann, August. *Catalogus Codicum Manuscriptorum qui in Museo Britannico Asservantur, Pars Tertia: Codices Aethiopicos Amplectens*. London, 1847.

—. *Veteris Testamenti Aethiopici, Tomus I: Octateuchus Aethiopicus*. Leipzig: Vogelius, 1853.

Dochhorn, Jan. 'Die Menschen als "Kinder der Mutter der Lebenden"—eine etymologische Parallele zu êm kol-chaj in Gen 3,20 aus dem Altäthiopischen'. *Zeitschrift für Althebraistik* 12 (1999): 2–20.

—. 'Die Ascensio Isaiae (JSHRZ II,1: Martyrium Jesajas)'. Pages 1–48 in *Unterweisung in erzählender Form: Mit Beiträgen von J. Dochhorn, B. Ego, M. Meiser und O. Merk*. Edited by G. S. Oegema. Jüdische Schriften aus hellenistisch-römischer Zeit 6.1.2. Gütersloh: Gütersloher Verlagshaus, 2005.

—. 'Menschenschöpfung und urzeitlicher Teufelsfall in Überlieferungen der Falascha: Der erste Teil von Teezâza Sanbat in der von Halévy veröffentlichten Version'. Pages 193–224 in *The Other Side: Apocryphal Perspective on Ancient Christian "Orthodoxies"*. Edited by Tobias Nicklas, Candida R. Moss, and Joseph Verheyden. Novum Testamentum et Orbis Antiquus / Studien zur Umwelt des Neuen Testaments 117. Göttingen: Vandenhoeck & Ruprecht, 2017.

Donadoni, Sergio. 'Un frammento della versione copta del "Libro di Enoch"'. *Acta orientalia* 25 (1960): 197–202.

Dryden, J. De Waal. *Theology and Ethics in 1 Peter: Paraenetic Strategies for Christian Character Formation*. Wissenschaftliche Untersuchungen zum Neuen Testament 2.209. Tübingen: Mohr Siebeck, 2006.

Dubis, Mark. *Messianic Woes in First Peter: Suffering and Eschatology in 1 Peter 4:12–19*. Studies in Biblical Literature 33. New York: Peter Lang, 2002.

—. *1 Peter: A Handbook on the Greek Text*, Baylor Handbook on the Greek New Testament. Waco: Baylor University Press, 2010.

Duensing, H. *Epistula Apostolorum*. Kleine Texte 152. Bon: Marcus & Weber, 1925.

Duensing, Hugo. 'Ein Stücke der urchristlichen Petrusapokalypse enthaltender Traktat der äthiopischen Pseudoklementinischen Literatur'. *Zeitschrift für die neutestamentliche Wissenschaft* 14 (1913): 65–78.

Duensing, Hugo and Christian Maurer. 'Apocalypse of Peter'. Pages 663–683 in *New Testament Apocrypha, Volume 2*. Edited by Wilhelm Schneemelcher and Robert McL. Wilson. London: Lutterworth, 1965.

Dunn, James D. G. *Christology in the Making: A New Testament Inquiry into the Origins of the Doctrine of the Incarnation*. Philadelphia: Westminster Press, 1980.

—. 'The Son of Man in Mark', *The Parables of Enoch: A Paradigm Shift*. Jewish and Christian Texts 11. Edited by Darrell Bock and James H. Charlesworth London: T&T Clark, 2013.

Ehrensperger, Kathy. 'The Pauline Ἐκκλησίαι and Images of Community in Enoch Traditions'. Pages 183–216 in *Paul the Jew: Rereading the Apostle as a Figure of Second Temple Judaism*. Edited by Gabriele Boccaccini and Carlos A. Segovia. Minneapolis: Fortress, 2016.

Elliott, John H. *1 Peter: A New Translation with Introduction and Commentary*. Anchor Bible 37B. New York: Doubleday, 2000.

Endres, John C. 'Prayer of Noah: Jubilees 10.3-6'. Pages 53–58 in *Prayer from Alexander to Constantine: A Critical Anthology*. Edited by Mark Kiley. London: Routledge, 1997.

Erho, Ted. 'The Ahistorical Nature of 1 Enoch 56:5-8 and its Ramifications upon the Opinio Communis on the Dating of the Similitudes of Enoch'. *Journal for the Study of Judaism in the Persian, Hellenistic, and Roman Periods* 40 (2009): 23–54.

—. 'Internal Dating Methodologies and the Problem Posed by the Similitudes of Enoch'. *Journal for the Study of the Pseudepigrapha* 20 (2010): 83–103.

—. 'Historical-Allusion Dating and the Similitudes of Enoch'. *Journal of Biblical Literature* 130 (2011): 493–511.
Esler, Philip F. *God's Court and Courtiers: Re-interpreting Heaven in 1 Enoch*. Eugene: Cascade. 2017.
Esler, Philip F. and Angus Pryor, 'Painting 1 Enoch: Biblical Interpretation, Theology, and Artistic Practice', *Biblical Theology Bulletin* 50/3 (2020): 136–153.
Falk, Daniel K., Florentino Garcia Martinez, and Eileen M. Schuller, eds. *Sapiential, Liturgical and Poetical Texts from Qumran: Proceedings of the Third Meeting of the International Organization for Qumran Studies, Oslo 1998*. Studies on the Texts of the Desert of Judah 35. Leiden: Brill, 2000.
Finneran, N. '(Town of) Lalibäla'. Pages 482–9 in *Encyclopaedia Aethiopica, Volume 3*. Edited by S. Uhlig et al. Wiesbaden: Harrassowitz, 2007.
Fletcher-Louis, Crispin H. T. *Jesus Monotheism, Volume 1: Christological Origins, The Emerging Consensus, and Beyond*. Eugene: Wipf & Stock, 2015.
Fredriksen, Paula. 'Judaism, the Circumcision of Gentiles, and Apocalyptic Hope: Another Look at Galatians 1 and 2'. *Journal of Theological Studies* 42 (1991): 532–564.
—. 'The Question of Worship: Gods, Pagans, and the Redemption of Israel'. Pages 175–201 in *Paul Within Judaism: Restoring the First-Century Context to the Apostle*. Edited by Mark D. Nanos and Magnus Zetterholm. Minneapolis: Fortress, 2015.
—. 'How Jewish is God? Divine Ethnicity in Paul's Theology'. *Journal of Biblical Literature* 137 (2018): 193–212.
Friedmann, Meir, ed. *Pesikta Rabbati: Midrasch für den Fest-Cyclus und die ausgezeichneten Sabbathe. Nebst einem Lexikon der vorkommenden griechischen und lateinischen Fremdworte von Moritz Güdemann*. Vienna, 1880.
Galling, Kurt. 'Jesaja-Adonis'. *Orientalistische Literaturzeitung* 33 (1930): 98–102.
Gaster, M. and B. Heller. 'Beiträge zur vergleichenden Sagen- und Märchenkunde 7. Der Prophet Jesajah und der Baum. Jüdische Baumsagen'. *Monatsschrift für Geschichte und Wissenschaft des Judentums* 80 (1936): 32–52.
Geerard, M. *Clavis Apocryphorum Novi Testamenti*. Turnhout: Brepols, 1992.
Gerö, Stephen. 'THE TA'ĀMRA 'ĪYASŪS: A Study of Textual and Source-Critical Problems'. Pages 165–170 in *Proceedings of the Eight International Conference of Ethiopian Studies*. Edited by Taddese Beyene. Addis Ababa: Institute of Ethiopian Studies, 1988.
Gieschen, C. A. *Angelomorphic Christology: Antecedents and Early Evidence*. Arbeiten zur Geschichte des antiken Judentums und des Urchristentums 42. Leiden: Brill, 1998.
Gilhus, Sælid. *Animals, Gods and Humans: Changing Attitudes to Animals in Greek, Roman and Early Christian Ideas*. London: Routledge, 2006.
Ginzberg, Louis. 'Die Haggada bei den Kirchenvätern, erster Theil: Die Haggada in den pseudo-hieronymianischen "Quaestiones"'. PhD Diss., Heidelberg/Amsterdam. 1899.
Gitlbauer. M. *Die Überreste griechischer Tachygraphie im Codex Vaticanus Graecus 1809*. Denkschriften der Kaiserlichen Akademie der Wissenschaften philosophisch-historische Klasse 28.2. Vienna: Gerold, 1878.
Goldschmidt, Lazarus, ed. and trans. *Der Babylonische Talmud mit Einschluss der vollständigen Mišnah, Vierter Band: Jabmuth, Kethuboth, Nedarim*. Leipzig: Harrassowitz, 1922.
Graf, G. *Geschichte der christlichen arabischen Literatur*. Studi e testi 118. Vatican City: Biblioteca Apostolica Vaticana, 1944.

Gray, S. W. *The Least of My Brothers: Matthew 25:31-46: A History of Interpretation*. Society of Biblical Literature Dissertation Series 114. Atlanta: Scholars Press, 1989.

Grébaut, S., ed. and trans. *Les trois derniers traités du Livre des mystères du ciel et de la terre*. Patrilogia Orientalis 6.3. Paris: Firmin-Didot, 1911.

—. 'Littérature éthiopienne pseudo-clémentine'. *Revue de l'Orient chrétien* 15 (1910): 198–214, 307–323, 425–439.

Guerrier L., with the assistance of S. Grébaut. *Le testament en galilée de notre-seigneur Jésus-Christ: Texte éthiopien, édité et traduit en Français*. Pages 141–236 in *Patrilogia Orientalis, Tomes Nones*. Paris, 1913.

Gundry, Robert H. *Matthew: A Commentary on His Literary and Theological Art*. Grand Rapids: Eerdmans, 1982.

Hagner, Donald A. *Matthew 14–28*. Word Biblical Commentary 33B. Dallas: Word Books, 1995.

Hahne, Harry Alan. *The Corruption and Redemption of Creation: Nature in Romans 8:19-22 and Jewish Apocalyptic Literature*. Library of New Testament Studies 336. New York: T&T Clark, 2006.

Haile, Getachew. *A Catalogue of Ethiopian Manuscripts microfilmed for the Ethiopian Manuscript Microfilm Library, Addis Ababa, and for the Hill Monastic Manuscript Library, Collegeville, Volume 2*. Collegeville: St John's Abbey and University, 1976.

—. 'The Legend of Abgar in Ethiopic Tradition'. *Orientalia Christiana Periodica* 55 (1989): 375–410.

Halévy, J. *Tĕ'ĕzâza Sanbat (Commandement du Sabbat), accompagné de six autres écrits pseudo-épigraphiques admis par les Falachas ou Juifs d'Abyssinie*. Paris, 1902.

Hammerschmidt, Ernst *Äthiopische Handschriften vom Ṭānāsee 1: Reisebericht und Beschreibung der Handschriften in dem Kloster des Heiligen Gabriel auf der Insel Kebrān*. Wiesbaden: Steiner Verlag. 1973.

Hamrick, James R. 'No Faithful Oaths: A Comparison of Esau's Speech in *Jubilees* 37:18-23 with Achilles' Speech in *Iliad* 22.260-272'. MA thesis, Trinity Western University, 2014.

Harrington, Daniel J., S. J. *The Gospel of Matthew*. Sacra Pagina 2. Collegeville: Liturgical Press, 1991.

Hartenstein, J. *Die Zweite Lehre: Erscheinungen des Auferstandenen als rahmenerzählungen frühchristlicher Dialoge*. Texte und Untersuchungen zur Geschichte der altchristlichen Literatur 146. Berlin: Akademie Verlag, 2000.

Hartman, Lars. 'The Functions of Some So-Called Apocalyptic Timetables'. *New Testament Studies* 22 (1975): 1–14.

Hays, Richard B. *Echoes of Scripture in the Letters of Paul*. New Haven: Yale University Press, 1989.

Heldman, Marilyn. 'Churches of Lalibäla,' Pages 484–489 in *Encyclopaedia Aethiopica, Volume 3*. Edited by S. Uhlig et al. Wiesbaden: Harrassowitz, 2007.

Heldman, Marilyn et al. *African Zion: The Sacred Art of Ethiopia*. New Haven & London: Yale University Press, 1993.

Helmer, Robert C. '"That We May Know and Understand": Gospel Tradition in the Apocalypse of Peter'. PhD diss., Marquette University, 1998.

Hempel, Charlotte, Armin Lange, and Hermann Lichtenberger, eds. *The Wisdom Texts from Qumran and the Development of Sapiential Thought*. Bibliotheca ephemeridum theologicarum lovaniensium 159. Leuven: Peeters, 2002.

Hill, J. V. *Tradition and Composition in the* Epistula Apostolorum. Cambridge, MA: Harvard University Press, 1990.

Hollander, Harm Wouter and Marinus de Jonge. *The Testaments of the Twelve Patriarchs. A Commentary*. Studia in Veteris Testamenti pseudepigraphica 6. Leiden: Brill, 1997.
Hornschuh, M. *Studien zur Epistula Apostolotum*. Patristische Texte und Studien 5. Berlin: De Gruyter, 1965.
Horrell, David G. and Wei Hsien Wan. 'Christology, Eschatology and the Politics of Time in 1 Peter'. *Journal for the Study of the New Testament* 38 (2016): 263-276.
Hubbard, Moyer V. *New Creation in Paul's Letters and Thought*. Society for New Testament Studies Monograph Series 119. Cambridge: Cambridge University Press, 2004.
Hurtado, Larry W. 'Summary and Concluding Observations'. Pages 159-177 in *Who is this Son of Man? The Latest Scholarship on a Puzzling Expression of the Historical Jesus*. Edited by Larry Hurtado and Paul Owen. London: T&T Clark, 2011.
Hutchinson, John and Anthony Smith, eds. *Ethnicity*. Oxford: Oxford University Press. 1996.
Isaac. E. '1 Enoch'. Pages 13-89 in *The Old Testament Pseudepigrapha, Volume 1: Apocalyptic Literature and Testaments*. Edited by James H. Charlesworth. New York: Doubleday, 1983.
James, M. R. *Apocrypha Anecdota. A Collection of Thirteen Apocryphal Books and Fragments*. Texts and Studies 2.3. Cambridge: Cambridge University Press, 1893.
—. 'Additional Notes on the Apocalypse of Peter'. *Journal of Theological Studies* 12 (1910): 157.
—. 'A New Text of the Apocalypse of Peter'. *Journal of Theological Studies* 12 (1911): 573-583.
—. 'The Recovery of the Apocalypse of Peter'. *Church Quarterly Review* 80 (1915): 1-36.
—. 'The Rainer Fragment of the Apocalypse of Peter'. *Journal of Theological Studies* 32 (1931): 270-79.
—. *The Apocryphal New Testament*. Oxford: Clarendon, 1953.
Kaplan, Steven. 'Te'ezáza Sanbat: A Beta Israel Work Reconsidered'. Pages 107-124 in *Gilgul: Essays on Transformation, Revolution and Permanence in the History of Religions Dedicated to R.J. Zwi Werblowsky*. Edited by Shaul Shaked, David Shulman, and Gedaljahu Stroumsa. Leiden: Brill, 1987.
Keener, Craig. *Acts*. 3 Vols. Grand Rapids: Baker Academic, 2014.
Kelly, J. N. D. *A Commentary on the Epistles of Peter and Jude*. Thornapple Commentaries. Grand Rapids: Baker, 1969.
Klauck, H.-J. *Apocryphal Gospels: An Introduction*. Translated by B. McNeil. London: T & T Clark, 2003.
Knibb, Michael A. *The Ethiopic Book of Enoch: A New Edition in Light of the Aramaic Dead Sea Fragments*. 2 vols. Oxford: Clarendon Press, 1978.
—. '1 Enoch'. Pages 184-319 in *The Apocryphal Old Testament*. Edited by H. F. D. Sparks. Oxford: Clarendon Press, 1984.
—. 'Hebrew and Syriac Elements in the Ethiopic Version of Enoch?' *Journal of Semitic Studies* 33 (1988): 11-35.
—. *Translating the Bible: The Ethiopic Version of the Old Testament*. Schweich Lectures. Oxford: Oxford University Press, 1999.
—. 'The Apocalypse of Weeks and the Epistle of Enoch'. Pages 213-219 in *Enoch and Qumran Origins: New Light on a Forgotten Connection*. Edited by Gabriele Boccaccini. Grand Rapids: Eerdmans, 2005.
—. 'Interpreting the *Book of Enoch*: Reflections on a Recently Published Commentary'. Pages 77-90 in *Essays on the Book of Enoch and other Early Jewish Texts and Traditions*. Edited by Michael A. Knibb. Studia in Veteris Testamenti Pseudepigrapha 22. Leiden. Brill, 2009.

—. 'Isaianic Traditions in the Apocrypha and Pseudepigrapha'. Pages 292–303 in *Essays on the Book of Enoch and other Early Jewish Texts and Traditions*. Edited by Michael A. Knibb. Studia in Veteris Testamenti Pseudepigrapha 22. Leiden: Brill, 2009.

—. 'The Book of Enoch or Books of Enoch? The Textual Evidence for 1 Enoch'. Pages 36–55 in *Essays on the Book of Enoch and other Early Jewish Texts and Traditions*. Edited by Michael A. Knibb. Studia in Veteris Testamenti Pseudepigrapha 22. Leiden: Brill, 2009.

Knight, Jonathan. *The Ascension of Isaiah*. Guides to the Apocrypha and Pseudepigrapha 2. Sheffield: Sheffield Academic, 1995.

Kraemer, Ross Shepard. *When Aseneth Met Joseph: A Late Antique Tale of the Biblical Patriarch and His Egyptian Wife*. Oxford: Clarendon, 1998.

Kraft, Robert A. 'The Pseudepigrapha in Christianity'. *Tracing the Thread: Studies in the Vitality of the Jewish Pseudepigrapha*. Edited by John C. Reeves. Early Judaism and Its Literature6. Atlanta: Scholars Press, 1994.

Kraus, Thomas J. and Tobias Nicklas, *Das Petrusevangelium und die Petrusapokalypse: Die griechischen Fragmente mit deutscher und englischer Übersetzung*. Berlin: de Gruyter, 2004.

Kuhn, Thomas S. *The Structure of Scientific Revolutions*. 4th edition. Chicago: University of Chicago Press, 2012.

Kvanvig, Helga S. 'The Son of Man in the Parables of Enoch'. Pages 179–215 in *Enoch and the Messiah Son of Man: Revisiting the Book of Parables*. Edited by Gabriele Boccaccini. Grand Rapids: Eerdmans, 2007.

Leicester, R. 'Exit the Apocalyptic Son of Man'. *New Testament Studies* 18 (1971–1972): 243–267.

Levin, B. *Die Griechisch-Arabische Evangelien-Übersetzung: Vatican Borg. Ar. 95 and Berlin Or. oct. 1108*. Uppsala: Almqvist & Wiksells, 1938.

Liebengood, Kelly D. *The Eschatology of 1 Peter: Considering the Influence of Zechariah 9–14*. Society for New Testament Studies Monograph Series 157. Cambridge: Cambridge University Press, 2014.

Linebaugh, J. A. 'Debating Diagonal Δικαιοσύνη: The Epistle of Enoch and Paul in Theological Conversation', *Early Christianity* 1 (2010): 107–128.

Lührmann, Dieter. 'Alttestamentliche Pseudepigraphen bei Didymos von Alexandrien'. *Zeitschrift für die alttestamentliche Wissenschaft* 104 (1992): 231–249.

Lundhaug, Hugo and Liv Ingeborg Lied. 'Studying Snapshots: On Manuscript Culture, Textual Fluidity, and New Philology'. Pages 1–19 in *Snapshots of Evolving Traditions*. Edited by Hugo Lundhaug and Liv Ingebord Lied. Texte und Untersuchungen zur Geschichte der altchristlichen Literatur 175. Berlin: Walter de Gruyter, 2017.

Lusini, Giangrancesco. 'Tradizione Origeniana in Etiopia'. Pages 1177–1184 in *Origeniana Octava: Origene e la Tradizione Alessandrina*. Edited by L. Perrone. Bibliotheca Ephemeridum Theologicarum Lovaniensium 164. Leuven: University Press, 2003.

Macaskill, Grant. 'Matthew and the *Parables of Enoch*'. Pages 173–217 in *The Parables of Enoch: A Paradigm Shift*. Jewish and Christian Texts 11. Edited by Darrell Bock and James H. Charlesworth. London: T&T Clark, 2013.

Macomber, William F. *Catalogue of Ethiopian Manuscripts from Abbā Garimā . . . from Microfilms in the Collection of Dr Donald Davies, De Land, Florida and Godfrey, Ontario, and of the Hill Monastic Manuscript Library, St John's University, Collegeville, Minnesota*. Collegeville, Minnesota: Privately reproduced.

Macus, J. *Mark 1–8: A New Translation with Introduction and Commentary*. Anchor Bible 27. New Haven: Yale University Press, 2002.

Marcus, H. G. *A History of Ethiopia*. 2d edition. Berkeley: University of California Press, 2002.

Marcus, J. 'Authority to Forgive Sins on Earth'. Pages 196–211 in *The Gospels and the Scriptures of Israel*. Edited by C. A. Evans and W. R. Stegner. Supplements to the Journal for the Study of the New Testament 104. Studies in Scripture in Early Judaism and Christianity 3. Sheffield: Sheffield Academic, 1994.

Marmardji, A.-J. *Diatessaron de Tatien*. Beirut: Imprimerie Catholique, 1935.

Marrassini, Paolo. 'L'Apocalisse di Pietro'. Pages 171–232. *Etiopia e oltre: Studi in onore di Lanfranco Ricci*. Edited by Y. Beyene et al. Studi Africanistici, Serie Etiopica 1. Napoli: Istituto Orientale di Napoli, Dipartimento di Studi e Ricerche su Africa e Paesi Arabi, 1994.

Martínez, F. García, ed. *Wisdom and Apocalypticism in the Dead Sea Scrolls and in the Biblical Tradition*. Bibliotheca ephemeridum theologicarum lovaniensium 168. Leuven: Peeters, 2003.

Mathews, Mark D. *Riches, Poverty, and the Faithful: Perspectives on Wealth in the Second Temple Period and the Apocalypse of John*. Society for New Testament Studies Monograph Series 154. Cambridge: Cambridge University Press, 2013.

McDonald, L. M. 'The *Parables of Enoch* in Early Christianity'. Pages 329–363 in *The Parables of Enoch: A Paradigm Shift*. Jewish and Christian Texts 11. Edited by Darrell Bock and James H. Charlesworth. London: T&T Clark, 2013.

McKenzie, Judith S., Francis Watson, Michael Gervers, eds. *The Garima Gospels. Early Illuminated Gospel Books from Ethiopia*. Manar Al Athar-Monographs 3. Oxford: Manar Al Athar. 2016.

Michaels, J. Ramsey. *1 Peter*. Word Biblical Commentary 49. Waco: Word Books, 1988.

Milik, J. T. *The Books of Enoch: Aramaic Fragments from Qumrân Cave 4*. Oxford: Clarendon. 1976.

Mingana, A. *Woodbrooke Studies*. Cambridge: W. Heffer & Sons, 1931.

Moreschini, C. and E. Norelli, *Early Christian Greek and Latin Literature: A Literary History*. 2 Vols. Translated by M. J. O'Connell. Peabody: Hendrickson, 2005.

Munro-Hay, S. *Aksum: An African Civilisation of Late Antiquity*. Edinburgh: University of Edinburgh Press, 1991.

Najman, Hindy. *Seconding Sinai: The Development of Mosaic Discourse in Second Temple Judaism*. Supplements to the Journal for the Study of Judaism 77. Leiden: Brill, 2003.

Nanos, Mark D. 'Introduction'. Pages 1–29 in *Paul Within Judaism: Restoring the First-Century Context to the Apostle*. Edited by Mark D. Nanos and Magnus Zetterholm. Minneapolis: Fortress, 2015.

Nanos, Mark D. and Magnus Zetterholm, eds. *Paul Within Judaism: Restoring the First-Century Context to the Apostle*. Minneapolis: Fortress Press, 2015.

Nickelsburg, George W. E. 'The Nature and Function of Revelation in 1 Enoch, Jubilees, and Some Qumranic Documents'. Pages 91–119 in *Pseudepigraphic Perspectives: The Apocrypha and Pseudepigrapha in Light of the Dead Sea Scrolls*. Edited by Esther G. Chazon and Michael E. Stone in collaboration with Avital Pinnick. Studies on the Texts of the Desert of Judah 31. Leiden: Brill, 1999.

Nickelsburg, George W. E. *1 Enoch 1: A Commentary on the Book of 1 Enoch: Chapters 1–36, 81–108*. Hermeneia: Minneapolis: Fortress, 2001.

Nickelsburg, George W. E. and James C. VanderKam, *1 Enoch 2: A Commentary on the Book of 1 Enoch: Chapters 37–82*. Hermeneia. Minneapolis. Fortress, 2012.

Nickelsburg, George W. E. and James C. VanderKam. *1 Enoch: A New Translation Based on the Hermeneia Commentary*. Minneapolis: Fortress, 2004.

Nickelsburg, George W. E. and James C. Vanderkam. *1 Enoch: The Hermeneia Translation*. Minneapolis: Fortress, 2012.

Nolland, John. *The Gospel of Matthew: A Commentary on the Greek Text.* Grand Rapids: Eerdmans, 2005.
Nongbri, Brent. *Before Religion: A History of a Modern Concept.* New Haven: Yale University Press, 2015.
Nordenfalk, Carl. *Die spätantiken Kanontafeln: Kunstgeschichtliche Studien über die eusebianische Evangelien-Konkordanz in den vier ersten Jahrhunderten ihrer Geschichte.* Göteborg: Oscar Isacsons Boktryckeri, 1938.
Nosnitsin, Denis. 'Dərsanä Sänbät'. Pages 141–142 in *Encyclopaedia Aethiopica, Volume 2.* Edited by S. Uhlig et al. Wiesbaden: Harrassowitz, 2007.
Norelli, Enrico. 'Pierre, le visionnaire: la réception de l'épisode de la transfiguration en 2 Pierre et dans l'Apocalypse de Pierre'. *Foi Vie* 106.4 (2007): 19–43.
Olson, Daniel C. *A New Reading of the* Animal Apocalypse *of 1 Enoch: "All Nations Shall be Blessed".* Studia in Veteris Testamenti Pseudepigrapha 24. Leiden: Brill, 2013.
Olson, Daniel C., in consultation with Archbishop Melkesedek Workeneh. *Enoch: A New Translation.* North Richmond Hills: Bibal Books, 2004.
Origen, *Homilies on Luke.* Translated by Joseph T. Lienhard. Washington, D. C.: Catholic University of America Press, 1995.
Origen, *On First Principles.* Translated by G. W. Butterworth. Notre Dame: Ave Maria, 2013.
Owen, Paul. 'Aramaic and Greek Representations of the "Son of Man" and the Importance of the Parables of Enoch'. Pages 114–123 in *The Parables of Enoch: A Paradigm Shift.* Jewish and Christian Texts 11. Edited by Darrell Bock and James H. Charlesworth. London: T&T Clark, 2013.
Pate, Marvin and Douglas W. Kennard. *Deliverance Now and Not Yet: The New Testament and the Great Tribulation.* Studies in Biblical Literature 54. New York: Peter Lang, 2003.
Pérès, J.-N. *L'Épître des Apôtres et le Testament de notre Seigneur et notre Jésus-Christ.* Turnhout: Brepols, 1994.
Perrone, Lorenzo. 'Ascensione di Isaia profeta: Versione etiopica'. Pages 45–129 in *Ascensio Isaiae: Textus.* Translated by Enrico Norelli. Edited by Paolo Bettiolo. Corpus Christianorum, Series Apocryphorum 7. Turnhout: Brepols, 1995.
Perruchon, J. and I. Guidi, eds. and trans. *Le Livre des mystères du ciel et de la terre.* Patrilogia Orientalis 1.1 Paris: Firmin-Didot, 1903
Phillipson, D. W. *Ancient Ethiopia. Aksum: Its Antecedents and Successors.* London: British Museum Press, 1998.
—. *Ancient Churches of Ethiopia: Fourth – Fourteenth Centuries.* London: Yale University Press, 2009.
Pierce, Chad T. 'Apocalypse and the Epistles of 1, 2 Peter and Jude'. Pages 307–25 in *The Jewish Apocalyptic Tradition and the Shaping of New Testament Thought.* Minneapolis: Fortress Press, 2017.
Piovanelli, Pierluigi. 'A Testimony of the Kings and the Mighty who Possess the Earth: The Thirst for Justice and Peace in the Parables of Enoch'. Pages 363–379 in *Enoch and the Messiah Son of Man: Revisiting the Book of Parables.* Edited by Gabriele Boccaccini. Grand Rapids: Eerdmans, 2007.
Polotsky, H. J. 'Aramaic, Syriac, and Geʿez,' *Journal of Semitic Studies* 9 (1964): 1–10.
Portier-Young, Anathea. *Apocalypse Against Empire: Theologies of Resistance in Early Judaism.* Grand Rapids: Eerdmans, 2014.
Quasten, J. *Patrology.* 3 Vols. Utrecht: Spectrum, 1962.
Quispel, G. and Robert M Grant. 'Note on the Petrine Apocrypha'. *Vigiliae Christianae* 6 (1952): 31–32.

Rahmani, I. E. *Testamentum Domini nostri Jesu Christi*. Mainz: Kirchheim, 1899.
Rahmer, Abraham. *Ein lateinischer Commentar aus dem IX. Jahrhundert zu den Büchern der Chronik kritisch verglichen mit den jüdischen Quellen, Erster Theil*. Thorn: Justus Wallis, 1866.
Ramelli, Ilaria L. E. 'Origen's Doctrine of Apokatastasis: A Reassessment'. Pages 660–669 in *Origeniana Decima: Origen as Writer*. Edited by Sylwia Kaczmarek and Henryk Pietras. Bibliotheca Ephemeridum Theologicarum Lovaniensium 244. Leuven: Peeters, 2011.
—. *The Christian Doctrine of Apokatastasis: A Critical Assessment from the New Testament to Eriugena*. Supplements to Vigiliae Christianae 120. Leiden: Brill, 2013.
Randal Chesnutt, '*Oxyrhynchus Papyrus* 2069 and the Compositional History of 1 Enoch'. *Journal of Biblical Literature* 129 (2010): 485–505.
Reicke, Bo. *The Disobedient Spirits and Christian Baptism: A Study of 1 Peter III.19 and Its Context*. Acta seminarii neotestamentici upsaliensis 13. Copenhagen: Munksgaard, 1946.
Reynolds, Benjamin E. and Loren T. Stuckenbruck, eds. *The Jewish Apocalyptic Tradition and the Shaping of New Testament Thought*. Minneapolis: Fortress Press, 2017.
Ruiten, J. van *Primaeval History Interpreted: The Rewriting of Genesis 1–11 in the Book of Jubilees*. Supplements to the Journal for the Study of Judaism 66. Leiden: Brill, 2000.
Runesson, Anders. *Divine Wrath and Salvation in Matthew: The Narrative World of the First Gospel*. Minneapolis: Fortress, 2016.
Sandmel, Samuel. 'Parallelomania'. *Journal of Biblical Literature* 81 (1962): 1–13.
Schäfer, Peter and Hans-Jürgen Becker, eds. *Synopse zum Talmud Yerushalmi, Band IV: Ordnung Neziqin; Ordnung Toharot: Nidda*. Tübingen: Mohr Siebeck, 1995.
Schermann, Theodor, ed. *Prophetarum Vitae Fabulosae, Indices Apostolorum Discipulorumque Domini Dorotheo, Epiphanio, Hippolyto aliisque Vindicata*. Leipzig: Teubner, 1907.
Schwemer, Anna Maria. *Studien zu den frühjüdischen Prophetenlegenden. Vitae Prophetarum, Band I: Die Viten der großen Propheten Jesaja, Jeremia, Ezechiel und Daniel. Einleitung, Übersetzung und Kommentare*. Texts and Studies in Ancient Judaism 49. Tübingen: J.C.B. Mohr (Paul Siebeck), 1995.
Schwemer, Anna-Maria. 'Review of *Ascensio Isaiae: Text und Kommentar*. ed. Enrico Norelli (Corpus Christianorum. Series Apocryphorum 7–8), Turnhout 1995'. *Zeitschrift für Kirchengeschichte* 110 (1998): 398–402.
Sellassie, Sergew-Hable. *Ancient and Medieval Ethiopian History to 1270*. Addis Ababa: United Printers, 1972.
Selwyn, E. G. *The First Epistle of St. Peter: The Greek Text with Introduction, Notes and Essays*. London: MacMillan, 1946.
Siegert, Folker. *Einleitung in die hellenistisch-jüdische Literatur*. Berlin: de Gruyter, 2015.
Six, V. *Äthiopische Handschriften vom Ṭānāsee 3: Nebst einem Nachtrag zum Katalog der Äthiopische Handschriften deutscher Bibliotheken und Museen*. Stuttgart: Steiner Verlag, 1999.
Sjöberg, E. *Der Menschensohn im äthiopischen Henochbuch*. Skrifter Utgivna av Kungliga Humanistika Vetenskapsamfundet i Lund 4. Lund: GWK Gleerup, 1946.
Sorabji, Richard. *Animal Minds and Human Morals: The Origins of the Western Debate*. London: Duckworth, 2001.
Sperber Alexander, ed., *The Bible in Aramaic Based on Old Manuscripts and Printed Texts, Volume 2: The Former Prophets According to Targum Jonathan. Second Impression*. Leiden: Brill, 1992.
Sperry-White, G. *The Testamentum Domini: A Text for Students, with Introduction, Translation, and Notes*. Nottingham: Grove Books, 1991.

Spitta, Friedrich. *Christi Predigt an die Geister (1 Petr. 3, 19ff.): Ein Beitrag zur Neutestamentlichen Theologie*. Göttingen: Vandenhoeck & Ruprecht, 1890.

Stuckenbruck, Loren T. "The Eschatological Worship of God by the Nations: An Inquiry into the Early Enoch Tradition". Pages 189–209 in *With Wisdom as a Robe: Qumran and Other Jewish Studies in Honour of Ida Fröhlich*. Edited by Károly Dániel Dobos and Miklós Kőszeghy. Sheffield: Sheffield Phoenix, 2009.

—. "'Apocrypha" and "Pseudepigrapha"'. Pages 179–203 in *Early Judaism: A Comprehensive Overview*. Edited by John J. Collins and Daniel C. Harlow. Grand Rapids: Eerdmans, 2012.

—. 'A Place for Socio-Political Oppressors at the End of History? Eschatological Perspectives from 1 Enoch'. Pages 1–22 in *Reactions to Empire: Sacred Texts in Their Socio-Political Contexts*. Edited by. John Anthony Dunne and Dan Batovici. Tübingen Wissenschaftliche Untersuchungen zum Neuen Testament 2.372. Tübingen: Mohr Siebeck, 2014.

—. '1 Enoch 1: A Comparison of Two Translations'. Pages 25–40 in *New Vistas on Early Judaism and Christianity* (Jewish and Christian Texts 22. Edited by Lorenzo DiTomasso and Gerbern S. Oegema. London: Bloomsbury T&T Clark, 2016.

—. *1 Enoch 91–108*. Commentaries on Early Jewish Literature. Berlin, New York: Walter de Gruyter, 2007.

—. *The Myth of Rebellious Angels: Studies in Second Temple Judaism and New Testament Texts*. Wissenschaftliche Untersuchungen zum Neuen Testament 335. Tübingen: Mohr Siebeck, 2014.

Stuckenbruck, Loren T. and Gabriele Boccaccini, eds. *Enoch and the Synoptic Gospels: Reminiscences, Allusions, Intertextuality*. Society of Biblical Literature Early Judaism and Its Literature 44. Atlanta: Society of Biblical Literature, 2016.

Suter, David W. *Tradition and Composition in the Parables of Enoch*. Society of Biblical Literature Dissertation Series 47. Missoula: Scholars Press, 1979.

Theisohn, J. *Der auserwählte Richter: Untersuchungen zum traditionsgeschichtlichen Ort der Menschensohngestalt der Bilderreden des Äthiopischen Henoch*. Studien zur Umwelt des Neuen Testaments 12. Göttingen: Vandenhoeck & Ruprecht, 1975.

Theophilus of Antioch, *Ad Autolycum*. Translated by Robert M Grant. Oxford Early Christian Studies. Oxford: Clarendon, 1970.

Tiller, Patrick A. *A Commentary on the Animal Apocalypse of I Enoch*. Early Jewish Literature 4. Atlanta: Scholars Press, 1993.

Tilling, Chris. *Paul's Divine Christology*. Wissenschaftliche Untersuchungen zum Neuen Testament 2.323. Tübingen: Mohr Siebeck, 2012.

Turcan, Marie, ed. *Tertullien: la toilette des femmes*. Sources Chrétiennes 173. Paris: Cerf, 1971.

Uhlig S. *Der äthiopische Henochbuch*. Jüdische Schriften aus hellenistisch-römischer Zeit 5.6. Gütersloh: Gütersloher Verlagshaus, 1984.

—. *Äthiopische Paläographie*. Stuttgart: Franz Steiner Verlag, 1988.

—. *Introduction to Ethiopian Palaeography*. Stuttgart: Franz Steiner Verlag, 1990.

Uhlig, S. and A. Baussi, eds. *Encyclopaedia Aethiopica*. 5 vols. Wiesbaden: Harrassowitz, 2003–2014.

Ullendorf, E. *The Ethiopians: An Introduction to Country and People*. 2d edition. London: Oxford University Press, 1965.

—. *Ethiopia and the Bible*. Schweich Lectures. London: Oxford University Press, 1968.

Underwood, Paul A. 'The Fountain of Life in Manuscripts of the Gospels'. *Dumbarton Oak Papers* 5 (1950): 41–138.

VanderKam, James C. 'Studies in the Apocalypse of Weeks (1 Enoch 93:1-10; 91:11-17)'. *Catholic Biblical Quarterly* 46 (1984): 511–523.

—. 'Righteous One, Messiah, Chosen One, and Son of Man in 1 Enoch 37–71'. Pages 169–201 in *The Messiah: Developments in Earliest Judaism and Christianity*. Edited by James H. Charlesworth. Minneapolis: Fortress, 1992.

—. 'Genesis 1 in Jubilees 2'. *Dead Sea Discoveries* 1 1994: 300–321.

—. 'The Exile in Jewish Apocalyptic Literature'. Pages 89–109 in *Exile: Old Testament, Jewish, and Christian Conceptions*. Supplements to the Journal for the Study of Judaism 56. Leiden: Brill, 1997.

—. 'The Angel Story in the Book of Jubilees'. Pages 151–170 in *Pseudepigraphic Perspectives: The Apocrypha and Pseudepigrapha in Light of the Dead Sea Scrolls*. Edited by E. G. Chazon and M. E. Stone. Studies on the Texts of the Desert of Judah 31. Leiden: Brill, 1999.

Vermes, Geza. 'The Son of Man Debate Revisited: 1960–2012'. Pages 1–17 in *The Parables of Enoch: A Paradigm Shift*. Jewish and Christian Texts 11. Edited by Darrell Bock and James H. Charlesworth. London: T&T Clark, 2013.

Vielhauer, Philipp. 'Geschichte der urchristlichen Literatur: Einleitung'. Pages 510–511 in *Das Neue Testament, die Apokryphen und die Apostolischen Väter*. Berlin: de Gruyter, 1975.

—. Historia de la literatura cristiana primitiva: Introducción al nuevo testamento, los apócrifos y los padres apostólicos. Salamanca: Ediciones Sígueme, 1991.

Vööbus, Arthur. 'Ta'āmera 'Iyasus: Zeuge eines älteren äthiopischen Evangelientypus'. *Orientalia Christiana Periodica* 17 (1951): 462–467.

Waddell, James A. *The Messiah: A Comparative Study of the Enochic Son of Man and the Pauline Kyrios*. Jewish and Christian Texts 10. London: T&T Clark, 2013.

Walck, Leslie. W. 'The Son of Man in the *Parables of Enoch* and the Gospels'. Pages 299–337 in *Enoch and the Messiah Son of Man: Revisiting the Book of Parables*. Edited by Gabriele Boccaccini. Grand Rapids: Eerdmans, 2007.

—. *The Son of Man in the Parables of Enoch and in Matthew*. Jewish and Christian Texts 9. London: T&T Clark, 2011.

—. 'The *Parables of Enoch* and the Synoptic Gospels'. Pages 231–268 in *The Parables of Enoch: A Paradigm Shift*. Jewish and Christian Texts 11. Edited by Darrell Bock and James H. Charlesworth. London: T&T Clark, 2013.

Warde, Duane. 'The Prophets of 1 Peter 1:10–12', *Restoration Quarterly* 31 (1989): 1–12.

Watson, Francis. *Paul and the Hermeneutics of Faith*. London: T&T Clark, 2004.

—. *Gospel Writing*. Grand Rapids: Eerdmans, 2013.

Watson, W. Scott. 'A Syriac-Arabic Narrative of the Miracles of Jesus'. *American Journal of Semitic Languages* 16 (1899/1900): 37–46.

Wendt K, ed. and trans. *Das Maṣḥafa Milād (Liber Nativitatis) und Maṣḥafa Sellāsē des Kaisers Zar'a Yā'qob*, Corpus scriptorum christianorum orientalium 221–222, 235–236. Leuven: Peeters, 1962–63

—. *Das Maṣḥāfa Milād (Liber Nativitatis) und Maṣḥāfa Sellāsē (Liber Trinitatis) des Kaisers Zar'a Yā'qob*. Corpus Scriptorum Christianorum Orientalium, Scriptores Aethiopici 41–44. Louvain: Peeters, 1962–63.

Weninger, Stefan. 'Isaiah, Ascension of'. Pages 195–196 in *Encyclopaedia Aethiopica, Volume 5*. Edited by S. Uhlig et al. Wiesbaden: Harrassowitz. 2007.

Werman, Cana. '*Jubilees* in the Hellenistic Context'. Pages 133–158 in *Heavenly Tablets: Interpretation, Identity and Tradition in Ancient Judaism*. Edited by Lynn LiDonnici and Andrea Lieber. Supplements to the Journal for the Study of 119. Leiden: Brill, 2007.

Wessely, Charles. 'Les plus anciens monuments du christianisme écrits sur papyrus II'. *Patrologia Orientalis* 18 (1924): 482–483.
Wevers, Gerd A. *Sanhedrin. Gerichtshof*, Übersetzung des Talmud Yerushalmi 4.4. Tübingen: Mohr Siebeck, 1981.
Williams, Logan. 'Disjunction in Paul: Apocalyptic or Christomorphic? Comparing the Apocalypse of Weeks with Galatians'. *New Testament Studies* 64 (2018): 64–80.
Witakowski, Witold. 'The Miracles of Jesus: An Ethiopian Apocryphal Gospel'. *Apocrypha* 6 (1995): 279–298.
Wolter, M. '"Ihr sollt aber wissen . . .": Das Anakoluth nach ἵνα δὲ εἰδῆτε in Mk 2,10-11 parr'. *Zeitschrift für die neutestamentliche Wissenschaft und die Kunde der älteren Kirche* 95 (2004): 269–275.
Zuurmond, Rochus. *Novum Testamentum Aethiopice: The Synoptic Gospels: General Introduction: Edition of the Gospel of Mark*. Wiesbaden: Steiner Verlag, 1989.
—. *Novum Testamentum Aethiopice, Part III: The Gospel of Matthew*. Aethiopistische Forschungen 55. Wiesbaden: Harrassowitz Verlag, 2001.
—. 'The Textual Background of the Gospel of Matthew in Geʿez'. *Aethiopica* 4 (2001): 32–41.

Index of Authors

Acerbi, Antonio 90
Achtemeier, Paul J. 51
Allison, Dale C. 56

Barclay, John M. G. 25, 26, 28
Barrett, C. K. 80, 81
Barth, Fredrik 9
Barton, Carlin A. 9
Bauckham, Richard 125, 128, 129
Bausi, Alessandro 119, 120
Baussi, A. 154
Beck, Eric 7, 125, 165, 166
Becker, Hans-Jürgen 94
Beers, H. 34
Black, Matthew 44, 56
Boccaccini, Gabriele 23, 24, 32
Bock, Darrell 23, 27
Bockmuehl, Markus 134
Bouriant, Urbain 117
Boyarin, Daniel 9, 31
Brita, Antonella 145
Brock, Sebastian P. 56
Buchholz, D. D. 99, 117, 119, 120, 122, 123, 125–9
Burch, Vacher 87
Burke, Tony 133

Cameron, R. 12
Caquot, Andre 132
Chaîne, M. 114
Charles, R. H. 57, 62, 63, 74, 152, 155
Charlesworth, James H. 23, 24, 26, 27, 37
Chesnutt, Randal 56
Chialà, Sabino 32
Collins, A. Y. 31, 99
Collins, John J. 43, 48, 110
Cooper, J. 99, 110
Cowley, Roger W. 119, 120, 137
Crawford, Matthew 169

Daiber, T. 31
Dalton, William J. 39

Davenport, Gene L. 74
Davies, Donald M. 146
Davila, James R. 56
de Jonge, Marinus 56
DeSilva, David A. 56
Dibelius, Martin 87
Dillmann, August 65, 86, 151
Dochhorn, Jan 5, 29, 86–8, 108, 165
Donadoni, Sergio 56
Dryden, J. De Waal 49
Dubis, Mark 49, 50, 52
Duensing, H. 102, 118, 125, 127
Dunn, James D. G. 26, 46, 51

Ehrensperger, Kathy 13, 14
Elliott, John H. 39, 40
Endres, John C. 70
Erho, Ted 24, 81
Esler, Philip F. 3, 11, 20, 165
Falk, Daniel K. 43

Finneran, N. 108
Fletcher-Louis, Crispin H. T. 31
Fredriksen, Paula 16, 17, 18
Friedmann, Meir 93

Galling, Kurt 95
Gaster, M. 95
Geerard, M. 131
Gerö, Stephen 131, 133
Gervers, Michael 87
Gieschen, C. A. 102
Gilhus, Sælid 72
Ginzberg, Louis 94
Gitlbauer. M. 56
Goldschmidt, Lazarus 94
Graf, G. 102
Grant, Robert M. 127
Gray, S. W. 21
Grébaut, S. 99, 100, 117, 120, 132
Guerrier L. 98, 99, 102
Guidi, I. 100
Gundry, Robert H. 21

Hagner, Donald A. 21, 22
Hahne, Harry Alan 40
Haile, Getachez 114, 133, 138
Halévy, J. 86, 170
Hammerschmidt, Ernst 81, 118
Hamrick, James R. 4, 72, 163, 164, 165
Harrington, Daniel J. 21
Hartenstein, J. 102
Hartman, Lars 47
Hays, Richard B. 33
Heldman, Marilyn 108, 148
Heller, B. 95
Helmer, Robert C. 125
Hempel, Charlotte 43
Hill, J. V. 99
Hollander, Harm Wouter 56
Hornschuh, M. 102
Horrell, David G. 40, 49
Hubbard, Moyer V. 78, 79
Hurtado, Larry W. 31
Hutchinson, John 9

Isaac. E. 153

James, M. R. 56, 117, 118, 121, 124

Kaplan, Steven 86
Keener, Craig 79
Kelly, J. N. D. 51, 173
Kennard, Douglas W. 49, 50
Klauck, H.-J. 102
Knibb, Michael A. 44, 57, 58, 61, 82, 101, 152–5, 164, 165
Knight, Jonathan 85, 87
Kraemer, Ross Shepard 56
Kraft, Robert A. 56
Kraus, Thomas J. 118
Kuhn, Thomas S. 27
Kvanvig, Helga S. 33

Lange, Armin 43
Leicester, R. 31
Levin, B. 106
Lichtenberger, Hermann 43
Liebengood, Kelly D. 40
Lied, Liv Ingeborg 55
Linebaugh, J. A. 28
Lührmann, Dieter 93

Lundhaug, Hugo 55
Lusini, Giangrancesco 123

Macaskill, Grant 26, 42
McDonald, L. M. 26
McKenzie, Judith S. 87, 145, 146, 147
Maclean, A. J. 99, 110
Macomber, William F. 114, 146
Marcus, H. G. 101
Marcus, J. 31, 101
Marmardji, A.-J. 106
Marrassini, Paolo 120
Martinez, F. Garcia 43
Mathews, Mark D. 40
Maurer, Christian 118, 125
Michaels, J. Ramsey 51
Milik, J. T. 55, 57, 63, 64
Mingana, A. 117
Moreschini, C. 116
Munro-Hay, S. 101

Najman, Hindy 142
Nanos, Mark D. 16, 18, 19
Nickelsburg, George W. E. 11–13, 19, 24, 30, 33, 36, 40, 42–4, 48, 57, 58, 60–2, 152, 153, 155, 156
Nicklas, Tobias 118
Nolland, John 21, 22
Nongbri, Brent 9
Nordenfalk, Carl 146, 147
Norelli, Enrico 85, 110, 116, 128
Nosnitsin, Denis 86

Olson, Daniel C. 12, 13, 36, 57, 58, 62
Owen, Paul 23, 33

Pate, Marvin 49, 50
Pérès, J.-N. 99, 114
Perrone, Lorenzo 86, 87
Perruchon, J. 100
Phillipson, D. W. 107
Pierce, Chad T. 39
Piovanelli, Pierluigi 29
Polotsky, H. J. 101
Portier-Young, Anathea 47

Quasten, J. 110
Quispel, G. 127

Rahmani, I. E. 99
Rahmer, Abraham 94
Ramelli, Ilaria L. E. 121, 123
Reicke, Bo 39
Reynolds, Benjamin E. 40
Runesson, Anders 21

Sandmel, Samuel 24, 25, 28, 37, 164
Schäfer, Peter 94–6
Schermann, Theodor 93
Schwemer, Anna Maria 87, 93
Schuller, Eileen M. 43
Sellassie, Sergew-Hable 107, 108
Selwyn, E. G. 51
Siegert, Folker 55
Six, V. 99, 114
Sjöberg, E. 33
Smith, Anthony 9
Sorabji, Richard 72
Sperber, Alexander 94
Sperry-White, G. 110
Spitta, Friedrich 39
Stuckenbruck, Loren T. 3, 16, 39, 40–7, 52, 57, 63, 64, 73, 164
Suter, David W. 29

Theisohn, J. 27, 33
Tiller, Patrick A. 11, 12
Tilling, Chris 24, 29
Turcan, Marie 159

Uhlig S. 57, 58, 62, 108, 114, 145, 152, 155
Ullendorf, E. 101
Underwood, Paul A. 148

Van Aarde, Andries 140
Van Ruiten, J. 68, 80
Vanderkam, James C. 4, 19, 24, 29, 30, 33, 36, 44, 47, 57, 67, 68, 69, 74, 152, 163
Vermes, Geza 31
Vielhauer, Philipp 126
Vööbus, Arthur 133

Waddell, James A. 23, 24
Walck, Leslie. W. 26, 32–4, 36
Wan, Wei Hsien 40, 49
Warde, Duane 51
Watson, Francis 3, 28, 87, 110, 146, 147, 166
Watson, W. Scott 133
Wendt K. 100, 157, 158
Weninger, Stefan 85, 86
Werman, Cana 72
Wessely, Charles 117, 118
Wevers, Gerd A. 94
Williams, Logan 3, 45, 164
Witakowski, Witold 132–4, 138, 140, 142
Wolter, M. 31

Zetterholm, Magnus 15, 18, 19
Zuurmond, Rochus 101, 103–6, 146

www.ingramcontent.com/pod-product-compliance
Lightning Source LLC
Chambersburg PA
CBHW070641300426
44111CB00013B/2194